SECURITY COMMUNITY PRACTICES IN THE WESTERN BALKANS

In the early 1990s, the Western Balkans were the scene of prolonged and bloody inter-ethnic wars. Numerous issues remain unresolved; Bosnia is a dysfunctional state; Kosovo a disputed territory; Macedonia a fragile republic, however, it is hard now to imagine the renewal of inter-state armed conflict.

Investigating the causes and mechanisms driving peaceful transformation in the Balkans, this book examines developments in the region and contributes to discussions on security community building. Focusing on how different professional communities work together in the creation of regional peace and security, it sheds new light on how diplomats, policemen, soldiers and others brought about the transformation from conflict to peace through their everyday practices.

Conducted collaboratively by a research community based within the region, this volume will be highly relevant to scholars and researchers studying the Balkans, regional security, security communities and policymakers.

Sonja Stojanović Gajić is Director at the Belgrade Centre for Security Policy.

Filip Ejdus is Assistant Professor at the Faculty of Political Sciences, University of Belgrade.

SOUTHEAST EUROPEAN STUDIES

Series Editor: Florian Bieber

The Balkans are a region of Europe widely associated over the past decades with violence and war. Beyond this violence, the region has experienced rapid change in recent times though, including democratization, economic and social transformation. New scholarship is emerging which seeks to move away from the focus on violence alone to an understanding of the region in a broader context drawing on new empirical research.

The Southeast European Studies Series seeks to provide a forum for this new scholarship. Publishing cutting-edge, original research and contributing to a more profound understanding of Southeastern Europe while focusing on contemporary perspectives the series aims to explain the past and seeks to examine how it shapes the present. Focusing on original empirical research and innovative theoretical perspectives on the region the series includes original monographs and edited collections. It is interdisciplinary in scope, publishing high-level research in political science, history, anthropology, sociology, law and economics and accessible to readers interested in Southeast Europe and beyond.

For more information about this series, please visit: https://www.routledge.com/Southeast-European-Studies/book-series/ASHSER1390

Electoral Violence in the Western Balkans
From Voting to Fighting and Back
Michal Mocht'ak

Changing Youth Values at the European Periphery
Beyond Ethnic Identity
Edited by Tamara P. Trošt and Danilo Mandić

Security Community Practices in the Western Balkans
Edited by Sonja Stojanović Gajić and Filip Ejdus

Social Movements in the Balkans
Rebellion and Protest from Maribor to Taksim
Edited by Florian Bieber and Dario Brentin

SECURITY COMMUNITY PRACTICES IN THE WESTERN BALKANS

Edited by Sonja Stojanović Gajić and Filip Ejdus

LONDON AND NEW YORK

First published 2018
by Routledge
2 Park Square, Milton Park, Abingdon, Oxon OX14 4RN

and by Routledge
711 Third Avenue, New York, NY 10017

Routledge is an imprint of the Taylor & Francis Group, an informa business

© 2018 selection and editorial matter, Sonja Stojanović Gajić and Filip Ejdus; individual chapters, the contributors.

The right of Sonja Stojanović Gajić and Filip Ejdus to be identified as the author of the editorial material, and of the authors for their individual chapters, has been asserted in accordance with sections 77 and 78 of the Copyright, Designs and Patents Act 1988.

All rights reserved. No part of this book may be reprinted or reproduced or utilised in any form or by any electronic, mechanical, or other means, now known or hereafter invented, including photocopying and recording, or in any information storage or retrieval system, without permission in writing from the publishers.

Trademark notice: Product or corporate names may be trademarks or registered trademarks, and are used only for identification and explanation without intent to infringe.

British Library Cataloguing in Publication Data
A catalogue record for this book is available from the British Library

Library of Congress Cataloging in Publication Data
Names: Stojanović, Sonja, editor. | Ejdus, Filip, editor.
Title: Security community practices in the Western Balkans / edited by Sonja Stojanovic and Filip Ejdus.Description: New York : Routledge, [2018] | Includes bibliographical references and index.
Identifiers: LCCN 2017048608| ISBN 9781472453105 (hardback) | ISBN 9781472453136 (pbk.) | ISBN 9781315608082 (e-book)
Subjects: LCSH: Security, International--Balkan Peninsula. | Internal security--Balkan Peninsula. | Security sector--Balkan Peninsula. | Police administration--Balkan Peninsula. | Community development--Balkan Peninsula. | Peace-building--Balkan Peninsula. | Balkan Peninsula.--Politics and government.
Classification: LCC JZ6009.B35 S43 2018 | DDC 355/.0330496--dc23
LC record available at https://lccn.loc.gov/2017048608

ISBN: 9781472453105 (hbk)
ISBN: 9781472453136 (pbk)
ISBN: 9781315608082 (ebk)

Typeset in Bembo
by Taylor & Francis Books

CONTENTS

List of tables vii
List of contributors viii
Acknowledgements xiii
List of abbreviations xv

1 Professional practices of security community building: theoretical introduction 1
  Filip Ejdus

2 Diplomacy and the integration of the Western Balkans: evidence from Albanian diplomats 13
  Arjan Dyrmishi and Mariola Qesaraku

3 From community of practice to security community in the Western Balkans: a role for the armed forces of Bosnia and Herzegovina 28
  Kenan Dautović

4 Community of practice among Western Balkan police services in Montenegro: national politics vs. professionalism 41
  Dženita Brčvak and Emir Kalač

5 The police profession in Kosovo: caught in the quagmire between politics and a regional security community 57
  Florian Qehaja and Armend Bekaj

6	Croatia's police and security community building in the Western Balkans *Sandro Knezović, Vlatko Cvrtila and Zrinka Vučinović*	72
7	Norms and sovereignty: regional security cooperation in the Macedonian Police *Cvete Koneska*	88
8	International policy networks and security community building: the case of the Partnership for Peace Consortium *Filip Ejdus*	101
9	Conclusion: security communities of practice between national and regional fields *Sonja Stojanović Gajić*	121

Index *138*

TABLES

7.1 Types of regional police activities					96

CONTRIBUTORS

Armend Bekaj is Senior Programme Officer at the Democracy Assessment, Analysis and Advisory (DAAA) Unit at the International Institute for Democracy and Electoral Assistance (IDEA). He is a PhD candidate at the University of Sheffield. He holds BA Hons on International Studies, University of Leeds and MA on Conflict Resolution, Peace Studies Department, University of Bradford. Before starting his PhD, Armend has for several years worked in the civil society sector in England and the Western Balkans, as well as for various international organisations such as the OSCE Mission in Kosovo, USAID and UNDP. The focus of his research is the security sector reform in the Western Balkans, more specifically the horizontal relations between former combatants of intra-state armed groups across the borders of Kosovo, Serbia and Macedonia, and their vertical rapport with their respective state authorities.

Dženita Brčvak was a researcher at Centre for Democracy and Human Rights, think tank from Montenegro. She graduated from Faculty of Political Science, University of Montenegro and holds Spec. Sci diploma in International Relations. She currently attends an M.A. course in European Economic Integrations at Faculty of Economics, University of Montenegro. As a research fellow, she has been involved in many projects in the area of international relations, European integration and security policies. Main projects involvements: *Security Transition in the Western Balkans – from Conflict Zone to Security Community* (national coordinator/ project manager, researcher), *Monitoring of Regional Cooperation in the Western Balkans* (researcher), *Democracy Index* (junior researcher), *School of Gender and Security Sector Reform* (project manager), *Project Generation Facility* (associate), *Local Development Municipal Initiatives* (associate), and many others.

Vlatko Cvrtila is an external professor of security studies at the Faculty of Political Science, University of Zagreb. He has received his B.A, MPhil and PhD degree from the same faculty. He has taught courses such as political geography, and geopolitics. From 2004 to 2005 he was a Vice-Dean and from 2008 to 2010 the Dean of the Faculty of Political Sciences in Zagreb. Besides academic career, he served as adviser to Minister of Defence in the period 1996–1998, security adviser to Croatian President Stjepan Mesić and a Head of parliamentary Council for Oversight of Intelligence Services.

Kenan Dautović is Associate Professor at the Department for Security and Peace Studies at the Faculty of Political Science in Sarajevo and American Univerisy in BiH. He teaches courses on "Social Conflicts Prevention" and "Theory and Praxis of Conflict Prevention". After completing Air Defence Military Academy in 1989 in Sarajevo and Zadar he earned his master degree in 2005 and PhD in 2009 at the Faculty of Political Science of University of Sarajevo. He has worked as professional military officer in the Armed Forces of Bosnia and Herzegovina reaching rank of Brigade Commander. His research fields are social conflict analysis; peace philosophy; social conflicts prevention; unresolved conflicts, early warning, NATO alliance and BiH path towards its membership, strategic-doctrinal framework of BiH, security community, and military as a profession.

Arjan Dyrmishi is a senior researcher and the Head of the European and Security Research Department in the Institute for Democracy and Mediation in Tirana. He holds a bachelor degree in French History and Philology from the University of Tirana and a Master's Degree in Political Science from the University if Siena, Italy. Before joining the institute, he held various positions in Albanian government, including in the Prime Minister's office, the Ministry of Defence and the State Intelligence Service. His research interests include international relations, security studies, democratisation, political parties and European Union.

Filip Ejdus is Assistant Professor at the Faculty of Political Sciences, University of Belgrade. He acquired his Master's Degree at the Paris Institute of Political Studies (Sciences Po) (2005), at the London School of Economics and Political Science (LSE) (2006) and defended his PhD Thesis in the field of international security at the Faculty of Political Sciences, University of Belgrade (2012). Since 2015, he was Marie Curie Fellow at the School of Sociology, Politics and International Studies, University of Bristol working on a project titled Local Ownership in Security Sector Reform Activities Within CSDP Operations of the EU. In the period January 2007–March 2009, he was the Executive Director of the Centre for Civil-Military Relations (currently Belgrade Centre for Security Policy) and presently serves as a member of its Management Board. He co-chairs the Regional Stability in South East Europe Study Group (RSSEE) of the PfP Consortium of Defense Academies and Security Studies Institutes. He is the editor of the Journal of Regional Security and author of several books and academic articles in national and international journals in the field of European integration, international relations and security studies.

Emir Kalač was a researcher at Centre for Democracy and Human Rights think tank from Montenegro. He has M.A. from the Faculty of Political Science (University of Montenegro), where he has graduated in October 2010. He was working on projects dealing with security and defence, as well as human rights and EU integration issues. Some of the main projects he has been involved in are: *Security Transition in the Western Balkans-From Conflict Zone to Security Community, Monitoring Regional Cooperation in the Western Balkans, Civil Society Capacity Building to Map and Monitor Security Sector Reform in Western Balkans 2008–2011, Comparative Analysis and Country Papers on Independent State Institutions as Security Actors in the Western Balkans, Regional Project: Police Corruption*. Emir is co-author of: *Almanac on Security Sector Oversight in the Western Balkans*, published by DCAF, and *Security Sector Reform in Montenegro 2009–2012*, published by CEDEM.

Sandro Knezović is Senior Research Associate at the Department for International Economic and Political Relations of the Institute for Development and International Relations in Zagreb (Croatia). He holds a B.A. in International Relations, M.Sc. in Comparative Politics (thesis: European Union and Southeastern Europe: Comparative Analysis of Countries in the Region and the Union's Policy Towards Them) and a Ph.D. in Comparative Politics (thesis: Impact of External and Internal Factors on Regional Consolidation – The Case of Southeastern Europe) from the Faculty of Political Sciences, University of Zagreb. His scientific work is concentrated on international relations topics, especially those related to international and European security (CFSP/ESDP), the EU and NATO enlargement and its impact on the region of Southeast Europe. He is member of various international networks and expert working groups (Geneva Center for Democratic Control of Armed Forces – DCAF's Southeastern Europe Security Forum – Expert Drafting Group for Regional Security Strategy; UACES Specialist Group on EU Conflict Prevention and Crisis Management Policies etc.) that address these issues and has a noticeable experience in writing articles, giving lectures and attending numerous international conferences.

Cvete Koneska graduated from the American University in Bulgaria (AUBG) where she studied political science and international relations and European studies. Following graduation, she proceeded to a Master of Arts degree at the School of Slavonic and East European Studies (SSEES) in University College London, focusing on Politics, Security and Integration. Following the completion of the MA course, she returned to Macedonia to work as a Research Fellow in a young local think-tank (Analytica) in Skopje, where she was responsible for the Security and Foreign Policy programme as well as European Approximation research. Her interest in security issues in the Balkan region resulted with an interest in pursuing a doctoral degree in politics to further investigate these questions. In 2012 she completed a DPhil degree in Politics at University of Oxford, as a Weidenfeld Scholar. Her doctoral research focuses on how political elites accommodate across ethnic and ideological lines on various sensitive policy issues (military and police reform, decentralisation, language and education) in post-conflict context. It was published as a monograph *After Ethnic Conflict: Policy Making in Bosnia and Macedonia* by Routledge in 2014.

Florian Qehaja is Executive Director of Kosovo Centre for Security S and one of the co-founders of KCSS. He served previously in the position of Head of Operations (2008–2011). In addition to that, he has been an assistant lecturer at various universities in Kosovo. Florian is author of several scientific publications in the security field; as well as author/co-author of local, international publications regarding the field of security, rule of law and regional cooperation. Further, he is an international consultant on Security Sector Reform, Rule of Law and Good Governance cooperating with leading international governmental and non-governmental organisations. During the period of time 2005–2007, he has worked at the International Relations Office of the University of Prishtina in the position of Coordinator of the International Summer University of Prishtina. He holds Bachelor's Degree in Law at the University of Prishtina, MA in Contemporary European Studies from the the University of Sussex (United Kingdom) and the PhD at the Faculty of Social Sciences (Department of Security Studies), University of Ljubljana. His PhD research on local ownership and security sector development in Kosovo was published in the monograph in 2017.

Mariola Qesaraku is Program Coordinator at Friedrich Ebert Stiftung Albania covering the program area of European Integration, regional cooperation in Western Balkans and Media. She holds a BA degree in Political Sciences with a major in International Relations from the University of Siena, Italy and an MA degree in Contemporary European Studies from the University of Sussex, UK. She is winner of the European Union Erasmus scholarship and has spent six months at the University of Wales in Swansea, UK focusing on European Union Politics and Policies. Previously she has worked as senior researcher and program officer at the Institute for Democracy and Mediation, a think tank based in Tirana in the area of European and security issues. Her research interests are European integration, democratisation and security sector reforms, regional cooperation, anti-corruption policies, and media development.

Sonja Stojanović Gajić is Director at the Belgrade Centre for Security Policy. She has more than fifteen years' experience of working on security sector reform programs with particular focus on police reform, gender and security sector reform (SSR). Her original contribution is the development of methodology for measuring security sector reform (SSR) from the perspective of civil society tested in Albania, Bosnia and Herzegovina, Croatia, Kosovo, Macedonia, Montenegro and Serbia. She has published internationally on policing, women, peace and conflict resolution. Some of her recent publications are: *Women, Peace and Security in the Western Balkans* (ed. with Gorana Odanović), *Policing in Serbia: Negotiating the Transition between Rhetoric and Reform* (with Mark Downes) that appeared in the book *Policing Developing Democracies* (Routledge 2008). Prior to her current post, Sonja had worked for the OSCE Mission to Serbia and Montenegro in the strategic management program for the Serbian and Montenegrin police services. In the period of 2006–2011, Ms. Stojanović Gajić worked part-time as a teaching assistant for security studies at the Faculty of Political Sciences of the University of Belgrade. Sonja holds an MA in Politics, Security and Integration with distinction from the School of Slavonic and Eastern European Studies, University College London and she is currently a PhD candidate at the University of Belgrade.

Zrinka Vučinović was junior researcher in the Institute for International Relations (IMO) in Zagreb participating in a number of international projects. She holds MA in International Relations and National Security from University of Zagreb, Faculty of Political Science. Her master thesis was orientated towards region SEE, especially Bosnia and Herzegovina. As stipendist of European Commission she spent one year (2008) at University of Sarajevo, Faculty of Political Science, researching for final paper. She graduated in 2009 on "Ethnic Conflicts and Security Policy of Bosnia and Herzegovina".

ACKNOWLEDGEMENTS

The editors would like to acknowledge the support of the Research Council of Norway for the three-year project, *Security Transitions in the Western Balkans: from Conflict Zone to Security Community?*, that provided the resources for the research and collaboration behind this book. This support enabled intensive exchange between the Norwegian Institute of International Affairs (NUPI) and the research consortium from the Western Balkans run by the Belgrade Centre for Security Policy (BCSP) from Serbia and six independent research centres from the Western Balkans. They are Analytica from Macedonia, the Centre for Democracy and Human Rights (CEDEM) from Montenegro, the Centre for Security Studies (CSS) from Bosnia and Herzegovina, the Institute for Democracy and Mediation (IDM) from Albania, the Institute for Development and International Relations (IRMO) from Croatia and the Kosovar Centre for Security Policy (KCSS).

We would like to acknowledge the intellectual and professional support of our colleagues: Prof. Iver Neumann, Karsten Fris and Morten Andersen from NUPI who played critical roles during the development of research design and as peer reviewers of initial research products within this project. Iver and Morten inspired us to engage with practice turn in IR during our initial exploration into the research puzzle on why former enemies had started cooperating within regional security networks. Karsten provided encouragement and continuous support for the editors and contributors of this book to take a lead in its development. NUPI also assisted in preparation of this book by hosting a fellowship of seven researchers from seven Western Balkan think tanks in April 2011 at NUPI, as well as through involvement of NUPI staff as lecturers in research workshops. NUPI associate Hilde Haug provided feedback on the first versions of chapters within this book.

We want to thank our colleagues from partner think tanks for their contributions to the development of joint methodology, and engagement with security and diplomatic professionals in their countries both for the collection of empirical data and dissemination of the findings and collaboration. Our partners, and members of the BCSP team, Gorana Radovanovic and Isidora Stakic, deserve our gratitude for the support they provided to the organization over eight research workshops and three dissemination conferences (Belgrade Security Forum 2012 and 2013 and the closing workshop in Skopje). We also want to acknowledge the assistance of Matthew White and Ivan Kovanovic with language editing. At Routledge, we want to thank the series editor Florian Bieber for accepting the manuscript and Brenda Sharp, Claire Maloney and Richard Kemp for being so helpful and efficient in getting this book into print.

In sum, we believe that the collaboration has helped us develop this book and we hope it will give a credible voice to the emerging research community in security transformations from the Western Balkan region.

LIST OF ABBREVIATIONS

AFBiH	Armed Forces of Bosnia and Herzegovina
BiH	Bosnia and Herzegovina
BIA	Serbian Security Information Agency
CEEC	Central and Eastern European Counties
CSCE	Conference on Security and Cooperation in Europe
CoP	Communities of Practice
CoPs	Chiefs of Police
CSO	Civil Society Organization
CSS	Centre for Security Studies
DCAF	The Geneva Centre for the Democratic Control of Armed Forces
DEA	Drug Enforcement Administration
DPS	Democratic Party of Socialists
EAPC	Euro-Atlantic Partnership Council
EU	European Union
EUROPOL	The European Police Office
FBiH	The Federation of Bosnia and Herzegovina
FRY	Federal Republic of Yugoslavia
GFAB	General Framework Agreement for Peace
HDZ	The Croatian Democratic Union
IACP	International Association of Chiefs of Police
ICTY	International Criminal Court for former Yugoslavia
INTERPOL	The International Criminal Police Organization
IO	International organizations
IPNs	International policy networks
IR	International relations
ISOS	International Staff Officers Skills Course

JNA	Yugoslav People's Army
KLA	Kosovo Liberation Army
KPC	Kosovo Protection Corps
MARRI	The Migration, Asylum, Refugees Regional Initiative
MFA	Ministry of Foreign Affairs
MoI	Ministry of Interior
MTT	Mobile Training Teams
NATO	North Atlantic Treaty Organization
NGOs	Non-governmental organizations
OSCE	The Organization for Security and Cooperation in Europe
PfP	Partnership for Peace
PfPC	Partnership for Peace Consortium of Defense Academies and Security Studies Institutes
PSOTC	Peace Support Operations Training Centre
RACVIAC	Regional Arms Control Verification and Implementation Assistance Centre
RCC	Regional Cooperation Council
RSSEE	Regional Stability in Southeast Europe
SAA	Stabilization and Association Agreement
SDP	Social Democratic Party
SEE	Southeast Europe
SECI/SELEC	Southeast European Law Enforcement Centre
SEECP	Southeast European Cooperation Process
SEPCA	Southeast Europe Police Chiefs Association
SFRY	Socialist Federal Republic of Yugoslavia
SP	Stability Pact
SSR	Security Sector Reform
TTP	Technique tactics and procedures
UN	United Nations
UNHCR	United Nations High Commissioner for Refugees
UNMIK	United Nations Interim Administration Mission in Kosovo
UNSC	United Nations Security Council
USA	United States of America
WB	Western Balkans
WWII	World War II

1
PROFESSIONAL PRACTICES OF SECURITY COMMUNITY BUILDING

Theoretical introduction

Filip Ejdus

The conventional way of looking at security community building is to conceptualize it as a peace building process involving states and other actors such as international organizations (IOs). In this book we take a somewhat different approach, looking at how security communities are brought into existence by the talk and practice of communities of professionals bound by certain ways of doing things. Think of diplomats meeting on a daily basis at IO secretariats or policemen exchanging crime data with neighbouring countries. Think of soldiers preparing for a regional military exercise or intelligence officers making regional threat assessments. Think of regional networks of security experts meeting regularly to discuss how to achieve regional stability. Think of any other community of professionals who, by carrying out their work competently on a daily basis, actually contribute to a regional political constellation built on trust and 'dependable expectation of peaceful change', a security community. In particular, in this book we are interested in understanding how these various professional communities, through their day-to-day practices, are bringing about the transformation of the Western Balkans from a war-torn region into a security community. However, the case studies presented in this book are not 'objective snapshots' of a moving target taken by a detached group of scientists. Instead, the book presents a thick description produced by a regional network of scholars and experts who are themselves deeply involved in the process of security community building through the production of the academic discourse which is necessary both for regional transformation and in order to move away from the ethnic security dilemmas of the past.

In this chapter, the key literature which has illuminated our theoretical thinking will be brought together and discussed in order to set the stage for the empirical case studies which follow. However, this chapter will not set out a tightly coupled theoretical paradigm which will then bind all the case studies together in a single academic narrative. Instead, this chapter presents a quite diverse conceptual toolbox which has guided our empirical inquiry. Each chapter in this book was crafted with a similar but different set of analytical tools and instruments, as discussed at workshops convened in Tirana (Albania), Opatija (Croatia), Belgrade (Serbia) and Sarajevo (BiH) between 2010 and 2012. What follows is a summary of the literature which served as the backdrop to those memorable and thought-provoking meetings.

Security community

The concept of the security community was first introduced into IR in the 1950s by Karl Deutsch and his associates.[1] According to Deutsch, a security community can be defined by the existence of 'dependable expectations of peaceful change' (Deutsch et al., 1957: 5). The interest for security communities renewed following the end of the Cold War. Initially developed within the liberal paradigm, the concept was revived in the 1990s by social constructivists, in large part thanks to a volume co-edited by Emanuel Adler and Michael Barnett (Adler and Barnett, 1998). The book offered a sociological and path-dependent understanding of security community building. The authors proposed to study the emergence and deepening of security communities historically as a process of imagination and institutionalization of dependable expectations of peaceful change (ibid.: 49). In line with this, Adler and Barnett distinguished three types of security communities: nascent, in which states cooperate and coordinate policies without seeking a security community; ascendant, with increasing institutional and cooperation networks and an embryonic sense of 'we-ness'; and mature, with deep institutionalization, a well-articulated common identity and mutual expectations of peaceful resolution of disputes.

Following the publication of the Adler/Barnett volume, many constructivist scholars used the concept of security community to make sense of the changing world. Contrary to neo-realist predictions, the Euro-Atlantic security community did not collapse following the demise of the Soviet Union. Instead, it deepened and expanded geographically to envelop its former Eastern European adversaries. Understanding these developments required going beyond the neorealist distribution of material capabilities in the international system to include issues such as identity, norms and socialization (Neumann and Williams, 2000). Although the security community concept initially grew out of the North-Atlantic experience it was soon applied to a geographically wider Euro-Atlantic region (Pouliot, 2010; Adler 2008), the Persian Gulf (Barnett and Gause, 1998), Southeast Asia (Acharya, 1991, 1995, 2009; Garofano, 2002; Haacke, 2005), South America (Hurrell, 1998), Southern Africa (Ngoma, 2003; Nathan, 2006), and Southeast Europe (Vučetić, 2001; Cruise and Grillot, 2013; Kavalski, 2007). Only a relatively small number of works dealt with the geographical spread of security communities. Unsurprisingly, all these works were concerned with the spread of the liberal security community, institutionalized through the EU and NATO, to either Central and Eastern Europe (Adler, 2008) or Southeast Europe and more recently the Western Balkans (Vučetić, 2001; Kavalski, 2007; Grillot et al., 2010).[2]

The security community in the Western Balkans

Only three decades ago, most of the region which is today known as the Western Balkans still constituted the majority of Yugoslavia, a federal state which was thus itself already an amalgamated security community. At the time, the only region which was discussed in the dominant discourse was Southeast Europe (SEE). When Yugoslavia collapsed in 1991, the term Balkans gained dominance because it better captured the orientalist overtones of the Western portrayal of the ensuing conflict. Once the Eastern Balkan countries, Bulgaria and Romania, began EU accession talks in 1998, SEE was replaced by a narrower term – the Western Balkans (WB). It was coined by the EU and introduced during the Austrian presidency to denote the Western part of the peninsula which remained outside the European integration process. The term included all former Yugoslav republics minus Slovenia plus Albania. Although it was initially invented as a kind of Brussels speak for the purpose of EU enlargement policy, the term soon became a common political label, which ultimately outgrew its political meaning and entered the wider cultural discursive space. This is best exemplified by the 2006 publication of Lonely Planet's Western Balkans Travel Guide.

Today, however, to talk about security community (re)building in the Western Balkans makes perfect sense to academics and policy-makers alike. When Yugoslavia broke up in 1991, a decade of armed conflicts ensued, first in Slovenia (1991), then Croatia (1991–5), BiH (1992–5), Serbia/Kosovo (1999) and finally Macedonia (2001). By 2001, the Wars of Yugoslav Succession, as they are sometimes called, were put to an end with a robust military and diplomatic support of NATO and the EU. A security regime was installed through a set of peace deals, including the Dayton Peace Agreement for Bosnia (1995), the Erdut Peace Agreement for Croatia (1995), the Kumanovo Military-Technical Agreement and UNSC Resolution 1244 for Kosovo (1999) and the Ohrid Framework Agreement for Macedonia (2001).

The first progress in moving from this security regime to a nascent security community was made not by the Western Balkan states themselves but by the EU in devising the Stability Pact during Germany's presidency in 1999. Perhaps even more important were the June 2000 European Council meeting in Santa Maria De Feira, when it was decided to open the door to the potential future accession of the Western Balkan states, and the November 2000 Zagreb Summit, when the Stabilization and Association Process was endorsed. NATO followed suit by opening first its Partnership for Peace (PfP) program and then the prospect of full membership to Western Balkan states. Another step towards a nascent security community was made in April 2013 when Belgrade and Priština signed the EU facilitated Brussels Agreement thus setting in motion a normalisation process between Serbia and Kosovo. With the sole exception of Serbia, all countries in the region are either NATO members – such as Croatia and Albania – or have made significant progress towards joining the alliance. After Croatia's July 2013 accession to EU membership, the Western Balkan region has now shrunk as the EU expanded. Despite the enlargement fatigue caused by the Euro crisis, external region building and the expansion of the western security community into the Western Balkans will undoubtedly continue beyond this point, but the pace at which this will happen is yet to be established.

All this has so far been the object of analysis of a handful of academic studies. The first author to study security community development in Southeast Europe (SEE) and the Western Balkans was Srđan Vučetić (2001). In his piece, Vučetić demonstrated that at the outset of the twenty first century, the region well fitted Adler and Barnett's description of a 'nascent' security community. Vučetić identified the EU as the main extra-regional hegemonic region-builder and the Stability Pact (SP) as the main vehicle for the inclusion of SEE in the wider European zone of peace. More specifically, he argued that the SP was diffusing norms and practices of common and comprehensive security which were initially developed within CSCE rather than the EU and NATO (ibid.: 119). However, as Vučetić noted, the missing link preventing the SEE security community from moving into the 'ascendant' phase was the fact that regional identity was 'minimal' (ibid.: 124).[3] The main impediment to this is not only the lack of a common understanding of history but also the internalization of a negative self-image stemming from the Balkanist discourse, to use Todorova's term (ibid.: 125; Todorova, 1997). Vučetić rightly pointed out the role of external region-builders such as the EU and the CSCE as the formative practice producers. However, Vučetić's state-bias captured only part of the equation while leaving out societal interactions and professional practices which occur outside state bodies and their intergovernmental settings.

The next comprehensive attempt to approach the security dynamics of the Balkans through the security community concept was made by Emilian Kavalski (2003; 2004; 2007). Kavalski's main concern was not how security communities evolve and transform, but how they get off the ground in the first place. Combining liberal and constructivist paradigms in a single framework, he argued – much in line with Vučetić – that the expansion of the Western 'hegemonic peace order' to the Balkans after the 1999 Kosovo war was initiated by extra-regional actors such as NATO and the EU through the socialization of decision making elites in IOs. Kavalski pointed out an important difference between the deepening and the expansion of the liberal security community. While in the former IOs develop as a result of peaceful patterns of interstate relations in the Deutschian fashion, in the latter IOs are the cause of such peaceful relations.

Kavalski distinguished two types of international socialization. The first is the socialization of Balkan state-elites *by* NATO and the EU, which takes place as a result of conditionality policy. Backed by the prospect of membership, conditionality pushes prospective members to embrace regional cooperation, thus helping the embryonic security community get off the ground (Kavalski 2007: 62). In contrast, Kavalski posited socialization *within* those two organizations through various programs wherein Balkan states learn security community norms because they are in a situation similar to membership, such as the PfP program. Although his interest in hegemonic socialization is very useful and telling, Kavalski ignored the role of professions and communities of practice. By the same token, while focusing on the resources utilized to attain compliance with western hegemonic norms and practices (Ibid: 70) he failed to analyze how knowledge of those norms and practices is socially constructed and expanded geographically.

Further study of the promotion of the security community in the Western Balkans by NATO and the EU was undertaken by Grillot, Cruise and D'Erman (2010). The three authors' article confirmed Kavalski's thesis that the EU and NATO served as the key external third parties for the socialization of Western Balkan state-elites, thus precipitating the nascent phase of security community building in the region. In addition, they argued that IOs had socialized states individually into the European rather than into a Western Balkan commonality, at least at the very outset of promotion of the liberal security community. This changed in 2005, when the EU adopted a new policy insisting on regional cooperation as a precondition for future enlargement (European Commission, 2005). This external move in the direction of greater regional ownership created the potential for the security community in the Western Balkans to move from the 'nascent' to the 'ascendant' phase. However, as the authors noted, the practice of security community construction had yet to trickle down to the general populations and translate into a norm internalized by ordinary citizens. Unfortunately, as they argued, feelings of trust and belongingness are still very much lacking among the general population of the Western Balkan region, thus preventing further development and consolidation of the security community (Grillot et al., 2010: 62). Grillot, Cruise and D'Erman advanced an academic insight into the gradual inclusion of the Western Balkans into the Euro-Atlantic security community. However, their work suffered from similar limitation as the two above mentioned authors in assuming the central role of states and IOs.

The security community literature analysed thus far by and large focuses on what states and IOs do at the regional level of analysis. This is a valid approach in its own right. However, scholars investigating security communities have rarely gazed beyond and below states and IOs into professional and epistemic communities and their everyday competent practices of building regional trust. In order to fill this gap, this research brings to the table a discussion of the role of professional communities in the process of security community building. In order to do this, it is appropriate to examine the relevant literature on professional practices.

Professional practices of security community building

Systematic study of professions dates to the early twentieth century. Carr-Saunders and Wilson, pioneer authors of *The Professions*, defined professions as organized bodies of experts who apply esoteric knowledge to particular cases (Carr-Saunders and Wilson, 1934). The authors argued that professions have elaborate systems of instruction and training, along with entry examinations, formal prerequisites and peculiar codes of ethics. There are two distinct approaches to professions in sociology: functionalism and structuralism. Functionalists define a profession as 'a relatively homogeneous community whose members share identity, values, definitions of role, and interests' (Bucher and Strauss 1961). Structuralists, on the other hand, consider professions to consist of institutions, personnel, organizations, recruitment policies, standards and codes as well as their relations to the public (Abbott, 1988). This research will look at a number of professions, including the police, diplomats, the military and intelligence services and will examine the way the practices of these professions bring the security community into existence. But in order to capture the professional practice of security community building, this research will draw neither on functionalism nor on structuralism but rather on the 'practice turn' in social theory in general (Schatzki et al., 2001) and in IR in particular (Neumann, 2002; Adler, 2005; Pouliot, 2010; Adler and Pouliot, 2011a, 2011b; Andersen and Neumann 2012).

Instead of focusing either on practitioners' discourses or on their institutional setups, the 'practice turn' attempts to bring materiality back into the analysis of world politics, directing attention onto what practitioners do, in other words focusing on the quotidian unfolding of their professional life. Adler and Pouliot offered a definition of practices as 'competent performances' (Adler and Pouliot, 2011b: 4). In contrast to 'behaviour', which denotes any material doing, or 'action', which refers to meaningful behaviour, 'practices' are patterned actions 'socially developed through learning and training' (ibid.: 5). Practices are performances enacted more or less competently in a socially meaningful way; they rest upon background knowledge, on an unspoken know-how which is developed through practices and reified by them, thus bringing the discursive and material worlds together (Adler and Pouliot, 2011a: 16, 2011b: 7). International practices are defined simply as 'socially organized activities that pertain to world politics' (ibid.: 6). The practice approach, as argued by its proponents, following pragmatism in philosophy, promises to overcome deeply entrenched dichotomies in social science such as theory/practice, ideas/materiality, agency/structure and continuity/change (Dewey, 1920). In addition, although the 'practice turn' was initially confined to poststructural and constructivist paradigms, it has recently been enthusiastically suggested that it may also be used as an interparadigmatic focal point in the study of world politics (Adler and Pouliot, 2011a: 5; 2011b: 3). The 'practice turn' has thus opened up a new research agenda, maybe even a new debate in IR (Kratochwil, 2011).

On the mid-level, the practice turn was a fertile entry point for the translation of the concept of Communities of Practice (CoP) from cognitive anthropology (Wenger, 1998) into the study of world politics (Adler, 2005). For Wenger, a CoP is a group of people who share common competences, practices and skills (Wenger, 1998). Wenger challenged the traditional conceptualization of learning by conceptualizing it not as the transmission of abstract knowledge from one individual to another but rather as a process that takes place within a community through 'situated learning' or 'learning by doing'. However, while Wenger was dealing primarily with the formation of CoPs inside organizations, Emanuel Adler divorced the concept from the organizational environment and applied it to transnational and international relationships, thus adapting it for IR (Adler, 2005; Adler and Pouliot, 2011a; 2011b). He also proposed a concept of 'community constellations', which exist when a set of distinct CoPs overlap in a single process of cognitive evolution (Adler, 2005: 23).

Yet another similar concept which is useful in the study of professional practices of security community building is that of 'epistemic communities'. According to Peter Haas, who coined the term, an epistemic community is a 'network of professionals with recognized expertise and competence in a particular domain and an authoritative claim to policy-relevant knowledge within the domain or issue area' (Haas, 1992: 3). Members of an epistemic community may come from different professions, but they all share normative and causal beliefs, notions of validity and common policy enterprises. As the argument goes, the role of transnational epistemic communities in policy making is increasing in a world of growing complexity. This is so because epistemic communities produce knowledge, generate policy recommendations and serve as a powerful socializing vehicle under conditions of increasing uncertainty. Communities of practice and epistemic communities are both extremely pertinent concepts for the study of security community building. They both rest on the idea of a network, a community of practitioners that share access to limited knowledge and related views, language and values. This can lead to an increased sense of 'we-ness' among members and a sense of shared goals and purpose across national boundaries. Although the establishment of a security community is likely to result in an overall increased volume of interactions and cooperation across national boundaries, not all professions and sectors will be equally affected.

Related to the study of epistemic communities is the scholarly interest in the role of international policy and advocacy networks in world politics (Keck and Sikkink, 1998; Slaughter, 2001; Dupont, 2004; Aydinli and Yoen, 2011; Krahmann, 2005; Adler, 2008; Cross, 2011; Mérand et al., 2011). The development of networked modes of coordination among terrorists and criminals has been followed by networked responses of national and international security providers (Krahmann, 2005: 18–19). As mentioned earlier, according to Adler and Barnett the development of networks among states, societies and IOs is the central feature of the *ascendant* phase in the evolution of security communities. However, the role of international policy networks in the everyday practices of security community building remains understudied, and this book aims to fill that gap.

Summary of chapters

This introduction is followed by Chapter 2, written by Arjan Dyrmishi and Mariola Qesaraku. By examining the practices of Albanian diplomats, the authors analyse the embodiment of diplomacy in interstate relations between Western Balkan countries. The chapter argues that although diplomacy is practised extensively among the region's countries, and is widely accepted as the only way to solve interstate disputes, it has not become a self-evident practice. The main barrier is still the deep historical and cultural divisions which prevent the development of collective identity, the 'we feeling', which in effect constitutes the underlying factor holding security communities together.

Chapter 3, by Kenan Dautović, investigates how regional cooperation is understood, exercised, and learned by military professionals in BiH. Dautović's empirical findings identify a whole spectrum of possible ways, means and institutions through which the security community is reified, leading to the conclusion that BiH's military is fairly open to regional cooperation when the conditions which permit it prevail. This salient quantitative and qualitative transaction flow suggests that two key ingredients of a security community are first, expectations that peaceful change will reliably occur and second, the new social relations which these transactions initiate.

Chapter 4, by Emir Kalač and Dženita Brčvak, probes the practices of the Montenegrin police as part and parcel of security community practice in the Western Balkans. The authors' analysis is based on findings from their field research, which consisted of 20 qualitative interviews with police officers in Montenegro conducted between January and May 2012. In addition to this, the authors carried out field visits, non-participant observation and context analysis. The authors find that in high-profile cases the autonomy of the Montenegrin police is endangered by politics, while there is a good level of everyday apolitical cooperation within the region as a whole, for example over border policing.

Chapter 5 studies the role in the Western Balkans security community of police practices in the region's youngest state – Kosovo. Authors Florijan Qehaja and Armend Bekaj argue that the region's security community can be advanced through further professionalization of police services and a healthy detachment from negative politics when tackling security challenges of common concern. The authors use empirical evidence gathered through participatory observation in Kosovo between 2012 and 2014, as well as interviews with politicians, the police and other security sector informants. The chapter concludes with modest but unique empirical data which enriches the theory of security communities while highlighting the challenges set by the interplay between politics and the police profession and, by default, regional cooperation.

Chapter 6 examines the contribution of the Croatian police as a profession/epistemic community to the creation of a Western Balkan security community. The analysis of authors Sandro Knezović, Vlatko Cvrtila and Zrinka Vučinović is based on secondary sources and semi-structured interviews with Croatian police officers and MoI officials of various ranks. The authors conclude that regional cooperation in the field of policing has improved noticeably since 2000 and is successfully moving away from the work patterns of the 1990s. Nevertheless, they also conclude that there is limited empirical evidence regarding security community building in the region and the potential role of the Croatian police in the process.

In Chapter 7, Cvete Koneska examines how the professional practices of the police contribute to the adoption of non-violent democratic policing norms that are transforming the Western Balkans from a conflict zone towards regional integration and ultimately into a security community. Looking at the practices of regional cooperation in the Macedonian police, this chapter argues that regional cooperation in the Western Balkans remains predominantly externally driven by the requirements set by the EU and NATO for greater regional cooperation, while functional factors, such as the need to resolve common problems and address common needs, remain secondary. The author's empirical findings suggest that the vertical, hierarchical structure of the police and the lack of normative dislocation of old professional practices since the end of communism prevent the full adoption and internalization of cooperation norms.

In Chapter 8, the analysis moves away from professional communities at the national level and looks at a transnational community formation which acts as a security community at the regional level. In particular, the role of international policy networks (IPNs) in the process of security community building in the Western Balkans is analysed. IPNs are loose communities of government agencies, international organizations and CSOs that join forces to achieve commonly shared public policy goals. It is argued that IPNs play an important yet insufficiently studied role as intermediaries between states and civil societies in the evolution of a security community from the nascent to the ascendant phase. In particular, IPNs manage a security community's relevant knowledge, diffuse the norm of self-restraint, spread security policy influence and provide organizational flexibility. This is illustrated with arguments from an ethnographic case study of the Partnership for Peace Consortium of Defence Academies and Security Studies Institutes (PfPC) and its study group on Regional Stability in Southeast Europe (RSSEE).

In the final chapter, Sonja Stojanović Gajić summarizes the key insights of the project. In particular, the discussion considers how professional communities in the field of security across the region, have contributed to the security community building through mutual engagement, joint enterprises and a shared repertoire of routines, methods and tools of security cooperation. However, the limits of this situational peacebuilding in the Western Balkans are also pointed out, including ongoing securitisation processes, persistent mistrust and narrow and often diverging national interests as seen and constructed by political elites.

Conclusion

This book aims to contribute to both the theoretical understanding of security community building and empirical knowledge about it. It does this through the study of professional communities, cutting across the usual objects of security community building literature such as states, IOs or CSOs. The question of which professional communities or communities of practice qualify for such analysis should not, however, bear the burden of too much theoretical tinkering but rather ought to be left to empirical inquiry. In short, any community of practice which spreads the unspoken know-how and subjectivity of peaceful change potentially contributes to the transition from a conflict zone to a security community.

The book brings together 13 authors and seven case studies, theoretically informed by the 'practice turn' in IR and methodologically conducted through ethnographic research by culturally competent scholars who are themselves deeply embedded within the process of security community building in the region. This book also illustrates critical theory's assumption on the inseparability of theory and practice. In addition to being an exercise in theoretical and scholarly work, this book is also an exercise in security community building. While we studied other professional communities, including diplomats, the police and the military, our own scholarly network is also a small but distinct building block of regional transformation. All the scholars who participated in writing this book are active members of a nascent community of think-tanks, NGOs and academic institutions across the Western Balkan region, a community which could be an exciting research subject in its own right. However, another book will have to undertake this task.

Notes

1 Emilian Kavalski notes that the conceptual origins of the term were developed by Richard Van Wagenen (1952).
2 A number of studies deal with other aspects of EU and NATO enlargement without employing the concept of security community. For a theoretical overview see: Schimmelfennig, 2005.
3 Dimitar Bechev (2004) and Cvete Koneska (2008) have both made a similar point.

Bibliography

Abbott, A, *The System of Professions: An Essay on the Division of Expert Labor*, University of Chicago, 1988.
Acharya, A, "The Association of Southeast Asian Nations: 'Security Community' or 'Defence Community'?" in *Pacific Affairs* (1991): 159–178.
Acharya, A, "A regional security community in Southeast Asia?" in *The Journal of Strategic Studies* 18 (1995): 175–200.
Acharya, A, *Constructing a security community in Southeast Asia: ASEAN and the problem of regional order*, Routledge, 2009 (2nd edition), 2014 (3rd edition).
Adler, E, "The Emergence of Cooperation: National Epistemic Communities and the International Evolution of the Idea of Nuclear Arms Control" in *International Organization* 46:1 (1992): 101–145.
Adler, E, "Imagined (Security) Communities: Cognitive Regions in International Relations" in *Millennium: Journal of International Studies* 26:2 (1997): 249–277.
Adler, E, *Communitarian International Relations: The Epistemic Foundations of International Relations*, New York: Routledge, 2005.
Adler, E, "The Spread of Security Communities: Communities of Practice, Self-Restraint and NATO's Post-Cold War Transformation" in *European Journal of International Relations* 14:2 (2008): 195–230.
Adler, E and Barnett, M (eds), *Security Communities*, Cambridge University Press, 1998.
Adler, E and Haas, P, "Conclusion: Epistemic Communities, World Order, and the Creation of a Reflective Research Program" in *International Organization* 46:1 (1992): 367–390.

Adler, E and Pouliot, V (eds), *International Practices*, Cambridge University Press, 2011a.
Adler, E and Pouliot, V, "International Practices" in *International Theory* 3:1 (2011b): 1–36.
Andersen, MS and Neumann, IB, "Practices as Models: A Methodology with an Illustration Concerning Wampum Diplomacy" in *Millennium: Journal of International Studies* 40:3 (2012): 457–481.
Aydinli, E and Yoen, H, "Transgovernmentalism Meets Security: Police Liaison Officers, Terrorism, and Statist Transnationalism" in *Governance* 24:1 (2011): 55–84.
Barnett, M and Gause, FG, "Caravans in opposite directions: society, state and the development of a community in the Gulf Cooperation Council" in Adler, E and Barnett, M (eds) *Security Communities*, Cambridge University Press, 1998, 161–197.
Bechev, D, "Contested Borders, Contested Identity" in *Southeast European and Black Sea Studies* 4:1(2004): 77–95.
Bucher, R and Strauss, A, "Professions in Process" in *The American Journal of Sociology* 66:4 (1961): 325–334.
Carr-Saunders, AM and Wilson, PA, *The Professions*, Oxford: Clarendon Press, 1934.
Cross, Mai'a K Davis, *Security Integration in Europe: How knowledge-based networks are transforming the European Union*, Ann Arbor: University of Michigan Press, 2011.
Deutsch, K, Burrell, S, Kann, R, Lee, M, Lichterman, M, Lindgren, R, Loewenheim, F and Van Wagenen, R, *Political Community and the North Atlantic Area: International Organization in the Light of Historical Experience*, Princeton, NJ: Princeton University Press, 1957.
Dewey, J, *Reconstruction in Philosophy*, New York: Mentor Books, 1920.
Dupont, B, "Security in the age of networks" in *Policing and Society* 14:1 (2004): 76–91.
European Commission, "2005 Enlargement Strategy Paper", Brussels, 2005.
Garofano, J, "Power, Institutions and the Asean Regional Forum: A Security Community For Asia?" in *Asian Survey* 42:3 (2002): 502–521.
Grillot, SR and Cruise, RJ, "Regional Security Community in the Western Balkans: A Cross-Comparative Analysis" in *Journal of Regional Security* 8:1 (2013): 7–24.
Grillot, SR, Cruise, RJ and D'Erman, VJ. "Developing security community in the Western Balkans: The role of the EU and NATO" in *International Politics* 47 (2010): 62–90.
Haacke, J, "'Enhanced Interaction' with Myanmar and the Project of a Security Community: Is ASEAN Refining or Breaking with its Diplomatic and Security Culture?" in *Contemporary Southeast Asia* (2005): 188–216.
Haas, P, "Introduction: Epistemic Communities and International Policy Coordination" in *International Organization* 41:1 (1992): 1–35.
Hurrell, A, "An emerging security community in South America" in Adler, E and Barnett, M (eds) *Security Communities*, Cambridge University Press, 1998, 228–264.
Kavalski, E, "The International Socialization of the Balkans" in *The Review of International Affairs* 2:4 (2003): 71–88.
Kavalski, E, "The EU in the Balkans: Promoting an Elite Security Community" in *World Affairs* 8 (2004): 98–116.
Kavalski, E, *Extending the European Security Community: Constructing Peace in the Balkans*, London: Tauris, 2007.
Keck, ME and Sikkink, K, *Activists beyond borders: Advocacy networks in international politic*, Cambridge University Press, 1998.
Koneska, C, "Regional Identity: the Missing Element in Western Balkans Security Cooperation" in *Western Balkans Security Observer* 7–8 (2007–8): 82–89.
Krahmann, E, "Security governance and networks: New theoretical perspectives in transatlantic security" in *Cambridge Review of International Affairs* 18:1 (2005): 15–30.
Kratochwil, F, "Making Sense of 'International Practices'" in Adler, E and Pouliot, V (eds), *International Practices*, Cambridge University Press, 2011, 36–61.

Mérand, F, Hofmann, SC and Irondelle, B, "Governance and state power: a network analysis of European security" in *JCMS: Journal of Common Market Studies* 49:1 (2011): 121–147.

Nathan, L, "Domestic Instability and Security Communities" in *European Journal of International Relations* 12:2 (2006): 275–299.

Neumann, IB, "Returning Practice to the Linguistic Turn: The Case of Diplomacy" in *Millenium: Journal of International Studies* 31:3 (2002): 627–651.

Neumann, IB and WilliamsMC, "From Alliance to Security Community: NATO, Russia, and the Power of Identity" in *Millennium: Journal of International Studies*, 29:2 (2000): 357–387.

Ngoma, N, "SADC: Towards a Security Community" in *African Security Review* 12:3 (2003): 17–28.

Pouliot, V, "The Logic of Practicality: A Theory of Practice of Security Community" in *International Organization* 62:2 (2008): 257–288.

Pouliot, V, *International Security in Practice*, Cambridge University Press, 2010.

Schatzki, TR, Knorr-Cetina, K, and von Savigny, E, (eds) *The practice turn in contemporary theory*, London: Routledge, 2001.

Schimmelfennig, F, *The Politics of European Union Enlargement: Theoretical Approaches*, London: Routledge, 2005.

Slaughter, AM, *The Accountability of Government Networks*, in *Indiana Journal of Global Legal Studies*, 8: 2, Article 5, 2001.

Todorova, M, *Imagining the Balkans*, Oxford University Press, 1997.

Van Wagenen, R, *Research in the International Organization Field*, Princeton, NJ: Centre for Research on World Political Institutions, 1952.

Wenger, E, *Communities of Practice: Learning, Meaning, and Identity*, Cambridge University Press, 1998.

Vučetić, S, "The Stability Pact for South Eastern Europe as a Security Community-Building Institution" in *Southeast European Politics* 2 (2001): 109–134.

2

DIPLOMACY AND THE INTEGRATION OF THE WESTERN BALKANS

Evidence from Albanian diplomats

Arjan Dyrmishi and Mariola Qesaraku

Introduction

In the aftermath of the conflicts of the 1990s, the desire for peace and prosperity led Western Balkan countries to embrace Euro-Atlantic integration processes as a means of achieving stability and economic development. Despite the varying pace of progress, all of the region's countries have made considerable progress towards integration. Indeed, Albania and Croatia have been NATO members since 2009 and the latter joined the EU on 1 July 2013. However, despite the advances that have been made in integration processes and an increase in regional cooperation, the region continues to face problems which hamper more rapid internal and external integration.

Against this background, this paper examines the results of the cooperation and integration processes by looking at the extent to which diplomacy has become a self-evident practice in interstate relations between Western Balkan countries. This is useful for the task of understanding whether the region has made a break with the conflicts that have characterized its past and whether it is developing into a security community, that is a group of states which share common interests, values and interpretations of reality and seek non-violent means to settle their disputes.

The paper draws on interviews conducted with Albanian diplomats, and as a methodological tool for analysing the collected data employs the empirical indicators of the embodiment of diplomacy developed by Vincent Pouliot.

The study suggests that as a result of increased interactions between the region's countries diplomacy has become an extensive practice, and a platform for social learning for the region's diplomats. However, the fear of violence remains for Albanian diplomats, and despite increased interactions diplomacy is not yet a self-evident practice. Despite the absence of violent conflict for over a decade, the region's countries have not developed the meaningful sense of community and mutual trust which constitutes the fundamental aspect of security communities.

However, the shared desire to profit from the economic opportunities presented by integration and the identification of common transnational threats show that the Western Balkans may constitute a nascent security community. On the other hand, closer cooperation and interaction based on cultural and historical roots indicates the development of subregional Albanian and slavophone communities.

The findings also suggest that although the region's diplomats tend to have developed shared normative values, these values are not particularly influential in defining major policy decisions that could contribute to further improved relations, as these remain mostly the domain of politicians.

The paper is organized as follows: the first section presents an overview of the literature on security communities and diplomacy, followed by an outline of methodological and data collection approaches. The following section discusses the transformations in Albanian diplomatic practice and the embodiment of diplomacy in Western Balkan countries as a way of solving interstate disputes. The final section draws some initial conclusions.

Theoretical framework

The security community concept

As discussed in the introductory chapter of this book, in the case of the Western Balkans the security community is a relevant analytical tool because those countries which were once part of Yugoslavia, an amalgamated security community, are currently engaged in the process of joining pluralistic security communities, the EU and NATO. Since regional cooperation has been set as a key condition for attaining EU and NATO membership, it is of interest to examine whether such conditions have led to the development of mechanisms which are typical for security communities in the nascent and ascendant phase.

Emergence of diplomacy as a profession

Diplomacy has been central to communication between and among civilizations through the ages (Langhorne, 1998; Berridge, 2002; Hölsti, 2004; Neumann, 2005). The modern form of diplomacy has its origins in the Italian city-state system, which by the nineteenth century had grown into a profession requiring specialized knowledge and skills.

At the core of the concept of diplomacy is the idea of communicating, interacting, maintaining contact, and negotiating with states and other international actors. However, as Berridge points out, diplomacy is not simply the accomplishment of interacting and negotiating, 'instead it is the accomplishment of these tasks in such a way that it maximizes the moderating and civilizing effects on the conduct of the states' (Berridge et al., 2001: 5). Berridge stresses that diplomacy will remain essential to the difference between war and peace for as long as power is dispersed among a plurality of states (Berridge et al., 2001: 5).

The development of common diplomatic procedures, structures, routines and norms has led to the institutionalization of diplomacy as a fully-fledged international institution manned by professional diplomats (Bull, 2002; Jönsson and Hall, 2005; Neumann, 2012). The Congress of Vienna (1815) and the Vienna Convention on Diplomatic Relations (1961) rendered diplomatic practice thoroughly institutional and international (Jönsson and Hall, 2005).

The institutionalization of diplomacy has led to the development of a shared language and common practices that allow communication to take place with the minimum of unnecessary misunderstandings between different cultures, as well as establishing a diplomatic dialogue based on codes of interpretation and language shared by members of the diplomatic community (Jönsson and Hall, 2005: 95). Neumann conceptualizes diplomatic culture as an inter-subjective set of symbols and practices, or a 'third culture', which mediates between other cultures and practices, making specific interaction possible (Neumann, 2005). They can 'influence the processes and outcomes by binding decision-makers to a set of concepts and meanings that amount to a new interpretation of reality and also by becoming actors in the process of political selection of their own ideas' (Adler, 1992). Deutsch points out that in the process of the emergence of a security community, certain background conditions are necessary, such as the improbability of war between political units, the spread of intellectual movements that prepare the political climate and the development of the practice of mutual attention, communication and responsiveness (Deutsch, 1968: 281). In this process, diplomats can act to advance policies and ideas (Adler, 1992), while governments consider that coordinating their relations acts to increase mutual security and lower the transaction costs of their exchanges, as well as encouraging further exchanges and interactions (Adler and Barnett, 1998: 40). In nascent security communities, diplomats can play an important role, as they are able to identify areas where mutual benefits can be derived from the coordination of security policies. As agendas are created on the basis of new expectations and values, diplomats are not only in a position to communicate their understanding of issues to state leaders, but can also 'signal their intent on the particular issue at hand' (Adler, 2005: 73).

For instance, after examining NATO's transformation following the Cold War, Adler suggests that the expansion of NATO as a security community occurred via the diffusion of both democratic values and self-restraint subjectivities. This made violence unnecessary, as security officials from Partnership for Peace countries were well-versed in dealing with conflict through compromise, using legal and diplomatic means (Adler, 2008). He thus calls for practices to be placed 'in the driver's seat' when analysing the spread of institutions (Adler, 2008).

In the same vein, Pouliot analyses security communities by looking at the practical logic of day-to-day NATO–Russia diplomacy. He examines the practices of the NATO-Russia Council and suggests that diplomacy is not exclusive to security communities, pointing out that diplomacy is also used as a means of solving disputes in 'insecurity communities'. However, in such cases diplomacy is perceived as merely 'one possibility among others, including violent practices' (Pouliot, 2010: 42).

He stresses that the key distinction between diplomatic practice in security communities and insecurity communities lies in the self-evidence of diplomacy, as 'in a mature security community, diplomacy is the only thinkable way to solve disputes'. In a developed security community, then, states no longer live under the shadow of war (Pouliot, 2010: 42).

Thus, examining the embodiment of diplomacy through the practices of diplomats is relevant for two reasons. First, from their intermediary position between the policy makers of their respective countries and the diplomatic community which shares similar normative and professional values, the diplomats of Western Balkan countries can make a contribution to advancing policies and ideas that encourage interactions and cooperation and ultimately build trust. Second, analysing the practices of Albanian diplomats helps to understand the transition of Albanian diplomacy from the diplomacy of the communist era, which was seen as a means of spreading the communist revolution around the world, to mainstream western diplomacy.

Methodology and collection of data

Given the focus on the practices of diplomats as a professional group, this paper draws on practice theory as the methodological tool for analysing the collected data. Practice theory tends to bring background knowledge to the foreground of analysis and conceives of practices as 'embodied, materially mediated arrays of human activity centrally organized around shared practical understanding' (Schatzki et al., 2001: 11). Barnes points out that 'it is always necessary to ask what disposes people to enact the practices they do, how and when they do; and their aims, their lived experience and their inherited knowledge will surely figure amongst the factors of interest here' (Barnes, 2001: 30).

As discussed above, a new body of international relations literature has emerged which employs practice theory and observes practices performed by practitioners as tools for studying world politics (Neumann, 2002; Pouliot, 2010). The data used for this paper was collected in semi-structured face-to-face interviews conducted with 12 Albanian diplomats in June 2012.[1] The interviewees included senior, mid-level and junior diplomats. At the time of interview, the most senior official interviewed had been with the Foreign Service for 34 years, while the most junior diplomat had joined just four years previously. The average number of years in service was eleven and a half. Four of the interviewees had served at least once as Head of Mission. Nearly half of diplomats interviewed were female, reflecting the current gender balance in the Albanian diplomatic service. More than half of those interviewed either deal with the Western Balkans, covering bilateral or multilateral relations, or have done so in the past, either with the Ministry of Foreign Affairs (MFA) or at embassies. The interviewees were assured of their anonymity, and when quoted they are referred to simply as diplomats or interviewees. Apart from data collected from face-to-face interviews, our analysis also makes use of insights gained from several informal discussions and observations conducted at the Albanian MFA between November 2011 and June 2012.

Empirical evidence

Changes in Albanian diplomatic practice

Before turning to the embodiment of diplomacy in the Western Balkans through the practices of Albanian diplomats it is worth examining briefly the patterns of transformation observable in Albanian diplomatic practice over the past two decades. Thus, this section discusses the changes that took place in diplomatic practice following the end of the Cold War. Analysis of this transformation is relevant as the practices of diplomats during the communist period were determined by the different normative assumptions of communist diplomacy.

After WWII and the communist takeover of the government, Albanian diplomacy assumed the features of communist diplomacy. Promoted by the Soviet Union under Stalin and the Chinese during the Cultural Revolution, communist diplomacy sought to convert diplomats into purveyors of revolution and thus advance the cause of revolution (Hölsti, 2004; Sharp, 2009). Communist diplomatic practice was multifaceted and included party and state relations with communist governments; interstate relations with Western and Western-oriented Third World states; political alliances with states of socialist orientation; party-to-party relations with ruling and non-ruling communist and leftist parties and national liberation groups; and state representation in international organizations and forums (Zickel, 1991: 411–412).

Having almost entirely broken off relations with Western countries, Albania's diplomatic practice up to the mid-1960s was mostly centred on developing and maintaining relations with the countries of the Soviet sphere. The regionally limited diplomatic practice of this period was a combination of multilateralism and bilateralism. Following the split with the Warsaw Pact and the alliance with communist China, Albanian diplomatic practice became predominantly bilateral. With the exception of a limited presence at UN headquarters, Albania abstained from participating in active multilateralism in diplomacy until the end of the Cold War, condemning both NATO and the Warsaw Pact and refusing to participate in the Helsinki process launched in the 1970s (Bashkurti, 2005).

Thus, by the end of the Cold War, Albania had few embassies in Western European countries and kept a low profile in the international arena. It continued to remain faithful to communist diplomatic practice by maintaining relations and exchanges with communist parties in Third World countries and revolutionary factions around the world (Bashkurti, 2007: 313–314). One of the main implications of this foreign policy was a diminished role for diplomats (Bashkurti, 2004: 564) and a decline in the relevance of the diplomatic service, which by 1989 employed only 123 diplomats (Albanian MFA).

This legacy prompted the postcommunist government to undertake major reforms in 1992 with the aim of transforming the diplomatic service and implementing a new course in foreign relations (Starova, 2005: 11–12).

To mark a break with the past, communist-era diplomats were dismissed on a massive scale and replaced by newly recruited diplomats (Starova, 2005: 90).

However, this move produced a drop in professionalism throughout the 1990s and, as data from our interviews suggests, it took nearly one decade for the diplomatic service to regain stability in terms of numbers of staff with diplomatic training.

Our interviews suggest that Albanian diplomacy has broken with communist diplomatic practice and has fully embraced international norms and balanced participation in bilateral and multilateral diplomacy.

Analysis of recruitment and training practices reveals that diplomatic practice is driven by concern for the norms and rules of international law and diplomacy. In order to improve the knowledge base of diplomats, from early 2000 onwards there was a drive to recruit graduates in international relations and political science. The preference has been to recruit diplomats who have 'studied abroad', a recurrent narrative of line managers, who were keen to demonstrate that the professionalism of diplomats was increasing as a result of this recruitment pattern.

Another indication of the desire to change practices was revealed by the 'internationalization' of diplomatic training. Although the Albanian MFA has a diplomatic academy, all the diplomats interviewed pointed out that it mostly plays the role of 'coordinating' training with other diplomatic academies. A host of countries, including Austria, Germany, Italy, the Netherlands, Japan, China, Egypt, Turkey, Malaysia and more recently Brazil and South Korea, as well as international organizations, were mentioned as places where Albanian diplomats receive basic or tailored diplomatic training.

Analysis of the interview data shows a focus on Euro-Atlantic relations and regional cooperation. Currently, 38 of the 50 Albanian diplomatic missions abroad are located in Europe or North America. Regional cooperation has been prioritized by policy makers, and this has been reflected in promotion and posting practices. Despite their closeness and small size, Albania has embassies in all six of the region's countries. Interviewees revealed that successful diplomats now want to be sent to embassies in the region because they see it as an opportunity to further their careers. This represents a huge shift in Albanian diplomacy, which has traditionally viewed its neighbours as a threat, which it has continuously striven to counterbalance by establishing relations with larger world powers such as the Soviet Union in the early years of the Cold War, China in the 1970s and the USA in the 1990s.

Embodiment of diplomacy in the Western Balkans

Based on analysis of the interview data and the practices of Albanian diplomats, this section examines the embodiment of diplomacy in relations between the countries of the Western Balkans. The ultimate goal is to evaluate whether, from the point of view of practitioners, the region has left behind its predisposition to conflict and developed into a security community. As Adler points out, 'peace is the practice of a security community' when its 'members/inhabitants *practise* peaceful change and [the fact] that the use of force has become unimaginable has been internalized by individuals and embedded in practices' (Adler, 2005: 15).

In order to operationalize the data collected, we employ the empirical indicators for the embodiment of diplomacy developed by Pouliot. These are: (1) the unavailability of the option of using force, (2) the normalization of disputes and (3) daily cooperation on the ground.

The first indicator is concerned with examining the inaccessibility of mutual confrontation as a means of solving disputes, while the second is concerned with determining whether practitioners consider disagreements as part of normal practice and diplomacy as the best way to solve them, while the third indicator is concerned with the nature and focus of practitioner's interactions.

Our analysis is based on the dual assumption that diplomacy is not exclusive to security communities and that different degrees of embodiment of diplomacy lead to a variety of interstate relations in and through practice (Pouliot, 2010: 42). Pouliot makes the distinction between diplomatic practices in four communities by looking at the dimensions of intensity and self-evidence. In war communities, diplomacy is intense and goes hand in hand with organized violence; in insecure communities diplomacy is less intense, and remains under the threat of organized violence; in non-war communities diplomacy is extensively practised and becomes a normalized practice; in security communities diplomacy becomes a self-evident practice on the basis of which all further interactions take place, thus its intensity is reduced (Pouliot, 2010: 43).

Unavailability of the use of force option

In order to assess this indicator, we asked the following questions: Do you consider that the Western Balkans has passed into a phase where violence is excluded as a means of solving disputes? Is military confrontation still an option? Do you think that scenarios of mutual violence are still considered a possible means for Western Balkan countries to achieve foreign policy objectives? Does any country in the Western Balkans pose a security threat to the others? Do you think there are gaps between declared positions taken by the countries of the Western Balkans and practical actions taken by them?

The pattern observed in the interview data is that all diplomats consider that diplomacy has become a dominant practice in the Western Balkans. The engagement of Serbia and Kosovo in diplomatic talks was referred to recurrently by the majority of the diplomats as an illustration of this trend, along with the conviction that Serbia and Kosovo will 'engage further' in diplomatic talks with each other in the future. However, despite this trend, the diplomats do not think that diplomacy has become the only means for resolving interstate disputes. For example, interviewees' responses included: 'I wish it were the case but I don't believe that scenarios of violence can be excluded' (MD3, 13 June 2012); 'It is very difficult for the region to make a clean break with past conflicts' (FD1, 11 June 2012); 'The fear of violence is [still] there' (MD2, 8 June 2012); 'Any given society has elements that favour conflict, but I see that it goes beyond that' (FD5, 14 June 2012).

Many mentioned 'the difficulty of breaking with the past' as the main reason for their thinking. The diplomats questioned felt that it has been easier to use diplomacy as a means of dealing with issues pertaining to current developments or future prospects than to tackle issues which are rooted in the past. As one interviewee put it, 'History still matters a lot for the region's countries'. The majority of interviewees referred to relations between Serbia and Kosovo or Macedonia and Greece to illustrate this, as well as mentioning that nationalism remains strongly embedded in mainstream politics.

However, the majority of interviewees did not envisage military engagement or the outbreak of conventional war. Most interviewees gave the 'presence of NATO in the region' and the 'number of security cooperation formats' in which all the region's countries are engaged as arguments to explain the remoteness of the possibility that any country would resort to conventional warfare. The nature of the threats they discussed was the possible combination of the region's endogenous problems (including nationalism and economic recession) with exogenous factors, (such as influences and pressures from the outside world). These, they think, are what could lead to unpredictable developments.

Nevertheless, some variations in the thinking of the diplomats interviewed could be identified. This variation seemed to depend on the length of time they had spent dealing with regional affairs and their level of direct involvement with the region. Junior diplomats and those with less regional experience were inclined to consider such scenarios as being theoretical options rather than real threats to peace. Some of their answers included: 'Violence is disappearing from the vocabulary of the region's diplomacy' (MD6, 14 June 2012), 'Diplomacy in the region prevails independently of rhetoric' (FD4, 11 June 2012), or, as one put it to express the remoteness of the possibility of violence, 'Yes it can happen, but only if someone goes crazy' (FD3, 13 June 2012).

The main reason given by the majority of diplomats for this 'unprecedented' level of bilateral relations and regional cooperation was the shared goal of EU integration. However, a few diplomats were keen to point out that alongside the EU factor there has been also an increase in the countries' awareness stemming from lessons learned in past conflicts. As one diplomat asserted, 'none of the countries is interested in conflicts anymore' (MD1, 14 June 2012).

All of the interviewees affirmed that they do not see Albania as representing a threat to any of its neighbours. Many referred to Albania's position as a moderator and promoter of good neighbourhood policy. They also pointed out that steps have been taken to render Albanian minorities in neighbouring countries factors of stability. They referred to the new practice of tasking Albanian diplomats serving in the region with maintaining regular contact and communication with Albanian political parties and communities in neighbouring countries in order to promote this belief.

The interviewed diplomats also mentioned that the experience of cooperation has revealed 'more cooperative' and 'more reliable' countries. Croatia and Montenegro and, more recently, Kosovo are seen by Albanian diplomats as the most reliable partners, while Serbia is regarded as the most 'difficult to deal with' and at times 'unpredictable' (FD5, 14 June 2012). Similarly, mixed perceptions were expressed towards Macedonia and BiH.

Normalization of disputes

In order to assess this indicator, we asked the following questions: Why do you think disputes still occur in the Western Balkans? Do you think diplomacy will be the norm in solving disputes and in conducting interstate relations between Western Balkan countries? Do you think security cooperation has become normal practice in the Western Balkans? Why do you think Western Balkan countries cooperate with each other?

The main finding was that Albanian diplomats do not think that there will be a return to the way in which disputes were solved prior to 2000. Diplomacy is considered to have evolved as the norm for solving disputes, although this does not apply equally to all countries. The major normalising factors are considered to be 'NATO and EU integration processes', the 'lessons learned from the past' and the 'better economic prospects' that cooperation has produced. The reasons which still prevent disputes from being treated as the normal business of diplomacy are felt to be the 'lack of experience of cooperation' and the fact that political actors pursue actions that yield immediate 'political gains' in the domestic arena.

All of the interviewees were of the opinion that relations between the region's countries have improved steadily and that countries have already started to learn 'how to agree to disagree' when they interact with each other. As one diplomat put it: 'To have disagreements is normal business; in 80 per cent of cases we easily manage to find a common language, but then there is the other 20 per cent' (FD1, 11 June 2012).

Enhanced interaction and socialization between diplomats and political elites and the benefits of solving issues through diplomacy have meant that disputes increasingly belong to normal diplomatic business. Some diplomats recalled how they now 'treat as normal' any issue with their Croatian and Macedonian colleagues and pointed out how much things have changed compared with the difficulties they faced in the years immediately following the launch of the Adriatic Charter in 2003. Another diplomat referred to the way Albania and Macedonia handled the case of the murder of five Macedonian fishermen and the consequent damage to interethnic relations, highlighting that a few years earlier 'the countries would have dealt with such a case quite differently'.

However, they believe that not all of the region's countries treat disputes as normal business. With some countries the process has been slower or intermittent. One diplomat referred to the negotiations between Albania and Serbia for mutual recognition of university diplomas which stalled in 2002, although they described the issue as being 'purely technical and beneficial to both countries' (FD5, 14 June 2012). Yet diplomacy was referred to as a normalising factor even when cooperation is inhibited by politicized relations because, as one diplomat pointed out, 'It is part of a diplomat's job to moderate the rhetoric of statements made by political leaders' (MD2, 8 June 2012).

According to diplomats, a lack of 'previous experience of cooperation' and a 'lack of mutual trust' make cooperation more difficult from the outset. Many diplomats referred to a lack of prior cooperation not only to demonstrate the difficulties in normalising relations but also to highlight the progress that has been made. One of them pointed out that 'Balkan countries used to do things together very rarely … this is a new exercise, a new experience … we had no experience in communicating with Serbia before … the most important thing is to build trust … we are trying to identify common projects in order to start trusting each other'. Another diplomat referred to the opening of Albania's embassy in Sarajevo in 2010, and the 'pressure exerted by diplomats to convince decision-makers to open the embassy despite the financial constraints' by arguing that relations with BiH had remained underdeveloped compared with the other countries.

Some diplomats alluded to the negative consequences of political rhetoric even when it is used to promote cooperation. As one diplomat mentioned, 'Many political statements are made to impress which are not followed by concrete actions' (FD1, 11 June 2012), highlighting the risk that the credibility of commitments could be undermined by such overstatements.

One of the main achievements mentioned was security cooperation, which diplomats believe has advanced considerably in 'many areas' and has 'made a contribution to building trust' among the region's countries. Many of the interviewees considered Macedonia to be a 'de facto member of NATO' and felt that 'half of the region is now part of NATO'. Confidence built through arms control processes and participation in a number of security cooperation formats were mentioned as factors contributing to further consolidation of trust and practices through which diplomacy has gained more and more ground.

Confidence that NATO and EU membership are the final destination for all of the region's countries led some diplomats to refer to pragmatism as a reason for further normalization of disputes. With regards to the border dispute between Croatia and Slovenia, one diplomat pointed out that countries cooperate because they 'don't want to be blocked by others in membership processes' (MD7, 15 June 2012), while others mentioned Greece's veto on NATO membership for Macedonia (MD2, 8 June 2012; MD5, 14 June 2012).

Cooperation between diplomats

In order to assess this indicator, we asked the following questions: How does the interstate relations background affect interaction? Is the establishment of informal relations with diplomats from Western Balkan countries normal practice? What are the challenges facing Albanian diplomats when they deal with Western Balkan countries?

Throughout the cold war Albania remained a hard-line communist state with an isolationist foreign policy that led to underdeveloped relations with its neighbours, including Yugoslavia. Due to the ongoing conflict in former Yugoslavia these relations remained limited throughout the 1990s. Albanian diplomats' contacts with the region were confined to limited bilateral relations and some interaction within the framework of international organizations, mainly the UN, the Council of Europe and the OSCE. Thus, the launch of the Euro-Atlantic integration processes and the regional cooperation policy was an unprecedented opportunity for increased interaction between Albanian diplomats and their colleagues from the region's other countries.

Such interactions and socialization have led to a growing sense of common purpose among the region's diplomats and the emergence of a new type of relation that, as a number of interviewees pointed out, has been facilitated by 'cultural and bureaucratic similarities'. Given that EU and NATO integration processes have entailed a number of reforms in the domestic arena, the traditional division between internal and external domains has become blurred. As one diplomat put it, 'I never imagined that as diplomat I would deal with issues like organized crime, money laundering, finances or electoral reform' (FD3, 13 June 2012). The involvement of diplomats in internal as well as external domains, combined with a similar set of problems faced by the region's countries, has contributed to the identification of a set of problems that are seen as 'typical of the region'. Diplomats describe a sense of 'regional identity' that is stronger when 'we are away from the region' (FD2, 11 June 2012).

Moreover, analysis of our data suggests that diplomats have similar professional values to their counterparts and a tendency to distance themselves from the kind of politics that frequently obstructs faster and deeper regional cooperation. The manner in which one diplomat expressed his solidarity with a Macedonian colleague was revealing: 'I still remember the [sad] faces of my Macedonian colleagues at the Bucharest summit when Macedonia failed to get the invitation ... they had done so much [to get the NATO invitation] but ultimately they were let down by politics (FD3, 13 June 2012)'.

Analysis of our data suggests that diplomats enjoy increasing influence, chiefly as a result of the rising number of issues that, being 'technical' in nature, 'constrain' political decision-makers to either delegate decision making to diplomats or adopt the positions or suggestions which they make. As a result, as one diplomat put it, 'A group of untouchable diplomats has been created over the last few years as a result of their consolidated experience gained from serving both abroad and in the MFA' (FD5, 14 June 2012). These diplomats have been increasingly given assignments related to priority policy issues such as regional cooperation, NATO and EU affairs. Although the interviewees could not specify the extent to which this trend has spread, they confirmed that there are 'great similarities between the region's countries' (FD5, 14 June 2012) in this respect.

All of the interviewees mentioned the ease with which informal and personal relations have developed among the region's diplomats. They identified this tendency as one of the 'typical features of the region's diplomats' (MD4, 13 June 2012), regardless of nationality and ethnicity. The tendency to mix and socialize prevails even when the respective ministries require diplomats to maintain rigid positions.

The account of a junior diplomat about a regional seminar was revealing: 'When the Kosovar diplomat gave his business card to his Serbian colleague, the latter refused to accept it ... but later on in the pub the Serb told the Kosovar "I'm sorry for earlier ... but you know, I have nothing against you ... it's state policy"' (MD7, June 15, 2012).

However, the data shows that ethnicity remains relevant and continues to influence the way diplomats behave. Interviewees referred to cases when 'Macedonians and sometimes Bosnians' tended to support Serbian proposals in multilateral negotiations, 'just for the sake of Slavic solidarity' (MD1, 14 June 2012). Similarly, during seminar breaks or at formal gatherings, Albanian, Kosovar and Macedonian diplomats of Albanian heritage tend to group together and the same is true of Slavic speaking diplomats.

Conclusion

This chapter has adopted the embodiment of diplomacy as the key concept for tracking the emergence of a security community in the Western Balkans. The chapter shows that diplomacy has become normal practice among the countries of the Western Balkans and is widely accepted as the only way to ensure peace and social and economic development. Disputes between countries are viewed more and more as normal business, although deep disagreements remain on issues related to history and the use of nationalism as a means of pursuing political goals. The increased interactions between the diplomats that have taken place in the last decade within the framework of both bilateral and multilateral relations have significantly contributed to the development of interpersonal relations. This has led to diplomats identifying more strongly and on a professional level with the region as a community. Nevertheless, although improved interpersonal ties occasionally contribute to the pace of communication and interactions, the influence of diplomats still remains weak in terms of influence over the course of actions taken by governments. Yet, despite the fact that the countries are involved in a social learning process that has produced positive effects; the region has not developed into a security community where diplomacy is seen as the only option. The fact that the fear of violence has not fully disappeared from practitioners' sight reveals that diplomacy has not become self-evident and commonsensical, that is to say it is not yet the practice on the basis of which all further interactions take place (Pouliot, 2010: 1). Furthermore, our findings suggest that the possibility of using force has not entirely disappeared and practitioners reveal a sense of insecurity and unpredictability.

In terms of theoretical implications, the disaggregation of the concept of a security community reveals two different dimensions. Although the absence of war, accompanied by an unprecedented level of diplomatic interactions and engagement in various forms of security cooperation, has produced a certain level of assurances of peaceful change, the 'community' dimension remains less developed. Instead of a common regional identity, study of diplomats' practices sheds light on the emergence of subregional identities such as the Albanian and Slavic speaking communities, NATO and non-NATO members and the variety of geometries of interactions that stems from closeness or distance depending on the issues. In terms of security community formation, this is problematic because a collective identity (Adler and Barnett, 1998) or the 'we feeling' (Deutsch, 1968) constitutes the underlying factor that holds security communities together. Another aspect with theoretical implications relates to the conditions that precipitate the building of a security community. While the theory of security communities suggests that the point of departure in the building of a security community comes from the members of the community itself (Deutsch, 1968), evidence shows that in case of the Western Balkans it is mainly external factors that have spurred on and continue to steer the process. Rather than being motivated by the prospect of building a security community, the process is driven by the desire to become part of security communities that extend beyond the region. Thus, regional integration is perceived as a temporary process rather than the end goal. However, additional research into this subject that can integrate data from diplomats in the region's other countries is needed in order to cross-examine and further validate these findings.

Note

1 The authors conducted the interviews in the Albanian language between 8 and 15 June 2012. Transcription and translation of interviews were also carried out by the authors.

Bibliography

Adler, E, "The Emergence of Cooperation: National Epistemic Communities and the International Evolution of the Idea of Nuclear Arms Control" in *International Organization* 46:1 (1992): 101–145.

Adler, E, *Communitarian International Relations: The Epistemic Foundations of International Relations*, Routledge, 2005.

Adler, E, "The Spread of Security Communities: Communities of Practice, Self-Restraint, and NATO's Post-Cold War Transformation" in *European Journal of International Relations* 14:2 (2008): 195–230.

Adler, E and Barnett, M (eds), *Security Communities*, Cambridge University Press, 1998.

Albanian MFA, "Historiku i Krijimit të Institucionit të Ministrisë së Punëve të Jashtme të Shtetit Shqiptar [The History of the Establishment of the Institution of the Ministry of Foreign Affairs of the Albanian State]", available at: www.punetejashtme.gov.al/files/userfiles/historiku_shtator_2017.pdf

Barnes, B, "Practice as Collective Action" in Cetina, KK, Schatzki, TR and von Savigny, E (eds), *The Practice Turn in Contemporary Theory*, Routledge, 2001.

Bashkurti, L, *Diplomacia Shqiptare Ndërmjet të Kaluarës dhe të Ardhmes*, Tiranë:Geer, 2004.

Bashkurti, L, *Diplomacia Shqiptare* (Vol. 1), Tiranë:Geer, 2005.

Bashkurti, L, *Negociatat: Historia, Teoria, Praktikat*, Tiranë:Geer, 2007.

Bátora, J, *Foreign Ministries and the Information Revolution: Going Virtual?* (Vol. 2), Martinus Nijhoff, 2008.

Berridge, GR, Keens-Soper, M and Otte, TG, *Diplomatic Theory From Machiavelli to Kissinger*, Palgrave, 2001.
Berridge, GR, *Diplomacy: Theory and Practice* (Second Edition), Palgrave, 2002.
Bull, H, *The Anarchical Society: A Study of Order in World Politics*, Columbia University Press, 2002.
Deutsch, KW, *The Analysis of International Relations*, Englewood Cliffs, New Jersey: Prentice-Hall, 1968.
Haxhinasto, E, "Reforms in Diplomacy – the Challenges of the Ministry of Foreign Affairs for 2012", report presented by the Minister of Foreign Affairs to the Albanian Parliament, December 2011.
Hocking, B, "Multistakeholder Diplomacy: Forms, Functions and Frustrations" in Kurbalija, J and Katrandijev, V (eds), *Multistakeholder Diplomacy: Challenges and Opportunities*, Diplo-Foundation (2006): 13–29.
Hölsti, KJ, *Taming the Sovereigns*, Cambridge University Press, 2004.
Jönsson, C and Hall, M, *Essence of Diplomacy*, Palgrave Macmillan, 2005.
Kappeler, D, "Diplomacy of Tomorrow: New Developments, New Methods, New Tools" in Kurbalija, J (ed.), *Knowledge and Diplomacy*, DiploProjects, 1999.
Langhorne, R, "History and the Evolution of Diplomacy" in Jovan, K (ed.), *Modern Diplomacy*, Mediterranean Academy of Diplomatic Studies, University of Malta, 1998.
Neumann, IB, "Returning practice to the linguistic turn: The case of diplomacy" in *Millennium*, 31:3 (2002): 627–651.
Neumann, IB, "To be a Diplomat" in *International Studies Perspectives* 6:1 (2005): 72–93.
Neumann, IB, *At Home with the Diplomats: Inside a European Foreign Ministry*, Cornell University Press, 2012.
Pouliot, V, "The Logic of Practicality: A Theory of Practice of Security Communities" in *International Organization* 62:2 (2008): 257.
Pouliot, V, *International Security in Practice: The Politics of NATO-Russia Diplomacy*, Cambridge University Press, 2010.
Schatzki, TR, Knorr Cetina, K and von Savigny, E (eds), *The Practice Turn in Contemporary Theory*, Routledge, 2001.
Sharp, P, *Diplomatic Theory of International Relations* (Vol. 2), Cambridge University Press, 2009.
Starova, A, *Nëpër Hapësirat e Politikës së Jashtme e të Diplomacisë në Vitet 1992–2004*, Tiranë: Silver, 2005.
Zickel, RE (ed.), *Soviet Union, a Country Study*, Bernan Assoc., 1991.

Interviews

FD1, personal interview by authors with female diplomat, tape recorded, Tirana, June 11, 2012.
FD2, personal interview by authors with female diplomat, tape recorded, Tirana, June 11, 2012.
FD3, personal interview by authors with female diplomat, tape recorded, Tirana, June 13, 2012.
FD4, personal interview by authors with female diplomat, tape recorded, Tirana, June 11 2012.
FD5, personal interview by authors with female diplomat, tape recorded, Tirana, June 14, 2012.
MD1, personal interview by authors with male diplomat, tape recorded, Tirana, June 15, 2012.

MD2, personal interview by authors with male diplomat, tape recorded, Tirana, June 8, 2012.
MD3, personal interview by authors with male diplomat, tape recorded, Tirana, June 13, 2012.
MD4, personal interview by authrs with male diplomat, tape recorded, Tirana, June 13, 2012.
MD5, personal interview by authors with male diplomat, tape recorded, Tirana, June 14, 2012.
MD6, personal interview by authors with male diplomat, tape recorded, Tirana, June 14, 2012.
MD7, personal interview by authors with male diplomat, tape recorded, Tirana, June 15, 2012

3

FROM COMMUNITY OF PRACTICE TO SECURITY COMMUNITY IN THE WESTERN BALKANS

A role for the armed forces of Bosnia and Herzegovina

Kenan Dautović

Introduction

The term 'military' is most commonly used to talk about the exercise of state power and international relations in the broader sense. One particular aspect of this definition which rarely attracts much attention is the concept of civil-military relations. In this context the term 'military' refers to a profession which, while sharing a number of attributes with other professions, also has some specific characteristics of its own. It is generally believed that militaries exhibit a very high level of interoperability, which makes them highly suitable for all types of joint tasks. The notion of interoperability covers the possibility of conducting joint operations, but above all it provides the platform on which trust can be built. For example, this characteristic lies at the very heart of the concept of 'partnership for peace' through which NATO attempts to engage with its former adversaries.

Furthermore, the way the military routinely operates presupposes a high degree of interaction and practical work. Such routines or military practices are known as 'standard operational procedures' or 'techniques, tactics and procedures' (TTP), which implies that the military can be seen as a kind of community of practice. At the same time, this common knowledge and expertise reflects the very core of the military as a profession, which leads to the conclusion that the military profession represents a community of practice in its own right.

Anticipating the possible interplay between three key concepts, the 'military profession', 'community of practice' and 'security community', within the framework of the Western Balkans, this chapter therefore argues that regional military professionals, in practising daily cooperation, create a community of practice which consequently helps to foster a regional security community.

Relying on practice theory and looking at processes as well as at practice as a 'meaning in use and not using the meaning' (Andersen, 2011), this case study encompasses empirical research[1] on the Armed Forces of Bosnia and Herzegovina (AFBiH) through the means of semi-structured interviews and participant observations, supplemented by statistical data related to regional cooperation taking place at the Peace Support Operations Training Centre (PSOTC).

The AFBiH is a relevant unit of analysis as it developed from the three former warring armies which emerged from the terrible war of 1992–5. Consequently, regional cooperation in the case of Bosnia and Herzegovina (BiH) is a more a matter of internal than foreign affairs. The involvement of neighbouring countries in the conflict of the 1990s, and the level of influence they still exert on some elements in AFBiH, additionally accentuates this dimension. Also, AFBiH has a leading role in BiH's efforts to attain membership of NATO, and, to a lesser degree, the EU. Regional cooperation is one of the crucial requirements for this process.

The chapter starts with a theoretical discussion of the three main concepts, focusing on their common ground and mutual relations. This part is intended to facilitate better understanding of the theoretical framework surrounding these three concepts and determine whether a community of practice can serve as the meeting point between the military profession and the security community. The next section examines how military professionals in BiH understand, conduct and learn about regional cooperation. The main goal of this part is to comprehend the motivations which drive practitioners when they cooperate at the regional level and to determine when the practice of cooperation can contribute to security community-building. This section thus focuses on identifying practices which are performed because of practitioners' background knowledge, differentiating them from practices created and conducted by practitioners themselves. The concluding remarks then compares these practices with Deutsch's 'three tiers' of security community, in order to situate the Western Balkan security community within the theoretical framework.

Linking the three concepts

The military was originally considered to be merely a job, a way of earning a living, whether in a permanent or temporary capacity; organized or occasional. As a way of earning money, military service does not necessarily relate to the state, since there are plenty of services which can be offered on the basis of daily or hourly pay. However, if the term 'job' is qualified by the term 'organization' it becomes elevated to the next level – an 'occupation'. Finally, if an organized job (an occupation) is institutionalized and accorded expertise and jurisdiction by the state it becomes a profession.

A more scholarly definition classes a profession as a 'knowledge based occupation' (Macdonald, 1995: 160), describing it as 'a relatively homogeneous community whose members share identity, values, definitions of role, and interests' (Bucher and Strauss, 1961: 325) consisting of institutions, organization, personnel, recruitment policies, standards, codes and relations with the public.

Two important conclusions may already be drawn at this point. First, the military is simultaneously a job, an occupation and a profession. Second, it can be also said that the military profession falls into a 'domain of knowledge' that not only constitutes 'like-mindedness' but is also developed, shared, and maintained by a 'community of people that creates the social fabric of learning, meeting the requirements of being a typical community of practice' (Adler, 2008: 196; Wenger et al., 2002: 28–29). As such, the military has moved from being a community of practice whose members try to earn a living, to an organized and highly institutionalized community of people practising military skills as a profession.

Apart from these two features, it is necessary to briefly touch upon some of the military professional dimensions that are most relevant for the main topic of this chapter. In his 'essentialist' model', Huntington (1957: 7–8) suggests that what really differentiates the military from other professions is its expertise, responsibility and 'corporateness'.

Two main approaches to the concept of expertise have been defined. Huntington equates the military profession with 'officership', arguing that the very essence of officers' expertise is the 'management of violence'. On the other hand, Harries-Jenkins (1990: 122) and Janowitz (1974) insist on the diversity of the occupational tasks performed by the armed forces. These authors thus support Moskos (1986), who suggests that there is a trend in which officership shifts from a relatively monolithic professional group to a diverse conglomerate of specialized experts. Regardless of which approach is taken, this expertise, as it is broadly understood, makes background knowledge of the military an ingredient of the community of practice.

Huntington's (1957: 16) reading of 'corporateness' proposes that officership represents 'a public bureaucratic profession' which is open to a carefully prepared and limited body of potential members. It is thus placed in the category of 'an autonomous social unit' or, for Janowitz (1974), a 'social institution with extensive integration'. As well as the formal structures of the armed forces, officer corps includes societies, associations, schools, journals, customs and traditions, while military uniforms and ranks make a symbolic distinction between officers and civilians. Further, it represents a collective feeling of 'organic unity; of all members of the profession, articulated as a 'consciousness of themselves as a group apart from laymen' (Huntington, 1957: 10). This 'collective feeling' primarily serves the purpose of creating an internal group identity. However, it could also serve as the basis for trans-national understanding, thus articulating a kind of international group identity.

Following this short elaboration on the military as a profession, we can assert that the military is a group of people who share norms, values and understandings, possess common knowledge and expertise and are able to extend their 'we-feeling' across national borders, thus facilitating the process of international cooperation.

Linking the concepts of the military profession and the security community, it is important to highlight that Van Wagenen (1965: 819) accords particular significance to two aspects of the security community: cooperation, as the encouragement of 'closer compatibility of values', and security, as the environment of 'peaceful coexistence'. Another important aspect of this relationship was examined by Adler and Barnett (1996: 75), who stated that reciprocity relates to the attainment of a shared understanding of decision making that eliminates 'the use of violence as a means of statecraft'. This underscores the importance of cooperation and reciprocity when setting the stage for the next concept – the community of practice.

More specifically, analysis of international practices also faces the issue of corporate practices that are both 'structured and acted out by communities of practice', in which background knowledge is diffused among its agents (Adler and Pouliot, 2011: 9). Corporate practices are not the action of one corporate agent (a state, for example) but that of 'a community of representatives whose members enter in patterned relations, within an organized social context, thanks to similar background dispositions' (Adler and Pouliot, 2011: 10). This is exactly where the concept of security community meets the concept of community of practice.

When it comes to the ways certain practices are understood, performed, and/or learned there is a somewhat different dynamic. Building on Bourdieu's theory of practice as consisting of the triad of 'habitus', 'field' and 'practical sense' (Bourdieu, 1990; 2001; Bourdieu and Wacquant, 1992), Pouliot tried to develop a theory of practice for security communities, arguing that in social and political reality many practices suffer from a representational bias because they do not primarily derive from an instrumental rationality (logic of consequences), norm-following (logic of appropriateness), or communicative action (logic of arguing), focusing rather on 'what agents think about instead of what they think from' (Pouliot, 2008: 257). This 'thinking from' approach very often yields practices that are not instrumental but rather are self-evident or common sense. However, given that social reality is inseparably linked to background knowledge, it is almost inconceivable to imagine a situation which is purely commonsensical or belongs solely to one or more of the other three logics. In practice, these four logics are interwoven and their relationship is complementary rather than mutually exclusive.

Elaborating further on his theory, Pouliot criticizes Adler's argument that 'peace is the practice of a security community' (Adler, 2005: 15), asserting that there is 'more to peace than representations' and that peace is also a very 'practical relation' which is characterized, among other things, by 'nonviolent dealings' (Pouliot, 2008: 278). In the case of a security community, Pouliot reiterates Adler and Barnett's view of trust as the second constituent foundation of security communities, defining it as 'believing despite uncertainty'. This represents an excellent example of an 'inarticulate feeling derived from practical sense' (ibid.). Hence, Pouliot points out that because of their personal and collective history (habitus), and faced with a particular social context (field), security practitioners 'feel' (practical sense) able to believe despite uncertainty. Informed by the logic of practicality, they simply trust their security community counterparts (ibid.).

AFBiH and regional cooperation in the Western Balkans – practical experience

Before elaborating on the research findings, it is important to undertake a short methodological reflection on practice theory. Even though I have presented key theoretical considerations, the empirical part of the study will not seek a stable set of properties that confirm the existence of phenomena. Instead, in accordance with practice theory, it will look at processes where objects are continuously produced and where practices dominate participants' behaviour.

Understanding regional cooperation

In assessing the conditions which influence regional cooperation I have first identified 'intervening' factors. Although such factors may be closely allied with Deutsch's 'background' and/or Adler and Barnett's 'precipitating conditions', my conceptualization offers a somewhat wider framework, including not only 'permissive' factors, those that work in favour of regional cooperation, but also those that are perceived as impediments.

I have classified all the permissive factors identified during my research as either 'pushing' or 'pulling' factors, which I have then further subdivided into external and internal factors.

External pushing factors are mostly global security threats and challenges, while the most prominent internal pushing factor is the shrinkage of state budgets. Also, as suggested by respondent 7, in the case of the Western Balkans, regional cooperation is aimed at 'resolving many unresolved atavisms while reconciling formerly warring nations and teaching them how to resolve their conflicts in a peaceful manner'.

External pulling factors are mainly related to the attractiveness of Euro-Atlantic integration through the provision of a common security umbrella. Internal pulling factors are probably the most contested group of factors, since they are related to the least measurable values. Nevertheless, they are among the most frequently mentioned. For example, a rich history of coexistence in the Western Balkans is manifested by 'a similar culture, similar customs, and the same language background' (respondent 1), and by a situation in which 'the majority of people know each other, enabling personal contacts to facilitate cooperation' (respondent 16). Finally, regional cooperation is grounded in the natural desire to maintain good neighbourly relations and share experience, personally and professionally.

These internal pulling factors are confirmed to some extent by some findings from the two sets of observations of participants. For example, it was obvious that the use of a local language had a key role, regardless of whether participants were in mono- or multi-ethnic groups. Albanians tended to remain isolated because of the language barrier, although this may not be the only reason. Another influencing factor was the fact that most participants already knew each other as many of them attended unified military academies during Yugoslav times or from previous joint activities. This all contributed greatly to the creation of a relaxed atmosphere, where even body language was a strong sign of trust among regional participants.

Nevertheless, probably the most important factor, covering both the external and internal extremes of pulling and pushing factors alike, is national interest. Interviewees mentioned that most of the region's countries are relatively small, and thus have very limited capacity to develop their own defence and security capabilities. This is why they are very keen to pool resources, increase efficiency and exchange experience and knowledge in many fields. By doing so, the region's countries not only build mutual trust as *conditio sine qua non* for long lasting peace and stability, but they also help each other to meet the prerequisites for joining Euro-Atlantic structures, an official goal for them all. The only alternative to such an approach would be an 'out of area' approach, which would mean 'living in isolation and economic stagnation, either as a country or as a region' (respondent 20).

However, it would be misleading to list only permissive factors, as there is a whole array of constraining factors that are seen as obstacles to regional cooperation. These obstacles can be classified as political, financial, administrative, legal, cultural, social and historical issues.

Political factors represent an unparalleled challenge to the process of regional cooperation. For example, 'some political leaders lack sincerity in the way that they proclaim certain attitudes but do not follow this up with effective work' (respondent 13). They may also have 'different perceptions of how the region should look', while some still 'dream up (and pursue) irredentist projects' (respondent 3). There are also 'differences in the level of ambition regarding NATO membership' (respondent 15) which sometimes contribute to subtle disagreements. Since most of the region has not completed its transition process, respondent 18 suggests that 'insufficient democratization of the region' still has some negative political influence. Apart from inherently regional political dynamics, the 'influence great powers exert over the region' (respondent 17) should not be overlooked at any time.

The biggest administrative obstacle, according to respondents 2, 16, and 19, is found in slow and bureaucratic state apparatus, particularly those of the security and defence agencies, which are usually seen as bureaucratic organizations. The failure to 'bring all war crimes fugitives to justice' (respondent 13) probably represents the greatest legal impediment to the reconciliation process. The most prominent social obstacle is undoubtedly 'general poverty' (respondent 7). The historical dimension is dominated by the view of most respondents (3, 4, 5, 7, 8, 10, 11, 12, 13, 14, 19, and 20) that efforts to achieve a common understanding of the recent bitter experiences have failed to alter the prejudices and preconceptions of ordinary citizens. Course participants were observed to handle this sensitive topic by simply avoiding it.

This fairly extensive examination of intervening variables is intended to identify the factors which are relevant when discussing regional cooperation as a process. At the same time, the continuous interaction between 'pushing' and 'pulling' factors confirms that social relations change continuously in a manner which depends on the product of two opposing vectors. It seems that for AFBiH professionals, factors which are permissive for regional cooperation prevail. Nevertheless, underlying this big picture are layers of so-called national interest, which adversely affect any kind of simple generalization. In effect, then, all of the region's countries use regional cooperation only to the extent that it converges with national interest.

In order to complete the picture about general factors I have examined how practitioners interpret the roles of military professionals as conducive or impeding factors which influence regional cooperation. Interviewees conveyed thoughts about loyalty, professional solidarity and cooperation.

For our respondents, loyalty to their countries and the national interest is essential to military professionals, representing a precondition for their professionalism. This attitude is also a common component of the mindset of citizens of any country. In reality this is a multidimensional phenomenon, since loyalty is not only felt for the country served by the armed forces, but also for one's people or nation, region and family, among other groups. All these loyalties exist simultaneously. Further explaining the meaning of loyalty, interviewees stressed that although loyalty 'exists simultaneously in various spheres, the first priority is patriotism and loyalty to the state' (respondent 18). More precisely, loyalty to the country means loyalty to the state, to a civilian chain of command, to one's superior and to the ordinary soldier.

Cooperation and solidarity between the members of a profession is a potential influencing factor for establishing and conducting certain types of practices within the regional cooperation framework. According to interviewees, such practices include 'the working culture, readiness to cooperate and communicate within the profession and readiness to help each other' (respondents 10, 16, and 19). For respondent 14, solidarity begins 'when one or both sides exhibit full professionalism'. Respondents insisted that this is even more relevant in the military profession, as a uniform always projects a sense of affiliation to a certain profession and identity. The military is also governed by certain laws and regulations, of which professional solidarity is part. Furthermore, this is a very dangerous profession at times, and its members are highly dependent on each other. On missions in particular, a great deal of tolerance and a willingness to help one other are manifested. The same is true for certain sub-professions such as aviation or mine clearance.

Some comments from interviewees appear to affirm professional solidarity regardless of the political distance seen at the state level. This phenomenon was clearly manifested within the AFBiH group. For instance, it was particularly noted in conversations about potential cuts to AFBiH or those about common problems in BiH such as corruption, the lack of political will and the lack of organization.

Summarizing the role of the military in regional cooperation we may assert that the most important factor which propels the military profession to cooperate is its willingness to do so. The principles, organization, norms, and set of values of all the world's militaries (and consequently those of the region) are, if not the same, then very similar. As a result, when confronted with a purely external military challenge, all tend to cooperate, creating a synergistic effect, which is vital for accomplishing missions. This conclusion is confirmed by both theoretical elaboration and empirical findings, thus demonstrating the military profession's tendency to engage unproblematically in transnational communities of practice as and when so directed by political elites.

If we recall the definition of a community of practice and put it into the context of the military profession, it can be seen that practitioners understand how this process evolves in practice. It is clear that most regional cooperation takes place in certain professional fields, namely services, branches and particular operations. People working in the field establish contacts unproblematically and arrive together at certain ideas, all of which come 'from below', where expertise is the dominant factor. Within the military in particular, professional relations between armies and military professionals contribute to regional cooperation and the peaceful settlement of disagreements. Surprisingly, the warring parties from conflicts of the 1990s have become the strongest advocates of the peaceful resolution of conflicts. Defence mechanisms thus represent good environments for pilot projects in regional cooperation. Furthermore, defence structures are pioneers in regional cooperation, which paves the way for other institutions.

The last question pertaining to the way practitioners understand regional cooperation relates to the reasons for choosing AFBiH as the unit of analysis. Since I have already stated that regional cooperation is more a matter of internal than foreign affairs for BiH, it is necessary to look at the perceptions of BiH practitioners in this regard. Due to the complex political and social system of BiH, respondents generally view regional cooperation as having a positive influence on internal issues in the country, as many of the challenges faced have a regional dimension. Good neighbourly relations, especially with Croatia and Serbia, have a positive effect on stability in BiH and strengthen trust in the country. By the same token, regional cooperation also contributes to economic and cultural stabilization. In fact, regional cooperation helps the internal consolidation of BiH. Nevertheless, not all respondents viewed regional cooperation as positive for the internal situation in BiH, emphasizing that 'some partners have not yet sufficiently understood the political organization of BiH' (respondent 7). Other respondents pointed out that 'the two power centres in Belgrade and Zagreb have an immense impact on the situation in BiH' (respondents 3 and 13).

Regarding the military's role in regional cooperation, respondent 1 noted that 'a unified AFBiH now has one decision making centre' at the state level which certainly 'enables all kinds of cooperation'. However, respondent 3 believes that before Sarajevo can make decisions on some issues, 'authorization must still come from Zagreb or Belgrade'.

The General Framework Agreement for Peace (GFAP), otherwise known as the Dayton agreement, established BiH as a state consisting of two entities and one district and defined three constituent peoples: Bosniaks, Croats and Serbs. The composition of AFBiH reflects this arrangement, which has significant influence on BiH's relationships with its neighbours, particularly Croatia and Serbia. In practice the entities have special relationships with those neighbours: the Federation of Bosnia and Herzegovina (FBiH) with Croatia and the Republika Srpska with Serbia. Croats from BiH see themselves as part of a single Croatian nation living in two countries, while Serbs perceive the Serbian nation in a similar way. This complex internal structure affects regional dynamics, including all kinds of military activities.

Conducting regional cooperation

Turning to the ways this community of practitioners conducts itself in everyday life, I will now discuss the ways regional cooperation takes place.

The huge interest from the international community in stabilizing the region following the wars of the 1990s resulted in approximately 70 initiatives within the defence and security sphere alone. These initiatives have been implemented largely through workshops, meetings, roundtables, working groups and conferences ranging from those taking place at the ministerial level to those involving operative executors and experts. Respondents identified a whole spectrum of specific activities relating to regional cooperation in the area of defence, which are shown in the following list:

- **Political level**

    a   Regional forum for defence policy directors
    b   Religious services within military structures
    c   Meetings between defence ministry representatives
    d   Research projects
    e   Project supporting international activities
    f   Bilateral cooperation programmes
    g   Cultural events with a military background

- **Strategic/operative level**

    a   Forums for defence chiefs
    b   Forums for deputy defence chiefs
    c   Forums for heads of military intelligence services
    d   Subregional arms control, trust building mechanisms and open sky activities
    e   Air space control activities
    f   Logistical activities
    g   Exchange of experience activities
    h   Common missions
    i   Military cooperation aimed at aiding civil actors in instances of natural disasters
    j   Daily regional cooperation between regional states in Brussels

- **Tactical level**

    a   Various forms of education
    b   Joint exercises
    c   Mine clearance and explosives destruction activities
    d   Sports contests
    e   Regional training and education centres
    f   Instructor exchanges
    g   Mobile training teams
    h   Permanent instructors

i   Coordination cell
j   Daily communication and meetings of commanders of the centres within the region and wider

The above list of forms of regional cooperation identified by respondents clearly fits Adler and Pouliot's definition of international practices. They exhibit regularities in time and space and are socially competent, based upon background knowledge, corporate and related to world politics.

While we can assume that all respondents have taken part in the aforementioned regional activities, their exact contribution is difficult to measure. However, their reflections how much influence they themselves can have when participating in regional cooperation activities may be relevant. First and foremost, respondent 9 suggests, in agreement with most other respondents, that they 'act within the framework of the system, being allocated certain tasks and areas of responsibility'. However, almost all feel that, within certain boundaries, the individual has the 'opportunity to be creative, contemplating processes and providing meaningful proposals to management' (respondent 9). For respondent 4, individuals are able to have an impact, an opportunity to speak and an opportunity to propose ideas as well as to set an example. Actually, in the rare instances where methods are not imposed and there is enough flexibility, it is surprising what people may come up with. This was also noticed in observations of participants, where they all demonstrated a high level of professionalism in pursuing their allocated tasks, with no reference to their national or ethnic background.

Learning about regional cooperation

The extent to which the military profession is willing to cooperate provides practical confirmation that, when they are given enough room for manoeuvre, military professionals may go well beyond 'expectations', thus allowing new practices to emerge. This is precisely the case with the Peace Support Operations Training Centre (PSOTC), which is probably the best illustration of the majority of possible features of regional cooperation in the field of training and education. The PSOTC's achievements in conducting regional training and education may serve as a good indication of efficient regional cooperation. The data for regional participants from Albania, BIH, Croatia, Macedonia, Montenegro, Serbia and Slovenia presented in following description comes not only from their respective armed forces but also from various governmental institutions and organizations.

The data covers the time from the establishment of PSOTC in 2005 to May 2012. In this period, PSOTC trained a total of 921 participants from 35 countries, of which 62 per cent (570) were regional participants. Of the regional participants, 48 per cent (271) participated in residential activities, while 52 per cent (299) took part in Mobile Training Teams (MTT) activities.

PSOTC has been running residential courses since 2005, and has trained 80 regional students so far. These 80 students represent 13 per cent of all students (including domestic ones), and 54 per cent of international students.

Regional Mobile Training Team (MTT) activities though have been run since 2009 and so far 38 per cent students came from Albania, 37 per cent from Montenegro, 18 per cent from Serbia, and 7 per cent from Croatia.

PSOTC has some characteristics which make it unique in international practice. For example, three of the region's countries (apart from BiH) participate in the PSOTC management board as members of its partners' body. This body convenes twice a year and provides politico-strategic guidelines to the PSOTC commandant. Three of the region's countries have provided military officers as permanent staff members, while one country contributes financially to PSOTC's running costs. PSOTC regularly exchanges instructors with other regional centres as well as delivering modules that are part of the wider training package. Its Mobile Training Teams (MTT) continuously conduct tailored training in the region's countries and engage instructors from host training institutions, thus creating joint MTTs. Finally, the PSOTC conducts joint courses with one of its sister centres for a regional audience. These activities represent the whole spectrum of regional cooperation within the framework of defence training and education. It should be noted that representatives of the wider security sector take part in PSOTC deliverables alongside military personnel.

The case of the PSOTC represents an unfolding example of the establishment of a fairly new training and education practice within the defence and security sector.

Nevertheless, the reality is not only positive. Opinions of the experience of dealing with partner countries[2] and perceptions of regional cooperation range from very positive generalizations to a more cautious analysis. Positive opinions emphasize that people generally recognize the benefit of regional cooperation and that the majority of the partners have sincere intentions. Even more, respondents believe that partners try to contribute and respect each other while demonstrating a readiness to offer further cooperation within certain domains. Lastly, they think that the majority of people at lower executive levels believe that they depend on a mutual understanding that cooperation represents official policy. More cautious opinions suggest that while the representatives of the majority of partner countries support cooperation, it is unclear whether they are fully open in stating their opinions. Respondents also think that there is a lack of information or limited knowledge about the contemporary situation in BiH, which may result in some misunderstanding.

Furthermore, even though there is an ongoing learning process within the framework of regional cooperation, we cannot state that a Western Balkan military identity is emerging. This is best explained by our respondents, who assert that there is a general understanding of the need for cooperation and regional integration but emphasize that there is no common Western Balkan identity, nor are there any initiatives to build it. In the case of BiH, discussions about identity are even more controversial, since there is not even a 'state' identity, let alone trans-state or national ones.

Concluding remarks

Examination of the current scale of engagement by AFBiH institutions in regional cooperation leads to the conclusion that there is very close and intensive cooperation between Western Balkan militaries. The range of activities through which this cooperation is conducted basically represents a set of international corporate practices practised within the regional setting of the Western Balkans. Since these practices are performed by a group of people who have common interests and operate within the framework of the same background knowledge, it is obvious that this is an example of a community of practice.

By the same token, the fact that this community of practice is aimed at sustaining peace and solving problems without resorting to violence leads us towards the security community concept. Daily regional cooperation between military practitioners provides a flow of interactions which is sufficient to create dependable expectations of peaceful change. At the same time, the logic of practicality helps create new social realities based upon a collective identity and a sense of trust.

AFBiH finds itself at the forefront of regional cooperation, and so makes a significant contribution to stabilizing the security situation in the region. In addition, meeting NATO standards not only results in improvements in interoperability, but also enables the Euro-Atlantic security community to encourage the socialization process.

Notes

1 Semi-structured interviews were conducted between March and May 2012 with 20 representatives of the Ministry of Defence and Armed Forces of BiH at ministerial, assistant minister, chief of department, joint staff, operational command and regional training centre levels. Participant observation was conducted at two courses held at the PSOTC. Junior Centre for Security Studies (CSS) researchers attended the ISOS Course (International Staff Officers Skills Course) for a period of three days. The course group consisted of 28 military personnel of various ranks from eight different countries, aged between 20 and 40. Observation was carried out of interactions between the regional course participants from Albania, Macedonia, BiH, Croatia and Montenegro and the three instructors from Croatia, Serbia and Montenegro. The Regional Inter-Agency Seminar was also observed, again for a three-day period. This course group consisted of 46 individuals of which 28 were military and 18 civilian. Participants were from both the government and international and nongovernmental organizations, all of which deal with defence and security matters. The participants were of various ranks and were from seven different countries: BiH, Croatia, Montenegro, Albania, Macedonia, Serbia and Slovenia.
2 This study suffers from one serious limitation stemming from the lack of comparative data collected from military counterparts in other Western Balkan countries. This limitation was addressed by asking respondents how they feel their counterparts react during regional cooperation.

Bibliography

Adler, E, *Communitarian International Relations: The Epistemic Foundations of International Relations*, New York: Routledge, 2005.

Adler, E, "The Spread of Security Communities: Communities of Practice, Self-Restraint, and NATO's Post–Cold War Transformation" in *European Journal of International Relations*, 14:2 (2008): 195–230.

Adler, E and Barnett, M, "Governing Anarchy" in *Ethics and International Affairs* 10:1 (1996): 63–98.

Adler, E and Barnett, M (eds), *Security Communities*, Cambridge University Press, 1998.
Adler, E and Pouliot, V, (eds), *International Practices*, Cambridge University Press, 2011.
Andersen, M, workshop lecture, 27–29October 2011, Tirana.
Bourdieu, P, *The Logic of Practice*, Stanford University Press, 1990.
Bourdieu, P, *Masculine Domination*, Stanford University Press, 2001.
Bourdieu, P and Wacquant, L, *An Invitation to Reflexive Sociology*, University of Chicago, 1992.
Bucher, R and Strauss, A, "Professions in Process" in *The American Journal of Sociology* 66:4 (1961): 325–334.
Burrage, M, "Revolution and the Collective Action of the French: American and English Legal Professions" in *Law and Social Enquiry: the Journal of the American Bar Foundation* 13:2 (1988): 225–227.
Deutsch, K, Burrell, SA, Kann, RA, Lee, M, Lichterman, M, Lindgren, RE, Loewenheim, FL and Van Wagenen, RW, *Political Community in the North Atlantic Area: International Organization in the Light of Historical Experience*, Princeton University Press, 1957.
Deutsch, K, *The Analysis of International Relations*, New Jersey: Prentice Hall, 1968.
Harries-Jenkins, G, "The Concept of Military Professionalism" in *Defense Analysis* 6:2 (1990): 117–130.
Huntington, S, *The Soldier and the State: The Theory and Politics of Civil-Military Relations*, Cambridge, Massachusetts: Belknap Press, 1957.
Huntington, S, "Power, Expertise, and the Military Profession" in *Daedalus* 92 (1963): 785–807.
Janowitz, M, *The Professional Soldier: A Social and Political Portrait*, New York and London: Free Press – Collier Maximillian, 1974.
Macdonald, K, *The Sociology of the Profession*, London: SAGE Publications, 1995.
Moskos, C, "Institutional/Occupational Trends in Armed Forces" in *Armed Forces & Society* 12:3 (1986): 377–382.
Pouliot, V, "The Logic of Practicality: A Theory of Practice of Security Communities" in *International Organization*, 62 (2008): 257–288.
Van Wagenen, R, *Research in the International Organization Field*, Princeton, NJ: Center for Research on World Political Institutions, 1952.
Van Wagenen, R, "The Concept of Community and the Future of the United Nations" in *International Organizations* 19 (1965): 812–827.
Wenger, E, McDermott, R and Snyder, W, *Cultivating Communities of Practice: A Guide to Managing Knowledge*, Harvard Business School Press, 2002.

4

COMMUNITY OF PRACTICE AMONG WESTERN BALKAN POLICE SERVICES IN MONTENEGRO

National politics vs. professionalism

Dženita Brčvak and Emir Kalač

Introduction

Regional cooperation in the Western Balkans has often been discussed in the context of the region as one of the major sources of security threats in Europe. Since the beginning of the 1990s, and during the two-decade period which followed, the Western Balkans was often associated with ethnic conflicts, civil wars and violations of fundamental human rights. Nevertheless, the setting has changed; the foreign and domestic policy goals of Western Balkan countries today are largely complementary, resulting in rapprochement and joint work, reflected through regional cooperation initiatives and networks. The Western Balkans is now a region in transition, overcoming its violent past, where cooperation has, at least at first glance, become the obvious choice for political elites.

The research in this chapter builds upon the theory of practice originally posed by Pierre Bourdieu and later developed by Vincent Pouliot and others. Our starting hypothesis was that professional ties and cross-border cooperation by professionals in the Western Balkans have progressed over time, impacting the regional security environment. However, our field research indicates that the drivers for this regional cooperation are rather different than expected. This chapter thus tackles the question of what the enabling and disabling conditions are for forming a community of practice among police services in the Western Balkans. However, we are unable to offer generalizable conclusions, as our unit of our analysis was the Montenegrin police alone.

The study argues that, at the level of everyday apolitical cooperation in the region as a whole, in areas such as border policing, common professional interests exist which amount to a community of practice. However, the Montenegrin police service lacks the professional autonomy needed to continue cooperation in those high-profile cases that could potentially incriminate political elites and expose their suspected links with organized crime. These cases are securitized as a matter of defence of national sovereignty.

This chapter is structured as follows. The first section will outline the theoretical and methodological framework, while the second offers arguments and justification for the selection of the Montenegrin police as the object of research. The third section applies the main argument to three case studies: socialization through domestic police education and joint regional training; interaction in regional formal events; and political interference in high-profile cases. The chapter concludes with a general analysis of the professional autonomy of the Montenegrin police and the implications for the emergence of a security community in the Western Balkans.

Theoretical background and methodology

Having only recently regained its independence, Montenegro's chief focus is on resolving issues related to its sovereignty. Political decisions made in the period since independence in 2006 were often coloured by hasty decisions made by its leaders in order to demonstrate that the country was capable of making its own decisions and handling its own affairs. For example, Montenegro was among the first countries to recognize the independence of Kosovo in 2008, an act which caused serious riots in Podgorica and resulted in the Serbian government proclaiming the Montenegrin ambassador to Belgrade *persona non grata*. Nonetheless, on many occasions the Montenegrin government demonstrated its membership of a larger entity, the Western Balkans. The new state politics of the time had a major effect on the police, the main defence pillar of the country. Such a spillover of politics raises at least two important questions:

1. In which situations is the Montenegrin police an independent operating state body?
2. How and when does the government match its priorities to those of the region?

Our research began by analysing official data and documents. We then directed our attention to the normative dynamics of those directly involved in the process – police officers themselves. We encouraged police officers to elaborate on their own perception of the role of the police at the time. We used the anthropological approach suggested by practice theory in an attempt to decode the concepts of community of practice, professional identity and political interference in the specific case of Montenegrin police.

Rich in practice, the police provides wide scope for applying practice theory to research. Police practices are the most visible aspect of the state security apparatus and the aspect of the country's general security policy which springs to mind most readily. Thus, police practices require additional attention in scholarly research on regional security cooperation.

Further, the political legacy of the past 20 years in the Western Balkans, especially in Montenegro where the police forces were used as a central pillar of the defence system, makes the police a relevant case for testing regional security cooperation. In a region where the police are the face of the state in the eyes of people, any positive shift in the values of police professionals can indicate a transformation in the country's policies toward former enemies.

Very few studies approach the police as a professional community and almost none focus on the practices of police officers in the professional community. Neither do any studies map overlapping elements between the professional and security communities, but approach these as two separate spheres. On the contrary, this study argues that changes to the organizational norms, practices and patterns of one profession and its agents can contribute to a general transformation of the specific policy area and the way it is applied in relation to 'others'. Examining practices as suggested by practice theory allows analysis of various types of data and allows identifications to be made and gaps to be mapped between the evident and background knowledge. As Adler and Pouliot claim, practices are able to 'change the physical environment as well as the ideas that individually and collectively people hold about the world' (Adler and Pouliot, 2011).

Previous studies dealing with police reform in Montenegro have mostly provided general information about its role during the conflicts in BiH and Kosovo (Ponsaers, 2013), while some have addressed the period of security tensions and political distancing between Podgorica and Belgrade since 1997 (Ramet, 2006). However, no study has addressed the longer temporal context (from the conflict to the present), the internal dynamics between the region's countries or their relations when dealing with common problems.

Our analysis is based on the findings of field research conducted in Montenegro between January and May 2012. Our research consisted of 20 interviews with police officers and other professionals working at the Police Directorate, visits to the Police Academy and five border crossings, content analysis of the Montenegrin police official magazine *Policijski glasnik* and attendance at the major Cyber Crime Conference, organized by the International Association of Chiefs of Police (IACP) and the Southeast Europe Police Chiefs Association (SEPCA), held on 24–26 April, 2012 in Budva. We interviewed 10 police officers, two lecturers at the Academy and eight managers from various sectors and departments, including the National Bureau for Interpol at the Police Directorate. All interviews were conducted in the police working environment, from field offices across the country to the premises of the Ministry of Interior (MoI). Interviews were semi-open and anonymous and lasted approximately one hour. We were particularly interested in our interviewees' attendance at regional training, their experience at such events, their personal relations with their colleagues from the region and especially their views on the possibility of conflict occurring in the Western Balkans in future.

Introducing the Montenegrin police

There are two main reasons why the Montenegrin police is a litmus test for transformation of inter-state relations. First, it was involved in conflicts with neighbouring countries in the 1990s and was linked with the very organized crime it was supposed to fight. Second, it was one of the main nation-defending institutions during the quest for Montenegrin independence, and it is still perceived as a key institution for defending sovereignty.

An essential factor for understanding the role of the police in the past few decades is the fact that the social transition in Montenegro followed the pace of conflicts occurring in the neighbourhood. The police forces of all former Yugoslav republics took part in the wars of the 1990s, 'although their level of participation varied' (Sević and Bakrac, 2004: 250). Although precise data is lacking, Montenegro was no exception, as evidenced by judicial proceedings brought against former Montenegrin police officers who arrested BiH nationals and deported them to the Republika Srpska authorities, resulting in their execution.

In the mid-1990s Montenegro was still part of the Federal Republic of Yugoslavia (FRY). However, the country started building its own institutions independent of the federal authority when in 1997 the ruling Democratic Party of Socialists (DPS) took the first clear steps to distance itself from Slobodan Milošević, then FRY president. Until 2006, Montenegro formed a state union with Serbia. In various state arrangements, from being a faithful supporter of Belgrade's politics to aspirations for independence, Montenegro has largely defined its identity as separate from that of Serbia. Historical divisions between Montenegrins and Serbs have always had a negative impact on the political stability of Montenegro and have consistently applied to all strata of society. In other words, every issue, problem, discourse and discussion is usually ontologically reducible to this basic division, while the problem itself is an excuse to 'undermine' the opposing party (Bešić, 2011).

Further, the ruling party in Montenegro has not changed since the start of the transition process. The DPS, composed of ex members of the League of Communists of Montenegro, has ruled the country since 1990. This fact is very important for understanding the challenges Montenegro faces. The negative effect of an unchanged and powerful political elite spills over to other dimensions of social life in Montenegro, creating space for the politicization of institutions that should by default be free of political pressure. This particularly relates to the judiciary and police. In the new Montenegrin security system, the Montenegrin Police became the central security actor. Throughout the 1990s, and particularly after the adoption of the new constitution of the Republic of Montenegro in 1992, the police force vastly increased in number, and was characterized by a high degree of militarization. New military equipment for the police was imported.

During the 1990s, the police forces served primarily as the country's defence mechanism rather than as a service for the investigation and prevention of crime. 'Emphasising the creation of the police service as a defence mechanism meant the creation of a repressive militarized police structure, and not the police as a service for the citizen whose activities are controlled by democratic mechanisms and which aims to investigate crime and fight organized crime' (Radević and Raičević, 2011: 16). The period from the end of the 1980s through the 1990s was marked by an extreme rise in organized crime and corruption. This form of criminality was often openly tolerated and its suppression was not a priority for the police. Poor police work led to an increase in corruption at many levels, while the police itself remained the repressive arm of the regime, as in communist times (Schouten et al., 2006). Twenty years on, it is obvious that the formation of such a strong police structure narrowed the possibilities for change, contributing to the immutability of the elite during this period.

The Federal Republic of Yugoslavia formally ceased to exist with the Belgrade Agreement in 2003, and a new union of two semi-independent states, Serbia and Montenegro, was created. From November 2003 to January 2004 a very important process was completed – the passing of competencies over state borders from the armed forces of FRY to the Montenegrin Police (Radević and Raičević, 2011: 17–21). This meant that the Police Department officially gained a role as a state-building actor. Thus this institution was actually involved in the process of advocating for the country's independence. In 2006, the Military of Montenegro was created and took over responsibility for defence of the country.

Since re-gaining independence, a key debate regarding police reform in Montenegro has been about the police's level of autonomy within the Ministry of Interior.

It is important to note that, despite significant efforts aimed at increasing the professional autonomy of the Montenegrin police, this body has not been deprived of political impact. The decisive wave of security sector reform in Montenegro occurred in 2005 with the adoption of the Police Law and the Law on the National Security Agency. These laws separated the Public Security Service and the National Security Service from the Ministry of Interior and placed them directly under the aegis of the Government. The aim of this reform was to increase the independence and professionalization of these two institutions. With the adoption of the Police Law in 2005, the director of the Police Directorate became the state's 'first officer'. Doubts about whether the Police Directorate should remain independent or revert to the auspices of the Ministry of Interior (which would create a unified 'address' for fighting organized crime and corruption) were a key disagreement within the state-building coalition. The ruling coalition was composed of the Democratic Party of Socialists (DPS), led by current prime minister Milo Djukanović, and the Social Democratic Party (SDP) led by parliamentary speaker Ranko Krivokapić. This coalition had been running the country continuously since 1998 until 2016. Former police director Veselin Veljović was quite openly loyal to the DPS and was in favour of the Police Directorate being an independent body. On the other hand, the attitude of the SDP, of which the Interior Minister was a member, was that the police should operate under the aegis of the MoI. This 'conflict' was resolved with the adoption of a new Law on Internal Affairs in July 2012, which returned the Police Directorate to the Ministry of Interior (*Law on Internal Affairs*, 2012: art. 3). It is important to note the manner in which this service developed over the following years in order to understand how the Montenegrin police was always connected to high political affairs and how it has always served as the primary pillar in the defence of sovereignty.

However, the recent transformation of the Montenegrin Police from a militarized force to a decentralized and independent department raises the question of whether changes in the broader security context contributed to changes in the mutual perception of the region's police officers.

According to the police officers interviewed for this chapter, the recent intensification of cooperation and joint activities makes a renewed outbreak of conflict almost impossible. They believe that the international community, that is NATO and the EU, will not 'allow themselves to repeat the mistakes of the past' (border police officer, March 2012). Yet, 'different interpretations of the events of recent history', as well as the existence of potential 'crisis points', such as the still unresolved issues in relations between Serbia and Kosovo and between FBiH and Republika Srpska as well as ethnic problems in Macedonia still hinder neighbourly relations and the establishment of trust.

Further, given the existence of a widely dispersed regional criminal network, the region's police officers often need to approach to each other, and tend to cooperate regularly when dealing with suppression of various crimes. Such cooperation is further enhanced externally by the European Union. Once the EU began, through the Stabilisation and Association Process, to insist officially on regional cooperation as important precondition for accession, regional relations began to develop in a notably different pattern than was seen in the 1990s. Yet, in high profile cases, where organized crime is concerned, police work appears to still be under the influence of the various interests of political elites. This was confirmed by the flow of Operation Balkan Warrior, one of several cases which threatened the legitimacy of domestic political elites.

The fact that the police was used in conflicts with neighbouring countries in the 1990s, as well as that it was the nation-defending institution during the development of Montenegrin independence, the Montenegrin police is a salient test for interstate relations and security transitions in the Western Balkans.

Case study: socialization through domestic police education and joint regional training

In order to understand the habitus of a profession, it is essential to comprehend the way that newcomers become engaged in the service. Professional identity is created largely through occupational and professional socialization by means of shared education, training and vocational experience as well as by membership of professional associations (Evetts, 2006).

Socialization is conceived as the process through which a novice learns the skills, knowledge and values necessary to become a competent member of any organization or occupation (Chan, 2004). In the case of the police, this also includes learning and adopting organizational skills and attitudes that fit with those of other police officers. The competency gained through this process of developing skills and knowledge creates practice – a way of doing. 'Although practice is performed by an individual, it acquires meaning only through collectively shared understandings of competency, of what is well done or poorly done' (Gross Stein, 2011). The abundance of practices and activities in the police profession makes the practice-theory approach used in this study appropriate for this case study.

In Montenegro, police officers are educated at the Police Academy, formerly the Police Secondary School, which was founded in 2007 and is the country's sole institution for the education of current and future police officers. Although no foreign students are currently enrolled, lecturers exchange knowledge and experience continuously with colleagues from the region, while occasional visits by teachers from neighbouring countries also take place. Lecturers frequently attend regional and international training and workshops and value the opportunity to share experience and exchange literature and teaching guides with colleagues. In their opinion, this practice is not only helpful for their own work, but also enables their students to develop a similar modus operandi to their regional colleagues. Moreover, they explained how the use of common external material facilitated regional understanding:

> All Western Balkan states use DCAF's guides as their literature; we have access to a specially built literature database. Because of this, I think that students from regional Police Academies gain more or less the same knowledge, at least when it comes to the EU issues.
> *(Police Academy Lecturer, April 2012)*

So it seems that police academies are the places where professional we-ness is initially built. Recalling Adler's argument 'what creates like-mindedness is a domain of knowledge which constitutes shared practices and provides practitioners with a sense of joint enterprise' (Adler, 2008), this leads to the question: If all police recruits in the region are taught with the same literature, does this mean that they develop a common habitus?

Also important is that most of the officers interviewed graduated from the Secondary Police School in Serbia, where they studied with current police officers operating in various regional countries. Police officers share common experiences and special bonds developed during their education. The fact they have studied together consequently influences their 'way of doing':

> Many of those police officers from Serbia, Macedonia, Bosnia and Herzegovina and so on are actually my friends. For example, I can call my colleague in Serbia any time and ask for information. We can contact each other 24/7, without having to notify our superiors, if this will contribute to faster completion of the assignment and resolution of the case.
> *(Manager, Department for Foreigners and Illegal Migration, March 2012)*

Content analysis of police magazine *Policijski glasnik* from 2009 shows that Serbian and Croatian police officers most frequently attend joint gatherings with Montenegrin police. Training and workshops were usually run by an EU member state, most frequently Germany and Sweden (*Policijski glasnik*, April 2009).

Training now takes place frequently, and police officers who have had the opportunity to collaborate with colleagues from the region are unanimous that this cooperation is indispensable, even if it is initiated and usually supported by international entities such as the EU and various regional initiatives. No interviewee had ever had any unpleasant experience due to his nationality while at a seminar. We therefore argue that changes in the organizational and material aspects of police forces in Montenegro have effected a change in the attitudes of its officers.

> It is certain that many activities in the region were initiated by international actors. However, the problems we face at the everyday level are a key source of our interactions, and this is what encourages us to act together.
> *(Manager, Department for Combating Organized Crime and Corruption, March 2012)*

Western Balkan police departments have the will to cooperate, but lack the means necessary to conduct such activities. As a Lecturer at the Police Academy stated in April 2012, 'If it weren't for them [the EU and international organizations], we would not gather this often; especially due to the lack of financial means'.

The specificities of the police profession allow and require regional joint actions, regardless of the state of relations between the countries concerned. All departments within the Montenegrin Police Directorate rely on good communication and cooperation with colleagues from the region. When talking about police officers from another country, they do not speak of Albanians, Serbs or Croats; rather they speak of fellow colleagues, of professionals. They are interested in achieving the same goal – making their communities as secure as possible, thus, they share a common purpose. The means they use to make this possible are also similar.

Regional security cooperation activities take place at a number of meetings arranged under regional initiatives, such as SEECP, SECI/SELEC, RCC, RACVIAC, MARRI and so on.

These initiatives confirm the thesis of regional security complex theory originally developed by Barry Buzan, according to which the core of a system is the security interdependence of all the system's states. Buzan claims that insecurity is associated with proximity, since 'most political and military threats travel more easily over short distances than over long ones' (Buzan, 2000: 140). Given such an environment, security interdependence between neighbouring countries is much more intense than between more distant countries. Neighbouring countries can create regional security complexes, defined as a set of states whose major processes of securitization, de-securitization or both are so interlinked that their national security problems cannot reasonably be analysed or resolved separately from each other (Buzan, 2000). Such complexes can form various patterns depending on their background drivers, that is whether security interdependence is driven by amity or enmity. Interdependence can thus be positive or negative.

Given that all of the region's countries bar Albania were formerly part of one state, but also participated in the conflict which accompanied the dissolution of that state, we claim that security interdependence between these states indeed exists and that security threats can easily cross borders and thus affect each regional state's internal order. When it comes to the security agenda in the Western Balkans, no issue is a matter for a single country alone. Criminal groups are regionally and internationally connected; they endanger each state equally and thus push states and security institutions into acting together. In order to create good preconditions for police cooperation in the field, states have made efforts to define an adequate legal framework. Various agreements and protocols regulating bilateral or multilateral relations have been drafted and signed. The most important such legal documents are protocols on joint police patrols along Montenegro's borders with Albania, BiH and Serbia. These protocols have enabled direct contacts between officers from 'the other side' and direct exchange of information, knowledge and experience, as well as creating space for officers to meet and understand each other's stances. Our field research indicates that the region's police officers are building a professional community bound together by their expertise and practices.

Case study: interaction at regional formal events

During our field research, on 24–26 April 2012, Southeast European police directorates organized the IACP/SEPCA Cyber Crime Conference in Budva, Montenegro. This provided an excellent opportunity to observe police officers' interaction and see how they behave, with whom they spend their breaks and how they mingle.

The conference was attended by all relevant stakeholders from the regional police departments, as well as the Montenegrin Prime Minister and State Prosecutor, foreign ambassadors, representatives of international police and civil organizations, academics and civil society organizations. The atmosphere at the conference was rather *sterile*, with the setting strictly pre-arranged. All seats for participants were marked with flags and nametags. During the break, Western Balkan security officers mingled and spoke 'our language'. However, around halfway through the conference, most of the Western Balkan delegations left the room. Later, we discovered that there had been a series of bilateral meetings which resulted in some arrangements for joint operations.

Special focus was directed at the manner in which individuals from countries that less than two decades ago had fought large-scale conflicts interacted: whether there was separation or grouping among the participants and whether there was any kind of animosity or inconvenience. Language, as expected with at least the former Yugoslav countries, was the most binding element. Police officers and security professionals originating from former Yugoslavia assembled in several groups, and none openly expressed any form of animosity towards each other. To the spectator, it appeared that security officers from these countries mingled in a completely leisurely and natural way.

There is debate over why regional events are held so frequently. Some claim that these events are mostly imposed by the European Union integration process, and thus are initiated externally. Nevertheless, it is clear that interaction has greatly intensified over the past few years through various meetings and training events involving police officers from all the region's countries.

Although they sometimes discuss the 'difficult times and matters' during gatherings, police officers do not allow bigotry to encroach on their conversation. A very important 'consequence' of joint activities with colleagues from the region is the formation of friendships. As one interviewee put it, 'Given that many of us attend the same activities, as well as professional contacts we have managed to build friendly relations. This has significantly facilitated our activities, given that we now communicate on a daily basis' (Border Police Officer, March 2012).

When Western Balkan police officers attend courses alongside officers from a wider geographical area, they are often told not to spend so much time together during breaks. In addition, organizers frequently form working groups in a way which divides individuals from Western Balkan countries between different groups. When asked about their reasons for mingling with or avoiding individuals from specific countries, respondents replied that this usually occurs due to linguistic similarities rather than because of any prejudices or stereotypes about other nations.

Face-to-face cooperation: border police

Our initial assumption, which proved to be accurate, was that the majority of direct interactions between police officers occur at border crossings between employees of the Border Police sector. We visited five border crossings and talked to 10 officers, of which five were managers and five field police officers. Border police premises do not vary much from one to another. Offices are commonly located in old buildings and are furnished with old lockers, tables and chairs.

Interviews specifically addressed the protocol on conducting joint patrols along the common border, which enables practical application of regional cooperation. Border patrols are conducted jointly with Albania, Bosnia and Herzegovina and Serbia, and when on Montenegrin territory they are composed of two Montenegrin officers and one from the neighbouring country. Patrols are organized three to four times a month, although in case of emergency, additional patrols may be organized. This practice enables direct contact between police officers, making it possible for them to meet each other and creating space for most of them to become friends. These protocols were assessed by all respondents as highly valuable for the development of regional police cooperation: 'You don't have a clue what goes on the other side of the border until you start doing joint patrols. Participating in the joint patrol was a unique opportunity to see the border as a whole!' (Border Police Officer, March 2012)

All interviewees said that they are in regular telephone contact with their colleagues, while many have developed good friendships with police officers from the region. The only barrier to socialization during joint patrols appears to be language, and this primarily affects Albanian officers, since few Montenegrins speak Albanian and vice versa. However, some Montenegrin Border Police officers have attended an Albanian language course and thus learned the basics. During joint patrols, the presence of one bilingual mediator is obligatory, hence communication between police officers, although limited to a certain extent, is rather good. A very interesting practice was identified during the interview with Maritime Border Police officers. One Albanian-speaking officer wrote a message in Albanian, stating that something of 'security interest' was happening at the border. The message is kept in the Montenegrin Maritime Police premises so that if such a situation occurs it can be immediately typed and sent to the Albanian police commander. Apparently, this practice has been used, and has proved useful on several occasions.

According to interviews with the border police, all officers who had participated in at least one joint patrol believed that joint patrols represent the core of regional cooperation. Additionally, regional meetings are held regularly and are attended by high ranking managers. All of this enables continuous communication and information exchange between neighbouring police departments and contributes to more connected and effective police network.

Case study: high-profile case – drug boss Darko Šarić

Even though almost all levels of state government, including the police, claim that regional cooperation is excellent, there are some excesses which significantly call into question the professionalism of regional police services. The most intriguing recent excess occurred during Operation Balkan Warrior, a case involving Darko Šarić, a fugitive drug boss originally from Pljevlja, a small town in northern Montenegro. We have taken this operation as a case study as it demonstrates how politics continues to interfere with police work in the Western Balkans.

Darko Šarić became familiar to the public in 2009, when international agencies reported the seizure of 2.8 tonnes of cocaine near the Uruguayan border and the arrest of members of Šarić's group. This operation, which was given the name Balkan Warrior, was conducted through cooperation between the USA's Drug Enforcement Administration (DEA), the Serbian Security Information Agency (BIA) and the Uruguayan police. An international arrest warrant was issued in 2010 the day after Mr Šarić allegedly left Montenegro. The Montenegrin police soon reported that Šarić had left the territory of Montenegro illegally. This statement was published a few days before the National Interpol Bureau in Podgorica received notification of the arrest warrant. The Serbian Prosecutor's Office filed charges against Šarić's group a few months later. A statement from the State Secretary at the Serbian Ministry of Justice, Slobodan Homen, followed: 'The essence of the struggle against the Darko Šarić drugs clan and other criminal groups is to discover their connections with certain state officials from public enterprises and state officials in that country' (*Dnevne novine*, 2014). In October 2010, Duško Šarić, Darko Šarić's brother, was arrested by Montenegrin police on the basis of an Italian arrest warrant, after which the Montenegrin Prosecutor's Office also filed charges against Darko Šarić.

During the process of carrying out this operation, however, numerous contradictory statements were issued by the Serbian and Montenegrin authorities.

Although the drug boss had been born in Montenegro, in 2005 he officially became a citizen of Serbia. This further complicated the operation, as it led to discussions between Montenegro and Serbia over responsibility for and jurisdiction over the case. When the operation was launched, Montenegro's Ministry of Justice and Police Directorate, including the National Interpol Bureau, claimed that communication between Belgrade and Podgorica failed in this case because the Serbian judicial authorities did not submit the necessary information to the Montenegrin police in time. Reasons for this poor communication, in their opinion, should be sought in Serbia. Concurrently, the Serbian authorities frequently stated publicly that the fugitive drug boss was most probably in Montenegro.

These accusations grew even louder after Montenegro was hit by another scandal, the *Listing* affair, initiated in November 2011 when the daily newspaper *Dan* published the call log from Šarić's phone. The *Listing* affair showed that Šarić had communicated with numerous state officers, businessmen and security agency officials from Montenegro. Šarić had allegedly spoken several times to Montenegro's then Prime Minister, Igor Lukšić, and the Minister of Foreign Affairs, Milan Roćen. However, Lukšić and Roćen denied any connection with Šarić. Further investigation of the affair concluded that the call logs were fake. Nevertheless, the directors of the Police Directorate and the National Security Agency were replaced, while the entire affair was hushed up. The full details are yet to be revealed.

The mutual accusations and the manner in which the operation was conducted from the outset confirmed that the judiciary and police in both countries lack professional autonomy. Furthermore, political interference was evident throughout the entire process. The media constantly reported contradictory statements and efforts to evade responsibility by politicians. Thus, for example, Ranko Krivokapić, Speaker of the Montenegrin Parliament, accused Belgrade of trying to export its drug cartel problem to Montenegro. In his words, 'Serbia is the homeland of this crime and the seat of the octopus, one of whose legs reached Montenegro' (*Glas Srpske*, 2010). When the drug boss was finally arrested, Krivokapić then stated that 'cooperation between Serbia and Montenegro led to Šarić's arrest' (*KLIX*, 2014). The other side made similar statements.

A closer examination of this highly contradictory operation may establish whether or not the level of interstate cooperation depends on the various interests of each side. Thus far, however, the answer to this question remains unclear.

Conclusion: is regional police cooperation professional?

Based on the research presented in this chapter, everyday police work and police cooperation in the Western Balkans can be fairly assessed as professional. Because of the specificity of their work, police departments unproblematically establish cooperation and professional networks. Police officers are led by the premise that crime does not respect borders, hence cooperation and joint action are necessary if positive results are to be achieved. In doing so, although this takes place within certain limits, police departments effect a change in the security environment as well as in the ideas people hold about the region, as suggested by Adler and Pouliot. Here, the decoded habitus of the police matches Goode's principles of community within community, as its members are bound by a sense of identity, share common values, use a common language which is only partially understood by outsiders, are affected by the rules and power of their professional community and finally, although this professional community does not produce the next generation biologically, it does so socially through its control over the selection of professional trainees and through its training processes.

However, this regional professional network still has certain shortcomings in terms of its members' scope and the results in practice. The Montenegrin case has shown that even the level of cooperation varies from country to country. While close cooperation with Serbia and Croatia was often mentioned, interviewees made little mention of other countries in the region. For example, of all the region's countries, Macedonia was mentioned least in interviews. There are no unresolved issues with Macedonia, but the absence of a common border seems to diminish the necessity of joint police work, at least on the ground.

Also, while cooperation is fairly professional in most areas of everyday activity, there are cases which cast doubt on the intentions of the region's police services to cooperate fully. This particularly applies to the aforementioned Operation Balkan Warrior, in which both Montenegro and Serbia played political games, obviously trying to abdicate responsibility for the case and later trying to transfer the blame for bad results to the other side.

This being said, our core argument is that regional police cooperation in the Western Balkans depends on the specific problems faced daily by these countries, as long as this cooperation does not endanger their political interests. Regional cooperation is undoubtedly much more intensive than it was some 10 years ago, and the international community, or in other words the EU, has made a significant contribution to cooperation in the region. Joining the club of developed Western democracies has been set as a foreign policy priority for the region's countries. This necessarily involves overcoming past mistakes, and there are a number of regional activities aimed at realizing that process which are supported by various Western European countries.

Finally, although the region's countries are encouraged to cooperate by the problems they encounter, it must be said that a number of regional initiatives, meetings and training programmes would not have been organized if international support had been lacking.

Bibliography

Abbott, A, *The System of Professions: An Essay on the Division of Expert Labor*, University of Chicago, 1988.

Adler, E, "The Spread of Security Communities: Communities of Practice, Self-Restraint and NATO's Post-Cold War Transformation" in *European Journal of International Relations* 14:2 (2008): 195–230.

Adler, E and Pouliot, V, (eds), *International Practices*, Cambridge University Press, 2011.

Bechev, D, (2006) "Carrots, Sticks and Norms: the EU and Regional Cooperation in Southeast Europe" in *Journal of Southern Europe and the Balkans* 8:1 (2006): 27–43.

Bechev, D, *Constructing South East Europe – The Politics of Balkan Regional Cooperation*, Palgrave Macmillan, 2011.

Bešić, M, *Korupcija – praksa, iskustva, percepcija*, Podgorica: CEDEM, 2011.

Bucher, R and Strauss, A, "Professions in Process" in *The American Journal of Sociology* 66:4 (1961): 325–334.

Buzan, B, "Regional Security Complex Theory in the Post-Cold War World" in *Theories of New Regionalism*, Palgrave Macmillan (2003): 140–159.

Buzan, B and Wæver, O, *Regions and Powers: The Structure of International Security*, New York: Cambridge University Press, 2003.

Chan, J, *Using Pierre Bourdieu's Framework for Understanding Police Culture*, Sydney: School of Social Science and Policy, University of New South Wales, 2004.

Checkel, JT, *It's the process stupid! Process tracing in the study of European and international politics*, Oslo: Centre for European Studies, University of Oslo, 2005.

Delević, M, *Regional cooperation in the Western Balkans*, Institute for Security Studies, 2007.

Deutsche Welle, "Drugi 'nož u leđa' u Srbiji u roku od dva dana" (online, 2008) available at: www.dw.de/drugi-no%C5%BE-u-le%C4%91a-srbiji-u-roku-od-dva-dana/a-3704320

Dnevne novine, "Special issue – The case of Darko Šarić" (online, 2014) available at: http://issuu.com/dnevne-novine/docs/dnevne_a3f6c73698ec60/1?e=5189478/7150828

Enthoven, M and de Brujin, E, *Beyond Locality: The Creation of Public Practice-Based Knowledge through Practitioner Research in Professional Learning Communities and Communities of Practice. A Review of Three Books on Practitioner Research and Professional Communities*, Educational Action Research, 2010.

Ericson, RV, "The Division of Expert Knowledge in Policing and Security" in *The British Journal of Sociology* 45:2 (1994): 149–175.

Evetts, J, "Short Note: The Sociology of Professional Groups: New directions" in *Current Sociology* 45:2 (2006): 133–143.

George, AL and Bennett, A, *Case studies and theory development in the social science: Process tracing and historical explanation*, Belfer Center for Science and International Affairs, 2004.

Glas Srpske, "Balkanski ratnik zategao odnose između Srbije i Crne Gore" (online, 2010) available at: www.glassrpske.com/novosti/srbija/Balkanski-ratnik-zategao-odnose-izmedju-Srbije-i-Crne-Gore/lat/35669.html

Goode, WJ, "Community within a Community" in *American Journal of Sociology* 22:2 (1957): 194–200.

Government of Montenegro, "Potpisivanje sporazuma o policijskoj saradnji" (online, 2011) available at: www.gov.me/naslovna/najava-dogadjaja/104071/Ministar-Brajovic-potpisace.html

Gross Stein, J, "Background knowledge in the foreground: conversations about competent practice 'sacred place'" in *International Practices*, New York: Cambridge University Press, 2011.

Haas, P, "Introduction: Epistemic Communities and International Policy Coordination" in *International Organization* 41:1 (1991): 1–35.

Hughes, EC, *Education for a Profession*, University of Chicago Press, 1961.

Ikenberry, GJ and Kupchan, CA, "Socialization and Hegemonic Power" in *International Organization* 44:3 (1990).

KLIX, "Krivokapić: Saradnja Srbije i Crne Gore dovela do hapšenja Šarića" (online, 2014) available at: www.klix.ba/vijesti/bih/krivokapic-saradnja-srbije-i-crne-gore-dovela-do-hapsenja-sarica/140318054

Koneska, C, *Regional identity: The missing element in the Western Balkans security cooperation*, Central and Eastern European Online Library, 2008.

Merand, F, "Social Representation in the European Security and Defence Policy" in *Cooperation and Conflict* 41:2 (2006): 131–152.

Nezavisne novine, "Tri godine od Balkanskog ratnika, Šarić i dalje u bjekstvu" (online, 2012) available at: www.nezavisne.com/novosti/ex-yu/Tri-godine-od-Balkanskog-ratnika-Šarić-i-dalje-u-bjekstvu-162974.htm

Law on Internal Affairs, Official Gazette of Montenegro 44/2012.

Pobjeda, "Darko Šarić – profil: Anonimni milijarder" (online, 2012) available at: www.pobjeda.me/2011/12/05/darko-Šarić-%E2%80%93-profil-anonimni-milijarder/#.UzAXyahdW6N

Policijski glasnik, (online) available at: www.mup.gov.me/upravapolicije/Informisanje_javnosti/policijski-glasnik

Ponsaers, P, "Policing in Central and Eastern Europe as Epiphenomenon of Geopolitical Events" in *Handbook on Policing in Central and Eastern Europe*, Springer Science & Business Media, 2013.

Pouliot, V, *'Sobjectivism': Toward a Constructivist Methodology*, University of Toronto, International Studies Association, 2007.

Press Online, "Brajović: Srbija krivicu prebacuje u crnogorsko dvorište" (online, 2010) available at: www.pressonline.rs/info/politika/102247/brajovic-srbija-krivicu-prebacuje-u-crnogorsko-dvoriste.html

Radevic, R and Raicevic, N, *Context Analysis of the Security Sector Reform in Montenegro (1989–2009)*, Podgorica: Centre for Democracy and Human Rights – CEDEM, 2011.

Ramet, S, *The Three Yugoslavias: State-building and Legitimation, 1918–2005*, Bloomington: Indiana University Press, 2006.

Reiner, R, "Watching the Watchers: Theory and Research in Policing" in *The Politics of the Police* (4th ed.), London: Oxford University Press, 2010.

Republic of Montenegro Department of Police, *Annual Report* (online, 2010) available at: www.upravapolicije.com/crna-gora-uprava-policije-godisnji-izvjestaj_1570_7_33.html

Republic of Montenegro Department of Police, information on SEPCA Conference (online, 2012) available at: http://www.upravapolicije.com/index.php?IDSP=3210&jezik=lat

RTV, "Medojević i Knežević na 'savetovanju' u SAD" (online, 2010) available at: www.rtv.rs/sr_lat/region/sad:-crna-gora-tranzit-za-narkotike_176392.html?utm_source=feedburner&utm_m

Schouten, L, Gajić, N. and Riggle, S, *Reforma policije u Crnoj Gori 2001–2005: Ocene i preporuke*, Podgorica: OSCE Mission to Serbia and Montenegro, 2006

Sević, Z and Bakrac, D, "Reforma policije u Crnoj Gori" in Caparini, M and Otwin, M (eds), *Transforming Police in Central and Eastern Europe, Process and Progress*, Munster: Lit Verlag, 2004.

Stojanović, S and Gajić, N, *Reforma policije u Crnoj Gori 2006–2011*, Podgorica: OSCE Mission to Serbia and Montenegro, 2012.

Stojković, Z, *Korupcija u CG*, Podgorica: CEMI, 2009.

Vučetić, S, "The Stability pact for SEE as a Security-Building Institution" in *Southeast European Politics*, 2:2 (2001): 109–134.

Vreme, "Crna Gora dve decenije vlasti Demokratske partije socijalista: Sada i zauvek" (online, 2009) available at: www.vreme.com/cms/view.php?id=855733&print=yes

Youth Initiative for Human Rights, *Human Rights in Montenegro – 2011*, Podgorica: Youth Initiative for Human Rights, 2012.

Interviews

1 Officers and managers from the Border Police, Montenegro
a Branch Office of the Border Police, Tuzi, Podgorica, 14 March 2012
b Maritime Border Police, Božaj, Podgorica, 14 March 2012
c Branch Office of the Border Police, Goransko, Plužine, 19 March 2012
d Branch Office of the Border Police, Debeli Brijeg, Herceg Novi, 20 March 2012
e Branch Office of the Border Police, Bogaje, Rožaje, 21 March 2012
2 Lecturers (2) at the Police Academy, Danilovgrad, 25 April 2012
3 Manager at the Department for International Relations and European Integration, Podgorica, 9 May 2012
4 Officer and Manager at the Department for Combating Organized Crime and Corruption, Podgorica, 10 May 2012
5 Officer and Manager at the Department for the Fight against *Drugs* and Smuggling, Podgorica, 10 May 2012
6 Manager at the National Central Bureau of INTERPOL, 10 May 2012
7 Manager at the Department for Foreigners and Illegal Migration, 11 May 2012

5

THE POLICE PROFESSION IN KOSOVO

Caught in the quagmire between politics and a regional security community

Florian Qehaja and Armend Bekaj

Introduction

A police profession which is subject to democratic control is a relatively novel notion in postcommunist and post-conflict societies in the Western Balkans. A conventional approach to police and policing considers it to be part of a 'social contract', in which citizens surrender some of their powers and freedoms to the state (and by default also to the police) in return for a form of social order and rule of law. For the purposes of this chapter, the police profession is understood to encapsulate the institutions and personnel that comprise its service, a service that is buttressed by organizational rules, recruitment policies, standards, codes and public relations (Abbott, 1988; OSCE, 2008). Similarly, theories of Security Sector Reform (SSR) view the police as a structure mandated to provide public order and carry out security tasks for the purpose of the public good.

In Kosovo, the police force was established from scratch in the immediate post-conflict period in 1999, and thus it finds itself at a crossroads between creating its own legacy and consolidating a regional standing for itself. In fact, there is a strong link between the manner in which the police profession in Kosovo was developed and its positioning in the regional security community. The mixed composition of the police reflects a unique structure with three types of members: former combatants from the last armed conflict, former members of the socialist (Yugoslav) police force and new recruits from the post-conflict era. From a conceptual point of view, this composition can be viewed as a triangle of post-conflict, post-socialist and state-building elites. The complexity surrounding the police profession in Kosovo also results from the introduction of a myriad of foreign-driven techniques and methods, which have consequently become embedded in its organizational behaviour.

The authors approach the topic by testing it against theories of epistemic and security communities in the Western Balkan region. The chapter begins by examining the degree to which it is possible to talk of an existing and locally-driven security community in the region. It then analyses the internal capacities, as well as the challenges, that help or hinder the Kosovo Police in its quest for regional engagement. Next, the chapter explores external factors, such as Kosovo's political relations with its neighbours, that pose obstacles to the inclusion of its police in the wider regional security community. The chapter argues that the police in Kosovo can make a contribution to the further advancement of a security community in the region through the further professionalization of police services and a healthy detachment from negative politics when tackling common security challenges.

The chapter is divided into three sections. The first part delves into some of the main theories of epistemic and security communities to assist us in testing our empirical data. The second and third parts, which are empirically-based, are distinct from one another but are equally important for understanding the standing of the Kosovo Police *vis-à-vis* the wider regional security community. The second part explores the organizational structure of the police from its inception to its current state, and in so doing assists the reader in understanding its capacities for a cohesive identity and culture. The third part of the chapter provides some thoughts on epistemic communities and regional police cooperation from the perspective of the police in Kosovo.

Applicable theories of epistemic and security communities

In examining the police profession in Kosovo, and by extension its role in regional cooperation and regional security, we will use Haas's (1992) notion of epistemic communities. Such communities may have a transnational character as a result of the 'diffusion of community ideas through conferences, journals, research collaboration, and a variety of informal communications and contacts' (ibid., 17). Similarly, Sudgen (2006) highlights the importance of epistemic communities in tackling 'sources of violence' and thus advancing 'security sector governance.' In this way, academics can contribute to the formation and consolidation of 'epistemic communities', defined as specific collections of individuals who share the same worldview, or *episteme* (Haas, 1992). Haas further elaborates that the epistemic community is a 'network of professionals with recognized expertise and competence in a particular domain and an authoritative claim to policy-relevant knowledge within that domain or issue-area'. According to Haas, for such a community to be effective and consistent in its approach, its members must share certain principles and practices. Specifically, they must have:

1. a shared set of normative and principled beliefs which provide a value-based rationale for the social action of community members;
2. shared causal beliefs derived from their analysis of practices leading or contributing to a central set of problems in their domain and which then serve as the basis for elucidating the multiple linkages between possible policy actions and desired outcomes;

3. shared notions of validity – intersubjective, internally defined criteria for weighing and validating knowledge in their domain of their expertise; and
4. a common policy of enterprise – a set of common practices associated with a set of problems to which their professional competence is directed, presumably out of the conviction that human welfare will be enhanced as a consequence (Haas, 1992: 3).

The principles shared by an epistemic community are similar to security-related 'communities of practice', defined as 'likeminded groups of practitioners who are informally as well as contextually bound by a shared interest in learning and applying a common practice' (Adler, 2008: 196). In fact, the diffusion of ideas as a precursor to the creation of Haas's epistemic communities is well juxtaposed with the idea of 'likeminded groups of practitioners' that work together for an epistemic community. Security communities rest in part on sharing rational and moral expectations and dispositions of self-restraint. By taking as models the successful expansion of the West's security communities into Central and Eastern European countries (CEEC) during the 1990s, the issue at hand is how to successfully replicate this expansion and extend it into Southeast Europe. Indeed, if one is to discern the traces of the expansion of the so-called 'cooperative security' community, one can see that it grew from the Helsinki Process, henceforth endowing European institutions, in particular the EU and NATO, with the practices necessary for the spread of social structure (Adler, 2008: 197).

While it is important to create an epistemic security community that is transnational and scholarly in its approach, it is just as vital that there is functional police cooperation at the regional level. The key challenge for the police – but also for other security mechanisms – is how to intensify regional cooperation through across the board professionalization. Vučetić (2001) emphasizes three factors as preconditions for the above-mentioned expansion of cooperative security: socialization (high quantity and quality of exchange), reciprocity (trust and social learning) and intersubjectivity (shared identity, 'we-feeling' and mutual sympathy). He states that there is nothing to suggest that externally imposed arrangements cannot evolve into indigenous security bodies. 'The examples of NATO and the OSCE demonstrate that outside intervention can create the material conditions – a security environment – in which a special SP [Stability Pact] culture can arise and a regional security dynamics can develop, self-directed or as sheltered as a sub-community within a larger region' (Vučetić 2001: 118).

While the topic of this chapter fits well within the literature on security communities, the value it adds derives from the specificities of the Kosovo Police. These specificities begin with the founding of the force and continue through its interaction with the international community, and more recently its regional engagement, which is partially stalled due to regional political relations in the Western Balkans. Also, Vučetić's three factors are not easily accommodated into the Kosovo case, since there is a limited exchange and interaction at the regional level (socialization); trust constitutes an important part of communicating and sharing (reciprocity); while the sense of 'we-feeling' is detached from the so-called Yugosphere, as the (Albanian) language – predominantly spoken in Kosovo – potentially poses obstacles to reciprocity (intersubjectivity).

To echo Vučetić's clarion call, this chapter shares in common with other chapters in this book the question of whether such a security environment, or security community, can take root and grow in today's Western Balkan region. In assessing the probability of this scenario, we examine the level of interaction of professional communities – such as the police – and assess how far Deutsch's highly relevant definition of security communities as deriving from 'dependable expectations of peaceful change' (Deutsch et al., 1957: 5) is met. We define a security community as one which has made a convincing departure from a violent past and strives for peace. It is 'a social theory of IR in which shared identities play a crucial role in the construction of national interests, international practices, and regions' (Adler, 2005: 185). For the purposes of this chapter, we focus on the interaction of the Kosovo Police within the Western Balkan region. This geographical delineation is appropriate due to the common past shared by the case studies concerned and because 'in security terms, "region" means that a distinct and significant subsystem of security relations exists among a set of states whose fate is that they have been locked into geographical proximity with each other' (Buzan, 1991: 188).

In order to deconstruct regional security cooperation, it is useful to refer to Adler and Barnett's differentiation between three types of security communities: *nascent*, when states cooperate and coordinate policies without seeking a security community; *ascendant*, with increasing institutional networks and a sense of 'we-ness'; and *mature*, with deep institutionalization, a well-articulated common identity and mutual expectations of peaceful resolution of disputes (Adler and Barnett, 1998). This will be elaborated in the context of Kosovo in the last part of the chapter.

The authors of this chapter applied a number of mainly qualitative data collection methods. The data were collected throughout 2012 until 2015. In order to gain insight into the police profession from a practical and first-hand point of view, semi-structured interviews were conducted with current and former police officers. The intention was to conduct long structured interviews with key selected stakeholders with the aim of gaining an understanding of the strategic development of the institution rather than the operational side. Data were also gathered during the authors' involvement with security sector reform in Kosovo and the wider region between 2008 and 2014. Routine professional interaction with police officers, representatives of relevant parliamentary committees and the ministries overseen by those committees, as well as international organizations operating in the region, has helped in collecting research data pertinent for this topic. Respect for confidentiality and research ethics were observed at all times.

Developing a police profession from the ground

Following the 1999 war, Kosovo became submerged in a complex post-conflict system of governance, led by the United Nations Interim Administration Mission in Kosovo (UNMIK), supported by a number of organizations which assisted the latter in its work, including the Organization for Security and Co-operation in Europe (OSCE), the UN High Commissioner for Refugees (UNHCR), the European Union (EU) and others. With this system of governance, the whole security sector was reconstructed from scratch. The Kosovo Liberation Army (KLA) was disbanded and transformed into a civilian organization, the Kosovo Protection Corps (KPC). The new police structures absorbed within their ranks a large number of former KLA combatants. Under the executive competencies of the UNMIK chief, the OSCE was given primary responsibility for recruiting and training new police officers (O'Neill, 2004).

The first police officers were deployed in the immediate aftermath of the war, in July 1999. Their numbers peaked in March 2001, with over 4,500 members from all of Kosovo's communities (Bajraktari et al., 2006: 49). Concurrent with the development of a domestic police force, a large contingent of international police officers was also brought in. Their numbers decreased steadily with the increase of capacities of the Kosovo Police. The police thus began to perform the main security-related tasks as it was the only local security institution to be granted executive powers during UNMIK's governance (Kosovar Centre for Security Studies [KCSS], 2012).

The unique circumstances which dictated the development of Kosovo's security institutions in the late 1990s had a direct effect on its police service. The creation of the new security mechanisms was conducted without direct institutional correlations with the former security structures of socialist Yugoslavia. Therefore, considering that both the police and the security sector in general were built from scratch, the process was closer to 'development' than 'reform', and can be referred to as 'security sector development' (Qehaja and Vrajolli 2011). Although there is no clear definition of 'security sector development' as most sources refer to Security Sector Reform (SSR), the most relevant source summarizes it as 'a process dealing with the legacy of armed conflict, including the dissolution of military formations and their integration into new security structures and/or civilian life' (Bryden and Hänggi, 2004: 15). This definition can be applied convincingly to postwar Kosovo and its security mechanisms.

The development of the new police structure implied a number of challenges in creating a cohesive, standardized structure for all officers. In fact, the creation of a cohesive, sustainable and professional culture within the ranks of the police was particularly challenging. The complexities related to its development from zero, the role of international actors and regional political impasses have all made the police culture in Kosovo distinctively different from that of other police forces in the region.

According to interviews conducted for this chapter, there is general agreement that the composition of today's Kosovo Police is a result the existence of 'three categories' or elites of personnel (L. Neziri, pers. comm, 5 June 2012; R. Marmullaku, pers. comm, 25 May 2012):

- The first category is comprised of members educated in and with experience of working in the old Yugoslav system. These were either of former police forces themselves or were part of the reserve component of that force.
- The second category is comprised of former KLA combatants who joined the police force with a completely different type of experiential baggage to the first category. They were usually young men who had fought in the last armed conflict in the late 1990s and were reintegrated from the disbanded KLA into the newly created police.
- The third category of police personnel consists of new recruits whose experience with the police began from point 'zero', and who grew up professionally within the ranks of the new, post-conflict police.

The third category consists of a new wave of young men and women who have no direct links with past security structures. Their career often begins when they join the police. However, tension between the first two categories, especially in the immediate aftermath of the war, was quite palpable. On the one hand, the expertise and experience of the first category of police officers was undeniable and was very much needed during the initial phases of formation of the police. However, this category was often side-lined, looked upon with suspicion, or left out of decision-making structures due to their association with the old Yugoslav regime. To fill the void, former KLA combatants were recruited, joining the police with a completely different sort of experience: they had not been police officers in the past, and they had fought in 1998–99 and were now being 'transformed' into police officers. Further, their attitude and approach towards others was driven by postwar euphoria where the role of former combatants was more emphasized than that of other groups. At various points during the development of the Kosovo Police, between 25 and 50 per cent of the force were former KLA combatants. This was part of the North Atlantic Treaty Organization (NATO) led initiative to transform and reintegrate former combatants into post-conflict civilian life in Kosovo.

This mismatch between legacies of police officers has created friction over the years, and has subsequently resulted in delay in the formation of a cohesive police profession with a single identity and one culture. Paoline's reference to 'us' versus 'them' (Paoline 2003: 201) best illustrates such attitudes among police officers. The 'us' and 'them' dilemma reflects a lack of social cohesion within the police force, which consequently affects the overall performance of the institution. Hence, there was a need to increase uniformity, both physically and in attitude, starting from training and when out on patrol, to ensure that the organizational culture was instilled in the new recruits. There were setbacks in achieving this 'uniformity' in the attitude and profession of the Kosovo Police in its first few years, precisely because of the social and professional categorization of police officers depending on where they came from and the perceived baggage they brought with them. As a result, former KLA combatants who became police officers began to be perceived as slightly more trustworthy by their colleagues when compared to officers who had served under the old Yugoslav regime. However, while the first category might have enjoyed respect within their Kosovar Albanian community, the same was not true for the Kosovar Serb community, for instance, precisely because of their KLA legacy.

The second factor influencing the formation of police culture is what some interviewees referred to as the 'implications of various international organizational and managerial cultures' in its setup (I Azizi, pers. comm., 19 June 2012; B Selimi, pers. comm., 11 June 2012). The Kosovo Police is the recipient of multi-layered international assistance, which in consequence has affected the 'ethics and discipline of police officers' (I Azizi, pers. comm., 19 June 2012). There is also a clear inclination to state the prevalence of an 'American organizational culture in the development of the police'. This 'culture' can be discerned in the force's rules, regulations, grading and command procedures (R Marmullaku, pers. comm., 25 May 2012). However, the importation of such standard operating procedures comes with its own challenges. First, although the 'American organizational culture' is predominant, it is sometimes mixed with other training methods from Western European countries, which poses the problem of reconciling these methods. Second, the transplantation of foreign practices is often in conflict with local needs, which are not always compatible. Moreover, there is a wider incompatibility at play, a 'bifurcation of professional cultures', which affects the whole judicial system: while the police profession and standard operating procedures are largely based on American or British practices, the justice system is largely based on the practices of mainland Europe (B. Selimi, pers. comm., 11 June 2012).

Selimi also sheds light on the relationship between police executives and the international community in Kosovo. As a vestige of Kosovo's recent past as an international protectorate run by UNMIK, the Police continues to be occasionally too dependent on international assistance and advice. Selimi also stated that there is a culture of excessive loyalty, bordering on servility, towards either senior officers or the international community (B. Selimi, pers. comm., 11 June 2012). According to him, this culture was established so that officers could benefit from accelerated advancement in their careers.

While the effect of external support on Kosovo's security sector is generally positive, the import of myriad training cultures into police structures can have long-lasting effects. For example, this helps create a police identity which is distinctively different from that found in the wider region, with long term ramifications for the cohesiveness of the regional security community. Undoubtedly, international assistance has gone a long way towards shaping the professional culture of the police. However, a side effect is that there remain issues over the prioritization and localization of that assistance into a coherent and uniform professional service. Some authors point out the dangers of 'diverse cultural implications' present in the legislation. Benson argues that legal and procedural reform cannot be effective without deeper cultural changes and uniformity within the ranks of the police. 'Without reform of police culture, we could end up with merely a Potemkin village of legal reforms in which everything stays the same behind the scenes' (Benson,

2001: 681). As can be seen from the interviews quoted above, the challenge for the Kosovo Police is to transform those diverse cultural implications into a local context, with local 'buy in.'

Importing external expertise from the USA and Western European countries has played a crucial role in laying the foundations of a professional police culture which is still being cultivated and harnessed. With the formation and progressive consolidation of mechanisms of democratic control, particularly since independence in February 2008, the police have become further embedded within Kosovo's wider security sector. Consequently, notions such as 'further professionalization', 'police culture' and 'community policing', although very well taught and trained from best practice scenarios, require further adaptation to the context of the local culture. Efforts at rapid westernization of the security sector were not compatible with Kosovo's level of democratization and its sensitive circumstances. Kosovo is an example of an externally imposed security sector which has not proved conducive to sustainable reforms (Bryden and Hänggi, 2004) as a result of a lack of coherency in policing standards. This can be illustrated using the example of cases of discrepancies between policing techniques. Experts from various countries each presented their own domestic techniques, thus jeopardizing the uniform set of standards among the police, as the methods implemented were completely incompatible with each other (Qehaja and Vrajolli, 2011).

In addition to imported international practices and cultures, attention should also be paid to the role played by domestic politics in forming, shaping and giving direction to the profession and culture of the police in Kosovo. Because of the specific political circumstances under which the police force was created, we will use Reiner's (2010) proposition for probing the 'vexed conceptual relationship between policing and politics'. The politics-police dichotomy in the case of Kosovo is intriguing and requires particular attention. This is because in the Kosovo case, where the police force was created after 1999, the line between politics and policing as two separate professions remains quite blurred. Political control over the police is exercised through the appointment of the police director by the Minister of Internal Affairs. Appointments are made by public servants on the Commission for High Appointments, who have limited knowledge of security policy and are often under the influence of the political elite. In other words, political interference in senior police appointments and in the conduct of police operations reflects an institution that acts in the interests of the ruling parties. Examples of political interference have been noted in police operations, political appointments, promotion to higher ranks, empowerment through various means of support and other matters (Forum for Security, 2011).

There is also a notable trend for high-level police officials to move into politics. For instance, the former President of Kosovo, Atifete Jahjaga, took office in April 2011, having previously served as a police colonel, and then prior to gaining the presidency being Deputy General Director of the Police. Jahjaga was the most senior ranking woman in the police. Her appointment was the obvious result of political calculations between three political parties (two coalition partners and the biggest opposition party), in an agreement mediated by the US Ambassador to Kosovo. Jahjaga's appointment helped avoid a political deadlock and preceded the creation of a new coalition government in Kosovo in 2011. What is disconcerting, however, is the involvement of national and international politicians in the police hierarchy, resulting in the appointment of a top official to a high political post. Another high-profile example of a switch from the police profession to a political career occurred when the former General Director of the Police, Behar Selimi, became a Member of the Assembly of Kosovo in April 2011. But far from being considered interference, the move of former senior police officers into politics can be interpreted as an attempt at career progression by certain members of the force (B Selimi, pers. comm., 11 June 2012). Former senior police officers claim that once they have reached the top of the hierarchy, there are no further opportunities for advancement within the institution, therefore a number of them decide to join other sectors.

However, Selimi's opinion is not shared by other former colleagues who state that the police have been deliberately used as a platform for moving into politics. Some other stakeholders went further in arguing that the inclusion of former senior police officers in politics is just a switch from uniform to political party, claiming that these officers were affiliated with the respective political party in the first place. Any change of government leads to calculations by senior police officers over their potential inclusion in politics and the government (R Marmullaku, pers. comm., 25 May 2012). In other words, there is a structural hazard at play here, and the shift from police to politics is embedded in the culture of the institution.

Such a relationship between the police and politics has been described as a 'crisis of elites in Kosovo', with no clear distinction between 'political elites', 'academic elites', 'musical elites' and others. Such is also the case with the 'police elite', which struggles to establish its own identity. The elite within police ranks is still so fragile that whenever a senior police member makes the jump to the 'political elite', it disrupts the entire system.

Some argue that there has been tremendous investment in the police, and consequently knowledge is transferred from that institution to other sectors, including politics (L Neziri, pers. comm., 5 June 2012). The high turnover of police officers and their interest in applying to other sectors (perhaps due to low salaries) shows that former police officers are very competitive candidates when applying for civilian jobs. This certainly hampers the consistency of the institution. Over more than a decade, much has been invested in recruiting and training police officers in Kosovo. However, helping them reach a certain professional threshold of qualification does not resolve the issue of keeping them within the ranks. This is largely due to the very high demands of the job market and the poor economy. For many, enrolling in the police is a way of earning a living, of having a job. The downside to this is that after they have undergone training and obtained better qualifications, they sometimes leave the police and take up better job opportunities. As a result, since its establishment in 1999 around 2,000 officers have abandoned the police for other sectors (I Azizi, pers. comm., 19 June 2012).

Further, Kosovo's politics-police dichotomy corresponds to what some authors refer to as the institutional legitimacy. It is widely argued that discourse and public perception play a key role in shaping the nature of a police force (McClellan & Gustafson, 2012). Quantitative data show that the Kosovo Police has been repeatedly rated among the most trusted security providers, albeit with a marked decrease in recent years (KCSS, 2013). The high level of public trust in the institution could result from two factors, first social sympathy towards the uniform and second the police's democratic behaviour towards citizens. In other words, this level of legitimacy provides good grounds for certain individuals to advance further into politics and other domains of public life.

Regional police cooperation: where does Kosovo fit in?

As seen above, the police profession and its reform is not just a technical issue. It consists of a multitude of elements where politics, both local and international, plays a significant role in constructing identity. In fact, politics is often a determining factor for the level of reform and, by default, for the nature of cooperation in the wider regional context. More than a decade after the end of the wars in former Yugoslavia, the level of regional interaction between security mechanisms, and specifically the police, continues to be frequently obstructed by politics. Complex and sensitive decision-making processes happen under conditions of political uncertainty and are often stalled or remain stagnant due to power brokering at the most senior levels of governance.

In Kosovo, the police force plays a significant role in contributing to the professionalization and completion of a national security community. Its contribution to such a community at the regional level, however, continues to pose various challenges. At this point, it is useful to recall Deutsch's definition of the security community as the existence of 'dependable expectations of peaceful change' (Deutsch et al., 1957: 5). We concur with the other authors of this volume in stating that it was the international community, first and foremost NATO and the EU, that was the main proponent of a security community in the Western Balkans, successfully introducing conditionality as a mechanism for bringing all regional actors together (Bechev, 2006). This corresponds with some scholars' claims that cooperation in the region can be driven only as a result of outside intervention and under the auspices of foreign actors.

At this point, we will use Adler and Barnett's (1998) differentiation between three types of security communities – nascent, ascendant and mature – to examine the Kosovo Police's role in regional security cooperation. Examining the level of consolidation of a regional security community *vis-à-vis* the Kosovo Police, we place its cooperation with neighbours as generally between nascent and ascendant. It is ascendant and on the rise with those neighbouring police services with which it enjoys excellent working relations, such as Albania. However, it is stalled at the nascent stage with the Serbian police services, for example, largely due to the political situation. The expectation stemming from the Brussels Agreement reached in 2013 is that the Kosovo Police's relations with its counterpart in Serbia will move towards the ascendant phase. If this happens, then the region will have tackled one of the most serious impediments to creating a stable security community in the region.

The political dialogue between Prishtina and Belgrade, and the subsequent agreement initialled by the two Prime Ministers, may be ushering the region into a new chapter of regional cooperation, with positive effects on cross border police engagement. The EU has brokered an agreement on Integrated Border Management between Kosovo and Serbia. Although there are obstacles to this agreement being implemented on the ground, the political dialogue may have given the region a renewed impetus to intensify regional engagement. As a result, cooperation between the Kosovo Police and its counterparts in Serbia may gradually be moving forward and away from its nascent stage, where it has stagnated for more than a decade.

However, the reality on the ground is that the Kosovo Police is yet to become a real contributing actor in a wider regional security community. For example, although there are 33 regional security and justice related initiatives in Southeast Europe (Prezelj, 2013), Kosovo is not a fully-fledged member of most of them. Rather, it is either represented via the EU or has observer status, and that only in a handful of them. Although the EU, as guarantor of the Brussels agreement has not so far managed to ensure that the agreement is implemented, its success is based on the over-simplified assumption that the continuation of dialogue reflects significant progress in itself (Qehaja, 2014). Nevertheless, this type of cooperation always relies on political developments. So far, as mentioned above, Kosovo is restricted from participating fully in these initiatives.

In fact, political developments influence and shape Vučetić's (2001) three factors: socialization, reciprocity and intersubjectivity. But politics certainly constrains professional cooperation between police officers. The former commander of Kosovo's border police recounted how on one occasion he approached Serbian border police officers, openly explaining to them the need to cooperate and refrain from politics (B Selimi, pers. comm., 11 June 2012). He explained that his Serbian counterparts' response was positive, but the communication could not be formalised. There are also several specific cases that reflect 'cooperation without recognition' (V Elshani, conference, 24 January 2014). This illustrates that police interaction across borders is often politicized, or is kept hostage to political processes within host countries. The above example shows that there may be professional willingness at the technical level which is overridden by political decisions.

However, such pessimism about Kosovo's regional cooperation is countered by its better cooperation with its other neighbouring police services in Albania, Macedonia and Montenegro. Our interviewees particularly highlighted the excellent cooperation that exists between police officers in Kosovo and Albania (B Selimi, pers. comm., 11 June 2012; L Neziri, pers. comm., 5 June 2012). Cooperation between the two police services is shown by the example of Kosovo Police patrols operating and assisting the Albanian police deep inside the territory of Albania, as far as the vicinity of Tirana, especially during the summer holidays. In addition, there is joint crossing point border management where citizens are controlled and checked at only one border post (the so called enter-enter control).

Sound cooperation also exists with Montenegrin and Macedonian police officers, with a track record of good cooperation practice (L Neziri, pers. comm., 5 June 2012; B Selimi, pers. comm., 11 June 2012; R Marmullaku, pers. comm., 25 May 2012). While cooperation is not at the level of that with Albania, satisfaction was expressed over cooperation with both countries. A factor in this is language, as most Macedonian border police officers come from the Albanian community, which makes communication much easier. If communication takes place with ethnic Macedonian counterparts, then Albanian community police officers are present to facilitate communication (B Selimi, pers. comm., 11 June 2012). The situation is slightly different with Montenegro where the Albanian minority community has almost no presence at border crossing points. However, if communication is necessary, the Montenegrin police appoints Albanian speaking police officers who liaise with the Police HQ in Kosovo (B Sadriu, pers. comm., July 2012).

Two key dimensions are crucially important for police cooperation, and subsequently for a sustainable security community: trust and language. These are interconnected and have a significant role in ensuring cooperation. First, language poses a challenge to communication between the region's police officers. The fact that communication is conducted more easily with the Albanian Police than with other neighbouring police forces rests largely on the question of which language is used. Nevertheless, at least from Kosovo's perspective, the language dimension is not the primary obstacle to cooperation, as both a significant proportion of Kosovo Police officers speak Serbian or Montenegrin and some Albanian minority police officers serve at border crossing points on the other side. For example, Albanian minority community officers serve at three of Serbia's six border crossing points with Kosovo. The situation is similar on the Kosovo side, with officers from the Serbian community serving at up to five border crossing points. The situation at the border crossing points with Macedonia and Montenegro is similar.

Second, the impression provided by interviewees is that trust is a complex issue, meaning that it cannot be achieved quickly. Establishing trust requires more time, while the exchange of information must be tracked. But the issue of trust in police cooperation is not specific to the Western Balkans, as there are similar trust-related challenges within EU member-states. At a police conference, Cecilia Malmström, the EU's Commissioner for Home Affairs, mentioned more than fourteen times in a five-page speech the need to build trust in order to secure better cooperation between police services in the EU (Malmström, 2011). She went on to explicitly ask police representatives to trust each other when sharing experiences, information and know-how.

Conclusion

More than a decade after the establishment of the police force as part of the wider security sector, Kosovo faces ongoing challenges. Since 1999, Kosovo has been a melting pot of a diverse set of mechanisms for maintaining social control, law and order.

The previously existing myriad international and local police bodies – referred to by Reiner as the 'pluralization of policing' – have now given way to a more delineated structure, largely consisting of Kosovo's own institutions. In the case of Kosovo, the pluralization of policing refers to the importation of police traditions as best practice from the USA and Western European countries. It also refers to the mixed composition of the ranks of the police: former combatants, former officers from the socialist system and new recruits from the post-conflict era. Today's police service therefore results from a mix of police reform, with the practice of the police profession and community policing in the local context still to be consolidated.

A new police culture is being shaped, appropriate to the local context, while its police officers are being imbued with a sense of professionalism. However, creeping politicization of the police profession is causing setbacks to the latter. The dichotomy between the police profession and politics is especially critical in Kosovo. The police profession in Kosovo is at an important crossroads in its short history: internally, it continues to deepen its practice of democratic policing to serve all communities, while facing politically driven challenges, particularly in the north. At the same time, externally it faces hindrances to regional engagement due to the political situation, specifically Serbia's refusal to recognize Kosovo as an independent country.

However, on the other hand, the concept of security communities or communities of practice as described by Deutsch (1957), Adler (1998; 2008) and Vučetić (2001) relies precisely on the diffusion of a shared set of ideas and interests in a given region. Therefore, any hindrance of regional engagement imposed on the Kosovo Police is equally a setback for a fully-fledged regional security community. To illustrate the simple equation of this situation, the former cannot do without the latter and vice versa. In other words, the puzzle of the regional security community remains unsolved as long as any of its actors remain marginalized or not completely involved. The solution to this puzzle seems to require the resolution of seemingly larger political questions.

Such non-inclusive politics at the regional and international levels continues to condition the police's inclusion in a wider regional security community in line with those in other Western Balkan countries. Therefore, this insulation or isolation of the police does not assist the region as a whole to truly form regional mechanisms of cooperation, and continues to hinder the creation of sustainable and inclusive security communities. The April 2013 Brussels Agreement between Prishtina and Belgrade has the potential to open the door to more constructive cooperation between the two police services and, by default, help the region approach a more credible security community.

Bibliography

Abbott, A, *The System of Professions: An Essay on the Division of Expert Labor*, University of Chicago, 1988.

Adler, E, *Communitarian International Relations: The Epistemic Foundations of International Relations*, London: Routledge, 2005.

Adler, E, "The Spread of Security Communities: Communities of Practice, Self-Restraint and NATO's Post-Cold War Transformation" in *European Journal of International Relations* 14:2 (2008): 195–230.

Adler, E and Barnett, M (eds), *Security Communities*, Cambridge University Press, 1998.

Bajraktari, Y, Boutellis, A, Gunja, F, Harris, DY, Kapsis, J, Kaye, E and Rhee, J, *The PRIME System: Measuring the Success of Post-Conflict Police Reform*, Princeton (online, 2006) available at: www.princeton.edu/bobst/docs/WWS591b_FINAL_Police_Reform_Report.pdf

Bechev, D, (2006) "Carrots, Sticks and Norms: the EU and Regional Cooperation in Southeast Europe" in *Journal of Southern Europe and the Balkans* 8:1 (2006): 27–43.

Benson, RW, "Changing Police Culture: The Sine Qua Non of Reform" in *Loyola of Los Angeles Law Review* 681 (2001): 680–690.

Bryden, A and Hänggi, H, *Reforming and Reconstructing the Security Sector: Security Governance in Post-conflict Peacebuilding*, Geneva Centre for Democratic Control of Armed Forces, 2004.

Buzan, B, *People, States and Fear: An Agenda for International Security Studies in the Post-Cold War Era*, Harlow: Pearson Longman, 1991.

Deutsch, K, Burrell, S, Kann, R, Lee, M, Lichterman, M, Lindgren, R, Loewenheim, F and Van Wagenen, R, *Political Community and the North Atlantic Area: International Organization in the Light of Historical Experience*, Princeton, NJ: Princeton University Press, 1957.

Forum for Security, *Reforms in Kosovo Police*, Prishtina (online, 2011) available at http://www.fiq-fci.org/repository/docs/Reforms_on_Kosovo_Police.pdf

Haas, P, "Introduction: Epistemic Communities and International Policy Coordination" in *International Organization* 41:1 (1992): 1–35.

Kosovar Centre for Security Studies, *Kosovo Security Barometer: Second Edition*, (online, 2013) available at: www.qkss.org/repository/docs/Kosovo_Security_Barometer-The_voices_of_Kosovo_Insights_and_Perceptions_199745.pdf

Malmström, C, *European Police Cooperation: Tools, Training and Trust, 14th European Police Conference*, (online, 2011) available at: http://europa.eu/rapid/pressReleasesAction.do?reference=SPEECH/11/110&format=HTML&aged=0&language=en&guiLanguage=en

McClellan, SE and Gustafson, BG, "Communicating Law Enforcement Professionalization: Social Construction of Standards" in *Policing: An International Journal of Police Strategies and Management* 5:1 (2012): 104–123.

O'Neill, WG, *Police Reform and Human Rights*, New York: Hurist, 2004.

Organization for Security and Co-operation in Europe, *Guidebook on Democratic Policing*, (online, 2008) available at: http://www.osce.org/spmu/23804

Paoline, EA, "Taking stock: Toward a Richer Understanding of Police Culture" in *Journal of Criminal Justice*, 31:3 (2003): 199–214.

Peake, G, *Policing the Peace: Police Reform Experiences in Kosovo, Southern Serbia and Macedonia*, London: Saferworld, 2004, available at: www.saferworld.org.uk/downloads/pubdocs/Policing%20PA2.pdf

Prezelj, I, "Challenges of Multilateral Regional Security and Defence Cooperation in South East Europe" in *Journal on European Perspective of the Western Balkans* 5:2 (2013): 83–112.

Qehaja, F, "Kosovo-EU Relations: The Status-Neutral Dilemma" in Felberbauer, E and Jureković, P, *Croatian Membership in the EU: Implications for the Western Balkans*, Vienna: Federal Ministry of Defence, 2013, 89–103.

Qehaja, F and Vrajolli, M, *Context analysis of security sector reform in Kosovo*, Prishtina, DCAF, BCSP and KCSS, 2011, available at: http://qkss.org/new/index.php?section=news&cmd=details&newsid=198&teaserId=11

Qehaja, F and Vrajolli, M, (2012) "Kosovo" in Klopfer, F and Stojanović, S, *Almanac of Security Sector Reform in the Western Balkans*, Geneva: DCAF, 2010, 103–129.

Reiner, R, *The Politics of the Police* (4th edn), Oxford: Oxford University Press, 2010.

Sudgen, J, "Security Sector Reform: The Role of Epistemic Communities in the UK" in *Journal of Security Sector Management* 4:4 (2006).

Telegrafi, "Kosovës i mungojnë elitat politike" [Kosovo lacks political elites] (online) available at: www.telegrafi.com/lajme/kosoves-i-mungojne-elitat-politike-2-31557.html

UNMIK, *Regulation 1999/8 on the Establishment of the Kosovo Protection Corps*, available at: www.unmikonline.org/regulations/1999/re99_08.pdf

Vučetić, S, "The Stability Pact for South Eastern Europe as a Security Community-Building Institution" in *Southeast European Politics* 2:2 (2001): 109–134.

Interviews

Behar Selimi, member of the Assembly of Kosovo, former Director of the Kosovo Police, Prishtina, interviewed on 11 June 2012

Brahim Sadriu, spokesperson for the Kosovo Police, Prishtina, interviewed on 15 June 2012

Colonel Izet Azizi, head of the Kosovo Police Department for Discipline, Prishtina, interviewed on 19 June 2012

Latife Neziri, security issues analyst, Prishtina, interviewed on 5 June 2012

Rifat Marmullaku, security issues analyst, Prishtina, interviewed on 13 June 2012

Veton Elshani, head of ILECU at the Kosovo Police, quotation from the Conference Security Research Forum: Belgrade-Prishtina-Tirana, Tirana, 24 Jan 2014

6

CROATIA'S POLICE AND SECURITY COMMUNITY BUILDING IN THE WESTERN BALKANS

Sandro Knezović, Vlatko Cvrtila and Zrinka Vučinović*

Introduction

After the fall of the bipolar international political system, Europe faced an entirely different reality and was beset by numerous challenges to its developing foreign and security policy, of which the violent disintegration of former Yugoslavia was among those with the most significant impact. Following many years of war suffered by most parts of the former state, engagement by the international community ultimately led to a period of calm and stabilization. The disintegration not only created new borders and increased the number of bilateral problems but also posed a series of challenges to internal stabilization and democratization.

Security sector reform in post-socialist and post-conflict societies, especially those which were involved in war and violence, represents a crucial step in creating the conditions for developing peace and stability. The police, as well as the armed forces, were engaged in war activities and other forms of violence during and after the war. Police reform represents a difficult challenge for societies which have been through war and internal divisions which have both threatened stability and limited the development of democracy. The development of police forces which are capable of acting in the new democratic environment and are able to face all the dangers of transitional societies, such as organized crime and corruption, has been very difficult for all the states created since the fall of Yugoslavia.

In the last two decades, all of the region's countries have undertaken reform of the security sector and of the police in particular. Initially directed toward building capacity to fulfil national security needs, reforms later began to develop in the direction of creating regional networks which could encourage cooperation and strengthen security relations between the region's states.

While previous research has concentrated on the role of states and international organizations, this chapter attempts to introduce a somewhat fresh approach to the topic. It investigates the extent to which regional security cooperation has developed, focusing more on the everyday practice of security professions – specifically the Croatian police – and their potential role in the development of the security community in the region.

By examining empirical findings from semi-structured interviews carried during 2012–2013, this research attempts to analyse the potential role of the Croatian police as a profession in the process of creating a security community in the Western Balkans. We investigate how the practice of Croatian police officers has contributed to a move away from an unfavourable conflict environment and towards the creation of a community characterized by mutual confidence and 'dependable expectations of peaceful change'.

Our main argument is that while overall stabilization of the region and security cooperation formally progress, there is limited evidence to support claims that a regional security community exists. It is of course true that the changing security paradigm of the contemporary IR arena, where asymmetric threats require a cooperative approach, coupled with the impact of EU and NATO conditionality, has stimulated enhanced regional security cooperation. However, while evidence can be found for mutual relevance and the basic responsiveness of units, as well as for compatibility of values, there is hardly any which supports a generalized common identity and loyalty, which according to the theoretical framework represents the most important indicator. However, this should not be seen as an argument to 'de-energize' regional security cooperation in the forthcoming period, as it remains essential for the overall stability of Southeast Europe.

The chapter begins by presenting a short overview of the chosen theoretical-methodological framework and its general relevance for this analysis, outlining the combination of concepts used, positioning this research with regards to the existing literature and addressing the strengths and limitations of the methods chosen. A brief introduction to the police profession and argumentation about the relevance of the case of the Croatian police for this research follows. The paper then focuses on its main component, which offers an overall analysis of the empirical findings tested against the selected theoretical framework. After processing the empirical findings and testing them against the selected theoretical framework, the final section of this chapter presents our conclusions.

Theoretical-methodological framework

The two main pillars of the theoretical-methodological framework used for this research are the concept of the security community and the theory of professions. Their main postulates and general relevance for this endeavour will be elaborated in the following paragraphs.

The phenomena of security communities, according to its main proponents (Deutsch et al., 1957; Adler and Barnett, 1998), conceptualizes the new IR discourse, according to which community exists at the international level, profoundly shaping security politics. Existing within an international community, states may well develop a pacific disposition, and thus, in the climate of contemporary IR, a process of political integration leads to the creation of communities built on the idea of 'dependable expectations of peaceful change'.

Adler (2008) defines security communities as communities of practice with cognitive evolution, likeminded groups of practitioners who are informally as well as contextually bound by a shared persuasion and ultimately by their own rational calculation. Security communities spread through the co-evolution of background knowledge and subjectivities of self-restraint. Adler argues that the combined effect of communities of practice and the institutionalization of self-restraint accounts both for the social construction of rationality, in the sense that cooperative security practices related to self-restraint help constitute dependable expectations of peaceful change, and for normative evolution in the sense that self-restraint brings about security through cooperation. Security communities as communities of practice, more specifically, represent a 'configuration of a domain' of knowledge that constitutes like-mindedness, a community of people that creates the social fabric of learning and a shared practice that embodies the knowledge that community develops, shares and maintains. Hence, according to this argument, people function as a community through relationships of mutual engagement that bind members together into a social entity. Their engagement in a common practice means that they share an identity and feel they are 'we'. Furthermore, the argument is that collective identities entail that people not only identify (positively) with other people's fate but also identify themselves, and those other people, as a group in relation to other groups.

A lively scholarly debate on professions has continued for quite some time, but given the diverse approaches taken to the subject it is difficult to identify a general definition that can be broadly acceptable. However, two outstanding authors have shaped the debate on this issue, representing two opposite discourses.

The 'very loose definition' offered by Abbott (1988), working within the wider functionalist discourse, describes professions as exclusive occupational groups applying somewhat abstract knowledge to particular cases. Abbot's underlying questions concern the evolution and interrelations of professions and, more generally, the ways occupational groups control knowledge and skills. He argues that the evolution of professions in fact results from their interrelations. These interrelations are in turn determined by the way these groups control their knowledge and skills and he identifies two different ways of doing that: control involving techniques (crafts) and control using abstract systems of knowledge (professions) (Abbott, 1988). According to Abbott, the central problem with the existing concept of professionalization is its focus on structure rather than work.

On the other hand, the structuralist discourse predominantly sees professions as smaller communities contained within the larger community of society. According to Goode, broad inquiry into the structural relations between the contained community and the larger one may allow important hypotheses about the forces that maintain both communities to be derived. Characteristic of all established professions, and a goal of each aspiring occupation, is a 'community of profession', which differs significantly from other types of communities and the containing one in particular. Typically, a profession, through its association and its members, controls admission to training and requires far more education from its trainees than the containing community demands. Both of the foregoing characteristics allow professions to enjoy more prestige from the containing community than can other occupations (Goode, 1957).

While these two theoretical concepts have been widely discussed and developed in the international IR literature (Deutsch et al., 1957; Adler and Barnett, 1998; Abbott, 1988; Goode, 1957), there are very few authors who deal with the security community concept in the Western Balkan region (Vučetić, 2001; Kavalski, 2008). Furthermore, there is almost no record of previous efforts to combine this concept with the theory of professions, nor attempts to analyse the role of security professions in the creation of a security community in that part of Europe. This research will try to fill this gap and respond to the following research question: What is the role of the Croatian police as a profession in the process of the transition of the Western Balkans from a conflict zone to a security community? Of course, by formulating the research question in this way, we are by no means prejudging either the existence of any role for the Croatian police as a profession in the aforementioned process nor the actuality of the security community as a concept in the region. This will be an integral part of our research findings.

We have decided to focus our research on the empirical dimension. The selection of semi-structured interviews has provided a useful set of tools, helping us acquire a wide range of valuable information – empirical findings – to be tested against the chosen theoretical framework. More precisely, the semi-structured interviews have provided a framework which maintains a fine balance between well organized and loosely informative communication with the security practitioners who are the focus of our research.

The development of the police in Croatia

In early 1990, the Republic of Croatia held its first free democratic elections to the Croatian Parliament. The Croatian Democratic Union (HDZ) won the elections, and introduced changes to the organization of the security sector. The laws of the former Yugoslavia (the SFRY) gave republics full authority over the police. For one year, the new government continued to act under the existing law, while seeking personnel changes and increasing the number of police officers in order to change the structure and functioning of the police. The new government attempted to find ways to strengthen its influence over the security sector. The authorities in Croatia thus focused on strengthening the police according to Article 25 of the Law on Internal Affairs, which allows the Minister of the Interior, in the case that the situation deteriorates, to establish new police units.

This resulted in the focus shifting from the development of the police as a component of internal security, expected to deal with the usual police duties, towards greater emphasis on its ability to perform military tasks.[1] The aforementioned had a direct impact on the quality of development of the police profession, while the attention devoted to providing adequate training and education was significantly below acceptable levels.

A year after the first democratic elections in 1990, the Law on Internal Affairs was modified, significantly altering the structure of the police. The law clearly indicated that the tasks of the Ministry of Interior are: protection of law and order, state organization and defence of the inviolability of national territory and the territorial integrity of Croatia. In addition, employees were prohibited from membership of political parties, although it was not stated in what way it would be possible to determine this and applicable sanctions were not set out.

In order to minimize the influence of federal bodies, it was clearly stated that the Croatian police must operate in accordance with policy decisions made by the Croatian parliament and government. Changes in legislation provided for the establishment of the National Guard as a full military formation, regardless of its formal attachment to Ministry of Interior structures. The Republic of Croatia focused on the construction of military structures within police forces as this was obviously the only legal option for organizing units that could respond to the military threat posed by the former JNA.

In 1994 more amendments to the Law on Internal Affairs were adopted, which represented a further step in the professionalization of the police. These amendments strengthened the structure of the police within the Ministry of Interior and led to the organization of civil defence as an important component of the protection of people and material goods. Changes were also made to the field of education, with the establishment of the Police Academy, with two components: the Police College and the secondary police school.

Amendments to the Law on Internal Affairs adopted in May 2000 were focused solely on the counter-intelligence agency within the MoI – The Service for Protection of Constitutional Order – altering some elements of its organization and area of responsibility.[2] The aforementioned means that in fact there was no significant legislative modernization in the field of internal affairs for almost fifteen years. The law passed in 1994 was in place until 2009 when the existing law was divided into two new laws: the Law on Police Affairs and Authorities (2009) and the Police Act (2011). Even then, the motivation for change did not come from within the system, but rather represented a consequence of external conditionality. Both laws were in line with EU recommendations and were part of the conditions which the country needed to meet as a precondition for full EU membership.

From 1990 onwards, the police profession in Croatia developed in a very specific context. Due to growing tensions and needs, the new authorities wanted to establish proper control over the security sector. They directed their focus towards strengthening the capacity of police work, but due to the unstable political situation and military threats from the JNA, a unit with a military mission was in fact created.

Therefore, it is clear that the development of the police was dominated by factors that, rather than strengthening the police profession, actually undermined the professionalization of the police. It is interesting to note that the situation has not changed significantly since the switch of power in 2000 from the HDZ to the coalition of left wing parties. Security sector reforms were initiated within the armed forces and the security service, while changes to the police were very limited. Those elements of the 1994 Law on Internal Affairs which politicized police structures influenced the work of the police almost for 15 years. This was clearly not an environment in which police forces could develop independence in their work with the aim of fulfilling all tasks and assignments in accordance with professional ethics. Only in 2009, as a result of EU conditionality, was the relevant legislation cleansed of its limiting elements, finally paving the way for the creation of a professional and independent police service. The aforementioned has particularly influenced the development of the police as a profession in the last few years. That fact, alongside the role of the Croatian police in the military conflict of the early 1990s, coupled with the consequences it had for its image in Croatian society and its capacity to engage in regional cooperation, makes this case very interesting for our research and thus hopefully adds to its overall value and its contribution to the broader scholarly debate on this matter.

Empirical findings

In order to carry out comprehensive analysis of the development of the police as a profession, it must be taken into account that over the last two decades Croatia's police has been faced with numerous changes and challenges, which have also affected its cooperation with police structures in other countries. On the other hand, the fact that there are various interpretations of the importance of the police and the way its role should be assessed, coupled with its interconnectedness with other subjects of society, emphasizes the complexity of this study. Therefore, research on the police as a profession is a multidimensional task.

It is obvious that over the last decade the region has made a significant move away from being a zone of conflict which threatened the security of both its immediate neighbourhood and the wider world, including the EU and the international community. However, in order to comprehend the current state transitional processes in the region, the aforementioned theoretical frameworks must be tested in practice, which is precisely the focus of the empirical part of this research.

Semi-structured interviews were used for this purpose, as they are more flexible than structured interviews or surveys, and allow topics to be explored rather than keeping to concepts and questions defined before the interview, although some materials were prepared in advance. Furthermore, semi-structured interviews can ensure more detailed answers which were useful in the presentation of our findings as well as in reaching our final conclusions. For obvious reasons, derived from the nature of this method, it can be expected to be helpful in testing the theoretical concepts presented beforehand.

Due to the post-conflict character of Western Balkan states, and more specifically the fact that their police forces fought each other during the 1990s, establishing and intensifying cooperation between them was regarded as an innovation. Our interviews therefore generally began with a question about changes to or initiation of police cooperation. Furthermore, it was important to gather information about the reasons for changes in perceptions within the Croatian police about professional cooperation in the region. Such perceptions varied from almost no interest in cooperation in the late 1990s to a positive attitude to the current high level of bilateral and regional cooperation.

We were able to detect three main sets of motives or reasons[3] for the above-mentioned changes:

- Transformation of the security paradigm and new security threats;
- External conditionality;
- Increasing practical institutional and informal cooperation.

Analysis of these three sets of reasons or motives for changes in Croatian police officers' perceptions of professional cooperation in the region actually represents 'a summary of findings' from our empirical research and is drawn exclusively from the responses we obtained in interviews.[4] The first two sets are obviously driven from outside the region, while the third set develops internally, but as a consequence of the previous two.

Transformation of the security paradigm and new security threats

The contemporary threats that appeared in the international arena in the early 2000s – particularly terrorist organizations and organized crime networks with an increasing level of organizational sophistication and use of modern technology – have significantly altered the security discourse. Their ability to operate beyond the borders of the states where they were founded and the practical difficulties faced by the transatlantic community in attempting to efficiently contain them have meant that an increased focus on a cooperative approach to security has become necessary. These trends were also recognized by NATO in its 1999 Strategic Concept: 'The Alliance seeks to preserve peace and to reinforce Euro-Atlantic security and stability by … continued pursuit of partnership, cooperation, and dialogue with other nations as part of its co-operative approach to Euro-Atlantic security' (NATO 1999: 7). This is very relevant to the Western Balkans due to the fact that the region's newly established states have found it very difficult to fight organized crime networks on their own in this period.

As a majority of our interviewees stressed, the fact that criminality can now no longer be combated within national borders necessitates a common approach for the newly established post-conflict Western Balkan states. The well-known 'Balkan Route'[5] and the region's organized crime networks represent a significant security challenge for these relatively weak states with limited security sector capacity. In order to prevent the expansion of crime, it is of crucial importance to establish cooperation between states, as for matters such as organized crime, the trade in illegal weapons, human trafficking and the drugs trade, 'borders do not exist'.

Nevertheless, as our respondents point out, since the region's countries do not all face exactly the same security threats, it is difficult to envisage a uniform type of cooperation which is suitable for all regional actors. Moreover, analysis of police cooperation between Western Balkan countries leads to the conclusion that the level of cooperation depends on the extent to which the states face common security threats. As an example provided by our interviewees shows, the fact that Croatia has more than 1000 km of border with BiH implies that cooperation between border police units is important.[6] On the other hand, criminal police cooperation with Serbia is well developed due to the need to tackle various cases relating to organized crime, while there is a certain amount of cooperation with Montenegro on the specific issues of the illicit trade in tobacco products and vehicles and cooperation with Albania and Macedonia in the fight against drugs and human trafficking is notable.

It can be concluded from the above that the new forms of criminality put countries in a position in which cooperation between their security sectors was the only way to overcome the threats they faced.

External conditionality

Transition in the Western Balkans was rather complex and, unlike with Central and Eastern European countries, was a two-tier process: from authoritarian to democratic systems, and from conflict to post-conflict stabilization.

Undoubtedly, this was not the most conducive environment for consensual decision making, particularly as it was extremely difficult to achieve compatibility between the interests of external actors and local political elites, the latter rarely showing enthusiasm for carrying out the necessary reforms. As the majority of our respondents recognize, in such an environment the conditions set by external actors such as the EU and the assistance they provided was of significant importance.

Furthermore, they stressed that changes made at the regional level – in particular the affirmation by political elites of a positive attitude towards regional cooperation – were an important factor for the initiation and development of cooperation. The EU has played a crucial role in the process of stabilizing the region and has made a significant contribution to initiating and supporting cooperation. As previously mentioned, the conditionality mechanisms which were part of the enlargement process contributed immeasurably in that regard. The EU accession process also brought certain responsibilities, such as the adoption of the standards, procedures and practices found in developed Western countries. This included increased cooperation between the region's countries in the area of internal affairs as the only appropriate response to new forms of criminality.

However, it is important to note that our respondents stressed that there is an awareness that police cooperation is necessary at the regional level, especially in the fight against organized crime, and that such cooperation had already developed prior to the involvement of international actors. The major contribution of external actors is visible in the area of organizational framing, as well as facilitation of the development of personal contacts and experience sharing. Moreover, cooperation with the EU seems to have strengthened Croatia's position in regional initiatives and supported its role as a mentor to the other states, particularly in the field of internal affairs. On the other hand, the fact that individual states have made varying amounts of progress in integrating and implementing international norms and standards hinders the development of cooperation in this area. For example, in becoming an EU member state, Croatia was obligated to adopt the border control standards adhered to by all other member states, while other countries in the region do not have this type of border control, which presents an obstacle to border police on both sides.

Moreover, respondents argue that cooperation is expected to develop not only with the Western Balkan countries, but also on the wider European and global level, as this is the only effective way to address significant security challenges.

However, respondents seem to be aware that if these global trends are to be applied to the region, stabilization and a developed sense of confidence at the intraregional level are required. While it is clear that all of the region's countries are in the process of adopting the European values which correspond to those of the security community, and that they are fostering practical forms of cooperation, mutual trust and identification with the region are still lacking. In other words, while Croatian police officers find regional cooperation useful for various pragmatic reasons, they have not developed a sense of 'we-ness' with their colleagues in the region and prefer to be considered as a part of a wider transatlantic community. Their main objective argument is to point out that Croatia's membership of the EU and NATO represents an excellent example of the successful adoption of all relevant European values and benchmarks, including those relating to internal affairs. Croatia's Euro-Atlantic vocation is therefore both merit based and subjective, and a feeling of 'we-ness' with the other Western Balkan countries will be feasible only once they have acceded to the structures of the broader Euro-Atlantic framework.

Increased practical institutional and informal cooperation

Security dysfunctions in the Western Balkans, with police units playing a very important role in the 1990s conflict, have made both institutional and informal cooperation within this profession in the region a very demanding task. However, the factors discussed above in this chapter – the transformation of the security paradigm and external conditionality – have not only encouraged cooperation, but have also set higher standards, which must be met if cooperation is to be developed further.

Our research indicates that the establishment of police cooperation in the Western Balkans can be divided into three stages. In the first and second stages, the conflict itself and the post-conflict period, police cooperation was almost nonexistent. It is interesting, though, that organized crime groups cooperated at the regional level for the whole of this time. The third stage, from 2000, brought the initiation and development of police cooperation.

Moreover, at the beginning of the 2000s there was an obvious change of discourse within the framework of security debate in the region. Unlike in the 1990s, when security threats were analysed only through 'national lenses' and the region's states perceived their neighbours as the main sources of those threats, there was a noticeable understanding that some common threats existed, which required cooperation if they were to be tackled appropriately. Issues such as organized crime and corruption in particular, as the major security challenges for transitional post-conflict societies (not to mention weak states), proved to be a heavy burden for countries acting individually, and given their transitional character it became clear that there was no sustainable alternative to cooperation.

Thus, it was interesting to see how our respondents perceive bilateral cooperation with the region's other countries in the field of policing. Our findings show that, as would be expected, cooperation with countries which border Croatia is highly developed, especially those which also have to deal with organized crime networks (Serbia, BiH and Montenegro) and other challenges that affect the stability of those countries. On the other hand, there is an impression that cooperation with countries with which Croatia does not share a border (Macedonia, Albania and Kosovo) is less intense, as the nature of the threats and issues is somewhat different.

Being the 'Balkan route', the Western Balkan region represents an entry point into the European Union, thus it is clear that cooperation between all of the region's countries is essential in order to suppress threats such as organized crime, trade in illegal weapons and human trafficking. Everyday communication through INTERPOL or EUROPOL and the exchange of information not only reduces opportunities for organized crime groups but also improves the capabilities of the police officers who deal with this matter.

Another important factor for cooperation is the competences of police officers, and the fact that developing competences improves the system as a whole. This was confirmed by our research, as the majority of respondents noted that close cooperation in policing is often more visible and successful with neighbouring EU countries such as Italy, Hungary and Slovenia and even with EU states which do not border Croatia. Two factors explain this: first, Croatia's level of development and interoperability is much closer to that of bordering EU countries than to its 'eastern neighbours'; and second, EU membership (and especially the upcoming admission to the Schengen regime) results in a completely new context.

On the other hand, bearing in mind Croatia's experience with reform processes, it was stressed by the majority of our interviewees that cooperation with Western Balkan countries in recent times, given the obvious differences in the level of development, increasingly consists of experience-sharing and mentoring by Croatian police experts. However, despite the differences, police cooperation is perceived positively and is seen as increasing and as an appropriate tool for combating contemporary security challenges.

Alongside the influence of external actors, internal politics also has a significant impact on policing. While it is generally considered to play a positive role in defining guidelines, work framing and standardization, potential negative influences are also visible, particularly when political changes related to elections and the redefinition of political goals are expected. Even more uncertainty is created when changes occur in neighbouring countries, which has an unpredictable impact on the further development of regional cooperation. Nevertheless, political influence on policing is perceived as being in constant decline over recent decades, which may indicate that following the initial phase of intensive stimulation of reforms and context setting, police work is becoming standardized and settled in the internal and regional environment and so no longer requires such intensive input from the political stage.

Regional cooperation is generally assessed as functioning well, sometimes even exceptionally well, although significant space for further improvement is clearly visible. The areas of potential improvement are largely related to discrepancies in the progress made by the region's individual states in transition and integration with European structures. An important step was taken after 2000, when cooperation was significantly intensified both formally – within the framework of important international organizations such as INTERPOL, EUROPOL and, as frequently mentioned in interviews, the Southeast Europe Police Chiefs Association – and in less formal initiatives and personal contacts. The role of non-formal contacts, facilitated by the absence of a language barrier in the region, was very frequently mentioned by respondents as a crucial element of cooperation, as was the mentoring and experience-sharing model of Croatian participation in regional initiatives. Furthermore, according to our respondents, non-formal communication can also ensure rapid response in cases where an alarm is raised about the whereabouts of a felon or the location of a planned illegal operation. In such cases, fast reaction is essential, and as our findings indicate that the Interior Ministry's official procedures take too long, personal contacts are a key factor in obtaining a police job.

The fundamental prerequisites for cooperation are considered to have been satisfactorily fulfilled, while the fact that all of the region's countries have signed the most important international conventions facilitates common work and means that the situation is significantly better than 10–15 years ago. Although generally perceived as intensive and successful, cooperation seems to be significantly more developed with bordering countries, as they deal with the same issues. As previously mentioned, Croatia's most developed cooperation in the fight against organized crime is with Serbia, while border cooperation is more intensive with BiH. This leads to the conclusion that the level of cooperation between Western Balkan countries depends on the area in which cooperation takes place.[7]

While interviewees generally view cooperation as being at a satisfactory level and showing promise, when the question of potential improvements is considered, several crucial areas are mentioned. For example, some of the region's countries are yet to adopt information security laws, which seriously hampers cooperation with Croatia and other EU member states which are obliged to respect the normative requirements. The development of cooperation with EU member states – mainly with those which border, or are located close to, the Western Balkans – is another issue frequently highlighted by interviewees. The EU's Danube Strategy illustrates this issue. However, as organized crime remains a crucial challenge for the region, it is operational cooperation in that field which is considered to be fundamental for successful regional cooperation. Establishing a common centre for the fight against organized crime and terrorism, cooperation in the field of threat recognition and developing capacities and new tools are just a few ideas which interviewees raised as potential ways of improving the efficiency of cooperation. Moreover, it is not only a few specific fields of cooperation which are perceived as not sufficiently covered by cooperative actions, but rather cooperation per se is regarded by some respondents as actions undertaken merely on paper, while the practical dimension of police cooperation remains poor.

As already mentioned, personal contacts and the non-formal dimension of cooperation appear to be a key element of successful cooperation and should be developed intensively, as was the case par example within the framework of SEPCA. This relates *inter alia* to 'the gentle nature' of the issues with which police officers deal, as well as the huge importance of trust in the field of homeland security. However, not all people naturally have the ability to network and develop contacts with colleagues from other countries, therefore the selection of officers responsible for such contacts should be processed very carefully. Personal contacts make cooperation faster, easier and more effective. However, it should not be forgotten that officers remain servants of their country and must act in the interest of the nation and not themselves. Another problem resulting from the great importance of personal contacts is the lack of the continuity which results from the usual bureaucratic structure.

Our research shows that there is a very positive perception of the future development of regional cooperation in the field of policing and that mutual support among Western Balkan countries is expected to become more intense and more effective. The bilateral and multilateral agreements which have already been signed equip states with a broad set of instruments, of which only a few are currently in use, allowing cooperation to not only intensify but also widen and deepen. This deepening and widening should spread from operative cooperation, via tactical cooperation to the level of the ideas and approaches shared by the regional community. High level politics should be involved and cooperation is expected to be organized thematically and be developed by regional research teams and regional centres assigned to work on specific issues.

While it is evident that these empirical findings prove that regional security cooperation is progressing and is positively perceived by the interviewed professionals from the Croatian MoI and police, we could not fail to notice that we were unable to obtain empirical evidence for the development of a very important element of the theoretical concept of the security community, the so-called feeling of 'we-ness' – a generalized common identity and loyalty. While a large majority of respondents expressed a positive attitude towards the improved security cooperation in the region, almost all stated clearly that they identify themselves with and feel more loyal to the wider transatlantic community and can envisage a feeling of 'we-ness' with the rest of the region only within that wider framework, once the Western Balkan countries have met the criteria and joined the 'club'. Clearly, it is highly unlikely that substantial changes will take place in that regard, meaning that it would be very difficult to find empirical evidence for the tested theoretical concept in the coming period, not to mention the present.

Conclusion

Stability has proved to be the greatest challenge for the region over the last two decades or so. The region is still undergoing a long and painful process of, mainly externally stimulated, reforms. Progress in some areas is difficult to dispute – democratization, market reforms, respect for human and minority rights and so on. However, what still remains to be seen is whether the region has managed to move from being the conflict zone it was in the 1990s to meeting the theoretical criteria for a 'security community'.

Of course, having stated the research framework in this way does not necessarily imply that we assume the existence or nonexistence of a security community in the region. On the contrary, we strongly believe that the chosen theoretical framework and empirical methods are an appropriate way to test the proposition and hence contribute to security-related research in this part of Europe.

Given that it is highly unlikely to imagine that a single study of this scope could cover all aspects of security community in any region, we decided to focus our research on the police as a profession in Croatia and the way it contributes, or not, to the creation of a security community in regional terms.

So, despite the obvious limits of this study and its focus on the police as only one profession within the security sector of a single country, the methodological framework, and in particular the empirical methods at our disposal, lead us to conclude that our research is more than relevant for regional security studies. Moreover, it can contribute to the understanding of ongoing processes in the region that will define its 'shape' in the forthcoming period and determine its future stability.

Our findings show that regional cooperation in the field of policing is generally showing noticeable improvement and is successfully moving away from the patterns of work of the 1990s when conflict dominated the context. Obviously, the times when the security of one country in the region was defined against the threat posed by another are behind us, while political changes, EU and NATO accession processes and the detection of common security threats make the need for police cooperation self-evident.

This research has illustrated the perception that new political elites have brought an altered regional environment in which various types of cooperation (police cooperation included) are more likely to occur. As the benefits of this cooperation are visible, more energy is invested in various regional cooperation frameworks, while EU and NATO accession processes, with their accompanying conditionality, contribute significantly to the intensification of cooperation. The need for cooperation has been significantly increased by changes in international relations and the new threats thus brought to the region such as corruption and organized crime, threats which are commonly faced by transitional countries in this part of Europe. Personal contacts and informal cooperation, made possible by frequent regional events and communication forums, coupled with the absence of a language barrier, significantly improve overall regional cooperation and understanding, contributing directly to police efficiency at the national level.

Taking all the above into account, it is possible to conclude that police cooperation in the region is intensifying and developing. However, when the findings are tested against the theoretical framework of security communities, it is very difficult to detect all the necessary indicators and thus argue that a security community exists in the Western Balkans. While mutual reliance, compatibility of values and mutual responsiveness are clearly present, the researchers could not fail to notice the lack of a generalized common identity and loyalty. Our interviewees' identity and self-perception were rarely expressed in terms of the Western Balkans, but rather appear to be largely driven by the Europeanization process within the framework of EU and NATO accession, and thus corresponds to the European framework. Support for this argument in practical terms was largely sought in differences in the pace of reforms and the development of the police profession between Croatia and the region's other countries.

Furthermore, it is obvious that from the Croatian perspective the region lacks the core of one or several political units which are stronger, more highly developed and in some significant aspects more advanced and attractive than the rest to which the theory refers. In fact, the centre to which Croatia looks is Brussels, although given that Croatia is the region's most developed country, it may itself take that role for the other Western Balkan states.

Croatia's self-perception as being somewhat distinctive and the lack of a regional feeling of 'we-ness', mainly based on evident differences in development, do not necessarily imply that regional cooperation is less relevant and important for Croatia than for the region's other states. In fact, Croatia's wellbeing largely depends on the stability of the other Western Balkan countries and therefore practices of self-restraint that can help constitute dependable expectations of peaceful change remain of the utmost importance, while a regional feeling of 'we-ness' can be envisaged only within the framework of future common EU and NATO membership.

On the other hand, while the police as a profession represents a very important pillar of any country's security services, particularly in this region, it operates within a legal framework defined by political elites and its professional influence on decision making procedures at the state level should not be overestimated. In that sense, there is limited empirical evidence that the police is making a significant contribution to the formation of a security community in the region.

Of course, there is no doubt that the police remains an important institution in the security sector of any country in the Western Balkans, and cooperation remains crucial for the region's long term stability. Moreover, progress in reform processes in all of the region's countries will help them attain the same standards of democratic governance and functionality and hopefully contribute to a feeling of 'we-ness' in the wider framework of the transatlantic community.

Notes

* An earlier version of this text was published in Knezović, S., Cvrtila, V. and Vučinić, Z., "Croatia's police and security community building in the Western Balkans," *Eastern Journal of European Studies,* vol. 8 (2017): 167–184.
1 During the military conflict in the 1990s, in the absence of an established army, the police was the only armed force at the disposal of Croatian state. Hence, instead of performing police duties, police officers took part in armed conflicts at the local level to protect the territorial integrity of the newly founded state.
2 These changes were necessary due to proven violations of human and civil rights by the agency during the 1990s.
3 These elements dominated the discourse of the responses of the majority of our interviewees to our question about the motives for increased regional police cooperation.
4 There are no references to any particular interviewee – nor any information regarding their professional position – due to the fact that all interviewees were guaranteed absolute anonymity as a basic precondition for permission to conduct any interview with either MoI officials or police officers.
5 The Balkan Route has long been well known as a route for smuggling illegal goods and immigrants into Western Europe. It is best known for the smuggling of drugs, most notably of heroin from Afghanistan – the largest producer of the drug – to Western Europe – its biggest market. It has also been and still is a conduit for the trafficking of arms and the smuggling of goods and illegal immigrants (Foster, 2012: 1).
6 The length of the border and the intensity of both legal and illegal transfer of humans and goods make it very vulnerable to numerous criminal activities. Croatia's recent accession to the EU makes this question relevant for the Union as well, as this is now the EU's south-eastern external border. This is evident from the fact that the main EU body tasked with migration, asylum, security and border management dedicates significant attention to this issue in its Western Balkans Annual Risk Analysis 2014 (Frontex, 2014).
7 Furthermore, there are some specific fields of policing, such as forensic science, in which cooperation is less developed, but the reason for this is that newly adopted laws allow for the use of evidence collected during investigation by courts in other countries in the region, which has lessened the need for the direct cooperation in that particular area.

Bibliography

Abbott, A, *The System of Professions: An Essay on the Division of Expert Labor*, University of Chicago, 1988.
Adler, E, "The Spread of Security Communities: Communities of Practice, Self-Restraint and NATO's Post-Cold War Transformation" in *European Journal of International Relations* 14:2 (2008): 195–230.
Adler, E and Barnett, M (eds), *Security Communities*, Cambridge University Press, 1998.
Beck, J. and Young, MFD, "The Assault on the Professions and Restructuring of Academic and Professional Identities: A Bernsteinian Analysis" in *British Journal of Sociology and Education* 22:2 (2005): 183–197.

Bourgeault, IL, Benoit, C and Hirchkorn, K, "Introduction – Comparative Perspectives of Professional Groups: Current Issues and Critical Debates" in *Current Sociology* 57:4 (2009): 475–485.

Bucher, R and Strauss, A, "Professions in Process" in *The American Journal of Sociology* 66:4 (1961): 325–334.

Carr-Saunders, AM and Wilson, PA, *The Professions*, Oxford: Clarendon Press, 1934.

Checkel, JT, "International Institutions and Socialisation in Europe – Introduction and Framework" in *International Organization* 59 (2005): 801–826.

Dent, M and Whitehead, S, "Configuring the 'New' Professional" in Dent, M and Whitehead, S (eds), *Managing Professional Identities. Knowledge, Performativity and the 'New' Professional*, London and New York: Routledge, 2002.

Deutsch, K, Burrell, S, Kann, R, Lee, M, Lichterman, M, Lindgren, R, Loewenheim, F and Van Wagenen, R, *Political Community and the North Atlantic Area: International Organization in the Light of Historical Experience*, Princeton, NJ: Princeton University Press, 1957.

Dodsworth, FM, "The Idea of Police in Eighteenth Century England" in *Journal of the History of Ideas*, 69:4 (2008): 583–604.

Ericson, RV, "The Division of Expert Knowledge in Policing and Security" in *The British Journal of Sociology* 45:2 (1994): 149–175.

Faleg, G, "Evolution through Learning? – Epistemic Communities and the Emergence of Security Sector Reform in European Security Co-operation" in *European Union Studies Association 12th Biennial International Conference*, Boston, Massachusetts, 2011.

Foster, K, *Croatia: Corruption, Organized Crime and the Balkan Route*, Adriatic Institute for Public Policy, 2012.

Frontex, *Western Balkans Annual Risk Analysis*, European Agency for the Management of Operational Cooperation at the External Borders of the Member States of the European Union, 2014.

Goode, WJ, "Community within a Community – The Professions" in *The American Journal of Sociology* 22:2 (1957): 194–200.

Haas, P, "Introduction: Epistemic Communities and International Policy Coordination" in *International Organization* 41:1 (1991): 1–35.

Holgersson, S, Gottshchalk, P and Dean, G, "Knowledge Management in Law Enforcement: Knowledge Views for Patrolling Police Officers" in *International Journal of Police Science & Management*, 10:1 (2008) 76–88.

Hunter, V, *Policing Athens: Social Control in Attic Lawsuits*, Princeton University Press, 1994.

Kavalski, E, *Extending the European Security Community: Constructing Peace in the Balkans*, London: Tauris, 2008.

Larson, SM, *The Rise of Professionalism: A Sociological Analysis*, University of California Press, 1977.

NATO, *The Alliance Strategic Concept* (online, 1999) available at: www.mocr.army.cz/images/Bilakniha/ZSD/NATO%20The%20Alliance's%20Strategic%20Concept.pdf

Reiner, R, "Watching the Watchers: Theory and Research in Policing" in *The Politics of the Police* (4th edn), London: Oxford University Press, 2010.

Svensson, LG and Evetts, J (eds), *Sociology and Professions: Continental and Anglo-Saxon Traditions*. Goteberg: Daidalos, 2010.

Vejnović, D and Lalić, V, "Community Policing in a Changing World: A Case Study of Bosnia and Herzegovina" in *Police Practice and Research* 6:4 (2005): 363–373.

Vucetic, S, "The Stability Pact for South Eastern Europe as a Security Community-Building Institution" in *Southeast European Politics* 2 (2001): 109–134.

7

NORMS AND SOVEREIGNTY

Regional security cooperation in the Macedonian Police

Cvete Koneska

Introduction

The last two decades have seen fundamental changes in the countries of the Western Balkans. On the one hand, the end of the Cold War saw the East-West divide diminish in importance, while the region's states began the process of closer integration into the European mainstream. On the other hand, the dissolution of the Yugoslav federation and the accompanying ethnic conflicts reasserted the importance of state borders and exclusive group identities. Today, despite the rising popularity and legitimacy of EU and NATO integration, matters of sovereignty, territory and the use of force remain central to the discourse of statehood in the Western Balkans. The combined effect of these two trends – towards closer regional integration and towards a renewed focus on statehood – has been the emergence of a multitude of regional initiatives, although some have been more successful than others. By looking at regional police interactions, this chapter assesses the effects of regional security cooperation and aims to evaluate how far the region has progressed from being a conflict zone in the 1990s towards regional integration. Ultimately, the chapter reflects on the prospects for the Western Balkan region to become a security community, a model of security cooperation that precludes the use of violence in resolving mutual disputes, characteristic of a deep regional integration regime, as is the case with the EU and NATO.

Addressing the question of regional security integration and cooperation in the Western Balkans is important on at least two levels. First, focusing on the progress achieved since the end of the wars and ethnic conflicts in former Yugoslavia helps in understanding the nature and extent of the post-conflict transformation of these societies. Over the last 15 years, external influence, socialization in international organizations and domestic transitions have led to unprecedented transformation of the legal, political and identity structures which underlie politics in these states.

Examining security cooperation and integration reveals how these changes unfolded in an area traditionally under exclusive state control. Second, studying the progress of regional security cooperation in the Western Balkans allows the effectiveness and success of various efforts aimed at restoring peace, ethnic reconciliation, intra-regional confidence and post-conflict reconstruction in this region to be evaluated. Given the ongoing political and academic debates about the effectiveness of various forms of external intervention in conflict areas, findings about the experience of the Western Balkans can serve to illuminate the value of various initiatives and approaches to post-conflict security.

Norms and sovereignty

This chapter argues that most regional security cooperation in the Western Balkans is currently externally driven. Official rhetoric at both the political and professional levels is informed by the norms of cooperation, mutual trust and respect and peaceful conflict resolution, which are promoted by the various international organizations in which these states seek membership (the EU, NATO, OSCE and so on). However, compliance with these norms is largely ensured through instrumental means (Noutcheva, 2009). Although elite socialization (Checkel, 2005; Schimmelfennig, 2000) has led to increased commitment to EU norms of tolerance and cooperation at the highest political levels, among the political elites who are regularly exposed to and socialized into such norms, their dissemination and internalization among the police profession is lagging or lacking. Security cooperation is seen as a means to a higher end – NATO or EU membership – not as an end in itself. A related argument concerns the continued salience and importance of sovereignty and state security, despite the region's gradual progress with EU integration, which should render such concerns less relevant. Behind the official rhetorical layer, old practices of mutual distrust and inherited patterns of regional enmity and amity still shape the practices of security professionals. This prevents full domestication of norms of regional cooperation and opens a gap between rhetoric and practice that fractures the official discourse and undermines the regional integration process.

Turning to the case of the Macedonian police, this paper identifies two factors which explain the reluctance of the police profession to accept the new norms of regional cooperation: limited, top-down channels for norms dispersion and the lack of a normative crisis which could allow the penetration of new norms. In line with professional police culture elsewhere, the police in Macedonia features a strictly vertical, hierarchical structure, where respect for the chain of command and compliance with commands from superiors is crucial for the operation of the profession, even if compliance violates the dominant set of norms in society (for example, coercion and the use of force, see: Terrill, Paoline and Manning, 2003). Norms, therefore, spread vertically, from the top down, through specific chain of command channels, allowing limited space for normative diversity and for competing sets of norms to coexist. Moreover, unlike in some other states in the Balkans, and in the wider postcommunist space, the police in Macedonia did not face a normative crisis in the wake of democratic transition. Thanks to the transition to democracy occurring simultaneously with the establishment of an independent state, the old professional elites were not removed from the police, nor were the old set of norms dispensed with and replaced with more democratic ones. On the contrary, the image of the police as the defenders of state security and sovereignty was reinforced, narrowing down the opportunities for acceptance of cooperation and trust-building as the bases for police work in the region.

However, the normatively heavy discourse of EU integration that followed the end of the ethnic conflict in Macedonia in 2001 did not leave the police entirely untouched. The EU's police mission in the country between 2003 and 2005 directly targeted the police, aiming to introduce ethnically sensitive policies and make various police practices more inclusive and tolerant (Yusufi, 2004; Georgieva, 2007). While the top echelon of police managers has become more exposed to regional cooperation, with many regularly taking part in regional meetings, there is limited evidence that these norms have spread further down the professional structure of the police. Among rank and file police officers, old, entrenched attitudes and practices concerning outsiders and foreigners still persist.

The structure of this chapter is as follows. The next section discusses the role of the police in national security and the importance of police practices for establishing sustainable regional security cooperation. It also elaborates on the methodology and data used to analyse the empirical case study. This section is followed by a discussion of the regional practices of the Macedonian police in the present context in which post-conflict sovereignty concerns are combined with European integration aspirations. The findings reveal a gap between the official pro-European discourse and the closed, hierarchical structure and practices of the police. The paper concludes with a general discussion about the state of regional security cooperation in the Western Balkans, its drivers and its effects on domestic societies. It evaluates the progress achieved over the last two decades and the prospects for further cooperation and integration in the future as the region moves closer to NATO and the EU, while the features of a nascent security community are becoming more clearly discernible.

Police, security, practices

Although the main task of the police is domestic law enforcement, there are several justifications for focusing on police practices when studying regional security integration. First, for most citizens, the police are 'the face of the state' (Silver, 1967). That is, they are the state mechanism to which the public is most directly exposed and with which they interact on a daily basis. Interactions between the police and the public tend to shape the experience that both citizens and foreign visitors to the country have of the state and its approach to security. Indeed, police practices are the most visible face of the state security apparatus and the most powerful facet of state security policy in terms of public perceptions and reactions. As such, they have a direct impact on popular perceptions of domestic and regional security and require additional attention from scholarly research and in debates on regional security cooperation.

Moreover, the specific political legacy of the past few decades in the Western Balkans, which saw the police used as a tool of oppression by ruling political elites against ethnic minorities and political opponents, makes the police a particularly salient test case for regional security cooperation. Having taken part in violent conflicts and political intimidation, the police are an unlikely champion of regional security integration. Legacies of violence and mistrust of neighbours and minorities can persevere long after actual hostilities have ceased, preventing the adoption of new, tolerant values. Thus, any progress in regional cooperation among the police in the Western Balkans indicates the extent to which security integration in the Western Balkans region has advanced.

Finally, the particular organizational culture of the police – its hierarchies and chains of command; its pertaining practices, routines and standard procedures; its official rhetoric – makes it an additionally attractive subject for analysis. As a practice-rich area, the police provides a fertile subject for practice theory research – the methodological approach adopted in this book. While there is no lack of studies which focus on policing in post-conflict states, few approach the police as a professional community, and almost none examines the practices of police officers at various levels in the professional community. Rather, most studies of police reform approach the police as unitary receivers of external input from political elites and international actors who respond to these external stimuli. Such studies direct little attention to the internal dynamics of the police profession, and its employees and their interactions (Georgieva, 2007; Peake, 2004). This chapter aims to address this shortcoming and contribute further to better understanding of professional practices among the police and how they affect regional security cooperation.

Given the focus on the practices and routines of the police as a professional group, this chapter relies on practice theory as the methodological tool for analysing empirical data collected among the Macedonian police during 2012. Focusing on 'incorporated and material patterns of action … organized around the common implicit understanding of the actors' (Schatzki, 2000), practice theory enables the study of those implicit understandings between group members that are specific to a profession. Studying practices also allows the scope of analysis to be widened to include various types of data which are often neglected when the focus is placed on the institutional, political or discursive parameters of identity, as well as, more importantly, identifying and mapping the gaps between rhetoric and praxis. As Neumann (2002) points out, practices are performative, quotidian, reflective and improvisational. They provide information about agents' behaviour, identity and interests in multiple ways. Studying the practices of a specific profession at a specific point in history facilitates understanding of the processes of development of sets of national and regional interactions which pertain to professional identities, their regional transactions and influence, and how they contribute to greater regional security cooperation and integration.

The Macedonian police: legacies and continuities

When Macedonia declared independence from the Yugoslav federation in 1991, the police played a crucial role in the messy business of securing the new country's borders while the Yugoslav army was withdrawing from Macedonian territory. Until the new Macedonian army was established a year later, the police were responsible for performing the main tasks of state security and defence. This role in the country's independence anchored the police as one of the main pillars of the new state's sovereignty, a reputation further reinforced, at least among some groups in the population, with the role they played during the 2001 ethnic conflict. Their image as 'defenders' (бранители) has often been used to deflect criticism of their undemocratic practices and counter allegations of violations of human rights at home. Similarly, discussions over ensuring greater participation in and commitment to regional police cooperation have been dismissed as unimportant in the face of the need to fight threats to state security. By waving the patriotic flag, the police have withstood pressures to undergo internal democratic reforms, instead using patriotic rhetoric as a shield against unwanted external criticism.

Given these developments, in the first decade after independence and the fall of communism (1990–2000), no major reforms were implemented in the Macedonian police. The majority of police officers, as well as police management, remained in the profession, and the set of professional values and practices remained unchanged. Although cosmetic changes were made to the names of the various ranks of police officers, no new academic or professional institution was established to train and re-train police officers and managers, nor were new courses and curriculum changes introduced in the existing schools. The majority of the new intake joined the ranks of the police after completing specialized police secondary schools. Upon graduation they were socialized into professional norms through contact with older colleagues, during their initial 'probationary' period. Thus, there was no crisis leading to the dislocation of the dominant professional norms and practices in the Macedonian police after 1990. Rather, historical circumstances and training and initiation processes allowed the established routines and attitudes to be reproduced in the new, democratic political system.

However, things began to change gradually after the end of the ethnic conflict in 2001 and the Macedonian government's official adoption of EU and NATO integration as foreign policy priorities. The official political and security discourse changed to embrace the pro-EU rhetoric of regional cooperation and democratic governance, leading to additional attention being directed to the police and its role in society. In the aftermath of the conflict, one of the most urgent reforms was to reform the police, increasing the representation of ethnic minorities and introducing greater accountability and transparency in police work (Ohrid Framework Agreement, 2001). Until that time, the police was among the most ethnically exclusive public institutions, with minimal representation of ethnic Albanians and other groups (Teodosievska Jordanovska, 2006). Moreover, an EU police mission was set up to help the Macedonian police adopt principles and practices that would enable it to operate in an ethnically inclusive and tolerant manner, breaking with the previous culture of exclusion and oppression (EU Proxima, 2003).

As a result of external pressure for reform from EU and NATO officials and the intensified socialization of domestic political leaders into European ideas about security and democracy, a set of domestic legislative changes relating to the police was adopted between 2004 and 2008. The purpose of these legislative interventions was to adapt domestic legislation to the set of requirements stipulated by the Stabilisation and Association Agreement (SAA) with the EU and thus ultimately move closer to European Union accession. However, these activities appear to have been mostly aimed at an external audience in Brussels and at foreign embassies in Skopje. In practice, there were minimal efforts invested in actually implementing the new legislative provisions or building capacities within the police to enable the implementation of these changes. Thus, while the rhetoric of EU integration and related values of regional peace and cooperation took hold particularly among political elites and top ranking police officials, who were the most exposed to external influences from the EU, this was not accompanied by a change in the professional norms among rank and file police officers, whose professional practices and attitudes remained much the same as during the previous decade. The ultimate effect of these developments is a fractured police discourse in Macedonia today, in which rhetorical commitment to EU integration and compliance with European democratic norms and values is accompanied by a set of police practices that reproduce old antagonistic attitudes towards minorities and some neighbouring states.

Police practices today

The empirical data gathered from observations, interviews and questionnaires conducted during the first half of 2012 suggests that the police in Macedonia remains an overwhelmingly closed professional group. A strong professional identity, reinforced by symbolic and rhetorical devices, manifests itself through limited interaction with non-governmental and media organizations, while 'outsiders' have very limited access to information and opinion. Repeated attempts to gain permission to interview Interior Ministry officials and police officers failed, as requests were referred to superiors in the chain of command and eventually refused. The strictly hierarchical communication channels and strong in-group identity often appear to translate into mistrust of outsiders and defensive behaviour when approaches for information are made. Information was finally obtained by recourse to mechanisms for public access to information, however no direct face-to-face meetings with police officers and managers took place.

In general, the Macedonian police take part in most regional and bilateral initiatives on police cooperation, as witnessed by the country's being party to most regional initiatives and documents on security cooperation (RCC, SECI, MARRI and so on). There is high-level political commitment to regional security cooperation, which ensures participation, at the relevant political or professional level, in regional meetings and events. However, this hardly translates into a set of practices that favours regional interactions to supplement formal, official practices with a set of informal or semi-formal practices of regional interactions at the professional level. Strict adherence to professional hierarchical practices reinforces the closed group identity, visibly marked and distinguished by specific symbolic signs and behaviours (special uniform, ranks, salutations, language).

Data collected through participant observation of police officers during a regional police meeting illustrates the above claims. The behaviour of police officers during a meeting with regional police representatives and some members of international organizations and civil society organizations in Skopje in 2012 exhibited the practices that the police employ to reinforce their group's boundaries. Macedonian police officers strictly observed the professional hierarchy, following symbolic hierarchical practices such as saluting and standing up when a more senior police official entered the room (much akin to army practices). Strict adherence to one's group was observed even during breaks and meals, even though these were occasions when the official code could be abandoned in favour of interacting with members of other police forces or non-police participants. Nonetheless, Macedonian police officers sat together and chatted to each other instead. They displayed mistrust towards civil society representatives, especially upon discovering that some participants were members of local non-governmental organizations, thus marking a clear boundary between themselves and civil society representatives, who they saw as outsiders to their professional community who could not be trusted.

Yet, distinct group boundaries, thus reinforced by a set of symbolic signs and behaviours, need not necessarily present an obstacle to regional security cooperation. While they indicate that the Macedonian police are yet to be fully socialized into the norms of democratic (or European) ways of policing by embracing transparency and openness to citizens and civil society, the same exclusionary and defensive practices can serve as a confidence building, signalling factor that could enable cooperation with other police forces in the region. Similar institutional cultures and values, specific to the police and shared across police forces in the region, including similar distrust of civil society and external actors, could facilitate regional police interactions.

However, the rarity of such regional meetings as occasions for developing regional networks suggests otherwise. It seems that regional police interactions happen too infrequently to lead to any meaningful regional dynamic. Regional police training and workshops take place no more than a few times a year (no more than three bilateral meetings per year took place with each neighbouring state during 2010 and 2011) (Ministry of Interior, 2012), and are attended by only a few, usually high-ranking, police officers, which does not allow networks and contacts to be expanded to entire units on the ground. At the other end of the scale, few joint police actions involving regular police officers have taken place, since most cooperation between the region's police forces is through impersonal means – by exchange of information and consultation (Ministry of Interior, 2012). Regular police officers are almost never exposed to their counterparts in other countries though their work, which limits opportunities for professional bonding and development of mutual trust and respect. Moreover, there tends to be a high turnover of top level police officials, especially those who are politically appointed, which again limits the scope for disseminating norms of regional cooperation vertically from the top down. Unlike regular police officers, most of whom spend their career in the police, when ministers and state secretaries for police leave their posts they tend to sever the ties they have built with police officials from neighbouring countries, thus blocking the channels for dissemination of regional police cooperation norms.

The higher intensity regional cooperation seen at the higher official level further supports the argument that police cooperation in the region is top-down and externally driven. Even at this level, most visits and contacts are arranged through official procedures, through the Ministry's protocol or public relations unit, although there might be a set of additional informal high-level interactions that are not reported by the ministry. Nevertheless, even these practices do not seem to be reproduced at lower levels of the police profession. Finally, when discussing regional police cooperation, the Interior Ministry's official discourse also presents EU integration as the main reason for regional cooperation, thus providing additional support to the argument that the nature of the pro-EU security discourse is fractured, with a superficial rhetorical layer of democratic and cooperative norms coupled with a set of authoritarian professional practices and inherited attitudes of regional enmity.

The nature of regional police interactions further demonstrates that state sovereignty and security continue to shape the police's perceptions of regional security and regional cooperation. Analysis of data obtained from the Ministry of Interior on regional police cooperation between 2010 and 2012 suggests that regional interactions occur more frequently when they are not seen as a threat to state sovereignty or to exclusive police authority on the state's territory. As the table below shows, the most common types of regional police activities are ministerial and police management meetings – regional interactions at the highest political and managerial levels concerned with discussions about political and administrative issues and common goals – rather than moving police forces across international borders or getting police forces to work together. Based on existing legislation on regional police cooperation, such as the Convention for Police Cooperation in Southeast Europe, each of the activities listed below can be legally undertaken, yet no cross-border searches, 'hot pursuits' involving the pursuit of suspects across the country's borders or cross-border exercises took place in 2010 or 2011. Such activities can be seen as undermining the states' borders and a country's exclusive sovereignty over its territory and thus are less attractive forms of regional police interaction.

Overall, it appears that regional police interaction mostly involves high-level political and managerial officials, while the lower professional ranks in the police have far fewer opportunities to interact with their professional peers across the region. This perpetuates the old professional norms of the police, who lag behind the political and managerial elites in becoming socialized into the norms of

TABLE 7.1 Types of regional police activities

	2010	2011
Ministerial meetings	2	7
Police management meetings	4	9
Joint investigations	2	4
Joint training	0	5
Cross-border searches or actions	0	0
'Hot pursuits'	0	0
Cross-border exercises	0	0

cooperation, trust and peaceful conflict resolution. Moreover, the nature of regional police interaction suggests that the police and the country's political elites remain sensitive to issues of state sovereignty and territorial integrity, despite embracing regional and European integration as strategic political goals. This perpetuates old notions of state security and perceptions of regional threats to state security, in spite of the growing commitment to regional security initiatives.

Learning about cooperation: police education

Education and professional training, where students and professionals are socialized into a specific set of norms and values, are usually considered to be among the most powerful methods of normative learning. Therefore, considering police education and comparing its stated objectives to its educational outcomes among students provides insight into how future police professionals are socialized into professional norms and into the discursive assumptions that underpin those norms. However, analysis of empirical data about the effects of Macedonian police education through training and socialization does not lead to clear conclusions and fails to unequivocally support arguments about the replacement of existing professional norms through education. On the one hand, students at the Faculty of Security, where the country's future police officers are trained, are introduced to the principles of regional cooperation and contemporary theories of the trans-national nature of security threats and are taught the value of regional and international cooperation, which all predisposes graduates to multilateral responses to security threats, including regional cooperation. On the other hand, the educational system also seems to reproduce old regional stereotypes and prejudices about other Western Balkan countries, undermining and subverting the official curriculum.

The Faculty of Security (previously the Police Academy) is a relatively young institution. Although the institution was first established in 1977, it was closed in 1995 and it was only in 2004–5 that the current Security Faculty was re-opened. A decade of inactivity had seen most of its academic faculty leave, so a new team was formed with the opening of the new institution, including only a few staff who had taught at the old Police Academy. This ensured that the institutional culture and values of the old institution are not replicated and the new department will be more open to cooperation and regional interaction. Similarly, the curriculum and structure of the courses offered as part of training were substantially revised, allowing for the inclusion of new subjects and courses more attuned to novel developments in security studies and policing in particular.

A brief survey of the views and attitudes of undergraduate students at the Security Faculty conducted in early 2012 reveals mixed attitudes towards the region and regional cooperation. While in principle students have a good knowledge of the immediate region and know which countries are considered members of the Western Balkan region, their views of the rationale behind the region, the uniting factors that determine membership and the boundaries of the region reveals a mix of approaches and arguments. Many see membership of the Western Balkans region as defined by external factors – by aspirations to join the European Union, as a positive, shared goal – but some display resistance to the external drive behind the regional grouping, defining the region as an external creation for the benefit of more powerful countries, without regard to the needs of the Western Balkan states themselves. A few refer to shared problems and needs such as transnational crime as the driver behind the development of the Western Balkan region, but none referred to shared values and goals as the driving force. Such views suggest that regional cooperation is perceived as largely externally driven and legitimated by external factors. These views leave little room to consider the existence and effects of a local, national or regional rationale for regional integration or the existence of an epistemic community, as independent from the regional political leadership, that would pursue an agenda of regional cooperation in security or policing.

The survey also reveals that students have limited exposure to students and teachers from neighbouring countries. The Security Faculty has established official cooperation with three regional universities, one in Banja Luka, BiH and two in Serbia, in Pančevo and Novi Pazar, in addition to ongoing efforts to establish cooperation with a university in Kosovo. Despite this, only a small fraction of students goes on to spend a semester or a year in a neighbouring country. Study exchange with other European countries, especially those in Western Europe, is much more popular, while the curricula of the region's universities are more similar to those of universities in European Union member states than they are to each other, as Western Balkan governments are making an effort, through the Bologna Process, to harmonize their educational system to European Union requirements, while close to no attention is paid to harmonizing curricula with neighbouring states. Cooperation with universities in the region is used rather as an opportunity for teaching staff to give lectures and maintain academic links with staff in other countries, though the frequency of lectures by visiting or guest lecturers is also very low (between one and five per year), suggesting that such events are arranged in an ad hoc manner rather than being planned and integrated in the curriculum as a means of fostering better regional education cooperation and awareness of regional issues.

These findings are further supported by an overview of students' opinions of regional police cooperation. On average, students' opinions tend to reflect entrenched stereotypical views about traditional friends and foes in the region rather than being an extension of the theoretical arguments about regional cooperation that they encounter on their courses. When asked to rank the countries with which the Macedonian police should and should not cooperate, on average students most favoured cooperation with Serbia and Croatia, while cooperation with Kosovo and Albania was considered least desirable. Although such views cannot be directly attributed to what they learn as part of their studies, such attitudes among security studies students indicate that education about security cooperation and regional issues has not eradicated obsolete, quasi-geostrategic views of the region (Albanians as foes, Serbs and Croats as friends). Rather, prejudices about other countries and nations in the region appear to seep through educational channels and are reproduced with the new generations of graduates, existing in parallel with the EU-promoted values of democracy, cooperation and regional integration.

These findings suggest that police education in Macedonia can hardly be seen as providing an entry point for the socialization of new generations of police officers into a new set of norms of regional security cooperation and integration. Though the official curriculum, much like the official political rhetoric, has been revised to include courses about regional problems and regional security solutions, students on average display views that do not conform to these values. Rather, they reproduce the entrenched perceptions about regional friends and foes and external factors that shape the future of their country and its neighbourhood. Ultimately, the limited adoption and internalization of a new, democratic and regionally tolerant set of norms for policing during education contributes to the lag between the political norms associated with aspirations to NATO and EU membership and professional police norms, which focus on preserving state sovereignty and deterring threats from regional enemies.

Conclusion: what kind of regional security cooperation?

The aim of this paper was to examine the state of regional security cooperation in the Western Balkans in a bid to evaluate the success of the region's transformation from a conflict zone to a security community. Based on study of regional interactions and the adoption of regional cooperation norms by the Macedonian police, the empirical findings suggest that regional police cooperation is predominantly externally driven. Despite the intensification of interactions between police forces, especially at high-ranking political and managerial levels, as a result of the greater availability of regional security forums and initiatives, the main rationale behind police cooperation remains the desire to join the EU and fulfil the requirements for that goal. While externally promoted cooperation has spurred increased participation in regional initiatives in some areas, such as ministerial meetings and joint police training, full internalization by the police of the relevant values, norms and agenda is still lacking. Instead, the persistent hierarchical structure of the profession reinforces the vertical, top-down direction of communication among the police, limiting the scope for introducing normative and value changes at the topmost, political, level of police chiefs.

As a result, among regular police officers, regional and domestic security is still perceived through old, entrenched views about regional friends and foes. The closed and hierarchical nature of the professional community does not appear to allow for wider circulation and replacement of the norms that underpin everyday police practices. The police remain reluctant to engage in regional interactions that seem to undermine the salience of state borders – as emblems of state sovereignty and territorial integrity – limiting cross-border interactions to high level meetings of ministers and police managers. Joint operations, 'hot pursuits' and cross-border exercises do not take place, despite the existence of legislation allowing for such activities. At the wider strategic level, such findings indicate that the effects of regional and European integration are yet to counter the effects of the opposing trend of the growing importance of state borders and sovereignty in the Western Balkan region. The legacy of the break-up of the former Yugoslav federation and the ensuing ethnic conflicts still must be fully overcome before the region can move towards the creation of a community based on trust and a shared perception of common goals.

The empirical findings discussed above also provide insight into the entry points for norm dissemination among the police profession in Macedonia. Education, which is usually seen as the most appropriate and effective way of instilling new norms and values in a community, appears to be yielding mixed results, reproducing some of the old stereotypes and patterns of enmity and amity in the region. This indicates that the most important channel for norm dissemination among the police remains the top-down, hierarchical communication of professional norms. Given the large turnover of high-ranking police managers and home affairs ministers, such channels appear to have limited capacity to induce a full normative change among rank and file police officers. This perpetuates the fractured discourse on regional security cooperation, with rhetorical commitment to EU and NATO integration coupled with professional norms that are incompatible with such strategic goals.

Finally, taking Deutsch's definition of a security community as a group of people integrated to the point of 'real assurance that the members of that community will not fight each other physically, but will settle their disputes in some other way' (Deutsch et al., 1957), there is limited evidence of the formation of a security community among the countries of the Western Balkans. Nascent regional interaction patterns provide for increased cooperation across borders, but the core of the police professional community retains its distrust and enmity towards neighbouring states, preventing further integration. While there has been no recurrence of violent ethnic conflict in the region over the past decade, and some encouraging steps have been taken towards regional cooperation, the Macedonian police still have a long way to travel on the road to a Western Balkans security community.

Bibliography

Chekel, J, "International Organizations and Socialization in Europe: Introduction and Framework" in *International Organization* 59 (2005): 801–826.

Deutsch, K, Burrell, S, Kann, R, Lee, M, Lichterman, M, Lindgren, R, Loewenheim, F and Van Wagenen, R, *Political Community and the North Atlantic Area: International Organization in the Light of Historical Experience*, Princeton, NJ: Princeton University Press, 1957.

Finnemore, M, "International Norm Dynamics and Political Change" in *International Organization* 52:4 (1998): 887–917.

Fukuyama, F, *The End of History and the Last Man*, Free Press, 1992.

Georgieva, L, "Police Reform in Macedonia" in Ebnauther, AH, Fluri, PH and Jureković, P (eds), *Security Sector Governance in the Western Balkans: Self-Assessment Studies on Defence, Intelligence, Police and Border Management Reform*, Vienna: National Defence Academy, 2007.

Haas, P, "Introduction: Epistemic Communities and International Policy Coordination" in *International Organization* 41:1 (1991): 1–35.

Neumann, I, "Returning Practice to the Linguistic Turn" in *Millennium: Journal of International Studies* 31:3 (2002): 627–651.

Noutcheva, G, "Fake, Partial and Imposed Compliance: The Limits of EU Normative Power in the Western Balkans" in *Journal of European Public Policy* 16:7 (2009): 1065–1084.

Ohmae, K, "Putting Global Logic First" in *Harvard Business Review* 73:1 (1995): 119–125.

Peake, G, *Policing the Peace: Police Reform Experiences in Kosovo, Southern Serbia and Macedonia*, London: Saferworld, 2004.

Schatzki, T, "Introduction: Practice Theory" in Cetina, KK, Schatzki, TR and von Savigny, E (eds), *The Practice Turn in Contemporary Theory*, Routledge, 2000.

Schimmelfennig, F, "International Socialization in the New Europe: Rational Action in an Institutional Environment" in *European Journal of International Relations* 5:1 (2000): 109–139.

Silver, A, "The Demand for Order in Civil Society: A Review of Some Themes in the History of Urban Crime, Police and Riots" in *The Police: Six Sociological Essays*, New York, 1967.

Teodosievska Jordanovska, S, (2006) "Constitutional, Legal and Other Measures Aimed at Promoting the Equitable Representation of Communities in the Civil Service and the Experience from the Ombudsman Office", Council of Europe, T-02–006.

Terrill, W, Paoline, E and Manning, PK, "Police Culture and Coercion" in *Criminology* 41:4 (2003): 1003–1034.

Yusufi, I, "Europeanising the Balkans through Military and Police Missions" in *European Balkan Observer*, 2:1 (2004): 8–13.

Primary sources

Survey of students at the Security Faculty, Skopje. February 2012.

Responses to access to public data requests by: Ministry of Interior (March 2012, April 2012).

Ohrid Framework Agreement (13 August 2001), full text available at: www.refworld.org/docid/3fbcdf7c8.html (accessed on 16 March 2014).

European Union External Action Services, 'EUPOL Proxima/FYROM', Mission and objectives (2003) available at: www.eeas.europa.eu/csdp/missions-and-operations/proxima-fyrom/index_en.htm (accessed on 16 March 2014).

Law on Police (2006), *Official Gazette of Republic of Macedonia*.

Code of Police Ethics (2007), *Official Gazette of Republic of Macedonia* No.72/2007.

Rulebook for performing police duties (2008); Rulebook for activities in conflict of interest with police duties (2007), *Ministry of Interior*.

8

INTERNATIONAL POLICY NETWORKS AND SECURITY COMMUNITY BUILDING

The case of the Partnership for Peace Consortium

Filip Ejdus

Introduction

The analytical primacy of states in the mainstream approaches to IR has been under systematic theoretical and empirical scrutiny over the past few decades. Critics of the state-centric approach posit that in order to understand world politics one needs to go beyond states and international organizations (IOs) and include a variety of other actors and polities including classes, races, clans, nations, civilization(s), religions, cognitive regions, ethnic and indigenous groups, epistemic communities, trans-national advocacy networks, multinational companies and so on. In this chapter I contribute to this debate by looking at one particular actor in world politics that brings together representatives of states, IOs and civil societies with the aim of understanding and influencing policies: International Policy Networks (IPNs). More precisely, the question I probe in this chapter is the following: 'What is the role of IPNs in the process of security community building?' Here I argue that IPNs play an extraordinary role as a transmission belt between states and civil societies in the evolution of security communities. They play a particularly important role in the transition from the *nascent* to the *ascendant* phase, during which elite level preferences for self-restraint and peaceful change are expected to trickle down to civil societies and create a sense of collective identification. To that effect, IPNs fulfil four functions: producing knowledge on regional peace, diffusing the norms of self-restraint, influencing security community policies and providing organizational flexibility.

The argument is illustrated in an autoethnographic account of the Partnership for Peace Consortium of Defence Academies and Security Studies Institutes (PfPC) and in particular its study group on Regional Stability in Southeast Europe – (RSSEE). This particular IPN has been of critical importance for the involvement of security and defence expert communities, military and civilian, in the expansion of the Euro-Atlantic security community into postcommunist Europe including Western Balkans. For many years, I have been an active participant in this process. This article builds on that first-hand participation but goes beyond it. In the first section I theorize the role of IPNs in the process of security community building and explain my methodology. The second section presents how one particular IPN in which I have taken an active part has been involved in the creation of no-war community in the Western Balkans.

IPNs and security communities

Security communities evolve from birth to maturity. According to Adler and Barnett, during the *nascent* phase states don't intend to build a security community but rather seek security cooperation because of their cultural and political proximity, common security threats or shared economic challenges. In the *ascendant* phase, the multiple interstate channels of communication that were laid down during the *nascent* phase are now extended to civil societies. The defining feature of the ascendant phase is that, as Adler and Barnett posit, 'states and their societies are increasingly embedded in a dense network of relations collectively portrayed as friendly' (Adler and Barnett, 1998: 53). Finally, in the *mature* phase, states and societies 'share an identity and, therefore, entertain dependable expectations of peaceful change' (Adler and Barnett, 1998: 55).

As was demonstrated in the introduction to this book, the literature on security community building in general and the peaceful transformation of Southeast Europe in particular has paid insufficient attention to the role of civil-society. In this chapter I plan to enrich these insights by shedding light on one of the mechanisms at work behind the gradual involvement of civil society in the evolution of regional 'we-feeling' and the security community. The mechanism which interests me is the IPN. For the purpose of my analysis of security community building IPNs can be defined as:

> loose alliances of government agencies, international organizations, corporations, and elements of civil society such as nongovernmental organizations, professional associations, or religious groups that join together to achieve what no one can accomplish on its own.
>
> *(Reinicke, 2000: 44)*

As such, IPNs neither belong to the state nor to civil society, but rather straddle the two spheres. IPNs are a specific form of community of practice, which learns by doing things in a certain way (Wenger, 1998; Pouliot, 2008; Bueger, 2013). The IPNs are similar to epistemic communities. However, while the former are motivated by shared values and policy ideas, the latter have stronger internal cohesion as they are also brought together by shared causal beliefs (Haas, 1989; Cross, 2011). What distinguishes IPNs as communities of practice is their composition, combining the governmental, intergovernmental and societal spheres. They are a 'community' for they are composed of a set of distinct CoPs which overlap in a single process of cognitive evolution (Adler, 2005: 23).

In this chapter I draw on my personal experience within the PfPC to theorise about the role of IPNs in the security community building. Methodologically, I rely on 'analytic autoethnography', meaning that I was part of the social world under study and that I was committed to theoretical analysis (Anderson, 2006). I first became involved in the work of the PfPC when I was invited to its 9th annual conference held in Zagreb in June 2007. A few years later, in May 2010, I was again invited to a meeting of the PfPC's RSSEE study group held in Reichenau (Austria). The following December I was asked to become one of the three co-chairs of the study group which meets three times a year: in Reichenau Castle in Austria in the spring, somewhere in the region usually in the autumn and in Vienna in the winter.

As one of the three co-chairs of the study group since 2010, I have eight years of experience as an insider with a strong rapport with this IPN. Formally, my field research encompassed three events. The first was the 24th workshop of the study group, held in Reichenau Castle on 3–5 May 2012. The second was the 14th annual convention, organized in Tbilisi on 18–21 June 2012. The final event was a regional workshop held in Skopje on 27–29 September 2012. I also conducted 12 in-depth interviews with various participants in the working group: veterans and novices, women and men, from Western countries and partner countries.[1]

The aim of the field research was not to establish a causal relationship between everyday practices within this particular IPN and macro regional patterns of peaceful resolution of conflicts in Southeast Europe. Instead, the purpose of the research was to describe the quotidian involvement of this particular IPN in the evolution of a security community and theorize this activity. As Patrick Thaddeus Jackson remarked, such a non-causal ethnographic account can 'identify patterns and arrangements but can say little about their likelihood of persisting into the future' (Jackson, 2008: 92).

Drawing on that experience, the central argument that I develop in this chapter is that IPNs serve as an important transmission belt between state elites and civil societies during the transition from the *nascent* to the *ascendant* phase of security communities. During this transitory phase, when an embryonic elite security community has to encompass the field beyond the state and trickle down to civil society, IPNs have at least four functions.

First, IPNs diffuse the norm of self-restraint from the liberal core outwards to the illiberal periphery and from state elites downwards to civil society. According to Norbert Elias, self-restraint is a subjective disposition associated with a civilizing process lasting several centuries in which state institutions gradually gained control over the use of physical violence while individuals learned to discipline and control their impulses (Elias, 1982). Emanuel Adler translated the concept of self-restraint into IR by arguing that it 'develops not only within intrastate political communities and networks, but also within transnational communities of practice' (Adler, 2008: 205). As 'communities of practice' launched, financed and maintained by liberal state elites, security community building IPNs are sites where self-restraint is learned and the identities of actors are 'negotiated and transformed' (Adler, 2008: 196). Through socialization and learning, IPNs serve to diffuse the norm of self-restraint from the liberal Euro-Atlantic core to its peripheries.

Second, IPNs produce and diffuse knowledge about conflict-affected regions and about their peaceful transformations. In order to be constructed as spaces which are governed peacefully, regions need to be imagined by region-builders as bounded entities (Neumann, 1994). As builders of peaceful regions, IPNs have an important role in this process of knowledge production about where the borders of regions should lie and what the key security dynamics that glue them together (or tear them apart) are. In addition, IPNs also produce and diffuse knowledge about liberal security practices such as democratic control of the armed forces, security sector reform, peaceful resolution of conflicts, human security, transparency and accountability, security cooperation and integration among many others. IPNs are thus sites of continuous learning for civilian security experts, enabling them to shape local security discourses or policies in accordance with the liberal peace paradigm.

Third, IPNs influence security policymaking in both a direct and indirect fashion. Direct influence exists when an idea generated and advocated within IPNs feeds directly into the policy process through 'upstream advocacy' directed at policy makers. IPNs indirectly influence security policymaking when they shape policy discourse through 'downstream advocacy', targeting expert communities and wider audiences. Some IPNs, such as lobby groups, will focus primarily on upstream advocacy, others will try to reach both policy makers and a wider audience. IPNs can influence all four phases in the security policy cycle: agenda setting, policy formulation, implementation and monitoring/evaluation (Perkin and Court, 2005: 14). IPNs influence security policy both within emerging security communities and among external region builders. In the former case, IPNs help the various actors involved in the emerging patterns of regional security governance to learn from the liberal core and adapt and apply what they have learned to their own environments. In the latter case, IPNs provide precious local insights into complex regional security dynamics to numerous stakeholders engaged in external region building.

Fourth, IPNs help state agents to avoid traditional bureaucratic protocols and allow them greater organizational flexibility. Track one diplomacy is official, hierarchical, formal, rigid and slow government to government interaction limited to state elites. Track two diplomacy is unofficial and informal transnational networking between civil society groups oriented towards policy change (McDonald, 1991; Kraft, 2000; Kaye, 2001). IPNs sit somewhere in between and can be treated as track one 1½ diplomacy: they combine government officials with civil society experts in order to retain political relevance but also to enjoy as much flexibility as possible. In the evolution of a security community from the nascent to the ascendant phase, governments and civil societies use IPNs instrumentally to avoid formal protocols and feed liberal rationality into security policy cycles in the post-conflict regions. Due to their composition and flexibility, IPNs are policy transmission belts with greater carrying capacity then other diplomatic formats. This is especially the case when a security community needs to evolve from an embryonic phase, in which state elites engage in rudimentary cooperative practices, to the ascendant phase, characterized by wider societal trust and a shared we-feeling.

NATO, PfPC and the eastward expansion of the Euro-Atlantic Security Community

In 2011, the George C. Marshall European Center for Security Studies hosted the 13th Annual Conference of the PfP Consortium in the mountain resort town of Garmisch-Partenkirchen situated in the picturesque alpine surroundings of southern Bavaria. As a co-chair of the study group on Southeast Europe I was invited to speak on Serbian public opinion about Euro-Atlantic integration (NATO and EU accession). Although the working language of the conference is English, one of the speakers decided to speak in Russian. Like many other people in the room I grabbed my earphones to hear the simultaneous translation. However, I noticed that the entire front row of the audience, where senior American military officers and the staff of the George C. Marshall Center staff were seated, did not reach to the headphones but kept on listening to the speech in Russian without the aid of translation. When I pointed out to a colleague sitting next to me what seemed an odd situation, it was immediately explained to me that there was actually nothing strange about it.

From 1964 to 1992, Garmisch Partenkirchen had been home to the U.S. Army's Russian Institute. Throughout the Cold War, the Institute was a key military education and research centre for study of the Soviet Union, sporting one of the largest archives on the subject in the world. One of its specialties was in providing advanced Russian language training for Army Foreign Area Officers.[2] When the Iron Curtain fell and the Soviet enemy disappeared, the Institute became the George C. Marshall European Center for Security Studies 'in order to rapidly develop opportunities to work with European and Eurasian defense establishments'.[3] The strategic environment had undergone a tectonic shift: instead of preparing for war, the re-invented institution needed to create the knowledge necessary for widening and deepening sustainable peace. The marginal value of knowledge of the Russian language significantly decreased as the 'old dog needed to learn new tricks'. This task not only required a new doctrine, but also a new form of power: direct coercive and disciplinary power needed to make space for indirect and capillary power. While the former is solely in the hands of the military, the latter can only operate with and through civil society. In the late 2000s, as a civil society activist and a public advocate of democratic security sector governance in Serbia, I found myself deeply involved with one of the many capillary networks deployed after the Cold War with the aim of governing the East and South European peripheries at a distance. What follows is the story of the PfPC and its Southeast Europe study group.

'Opening academic brains': *the story of the PfPC*

After decades of bipolar stalemate, the end of the Cold War ushered in a period of eastward expansion for the Euro-Atlantic security community. Nonetheless, despite the end of superpower rivalries, Russia still opposed NATO's eastern enlargement as a threat to its national security. In order to bypass this resistance, the USA initiated the Partnership for Peace (PfP) programme at the meeting of defence ministers held in Travemünde, Germany in 1993, and it was officially established at the NATO Summit held in Brussels in January 1994. The PfP programme is a bilateral programme of cooperation between NATO and non-NATO states in Europe and postcommunist Europe established in order to introduce an evolutionary approach to NATO expansion without antagonizing Russia. As the then US Secretary of Defense William Perry succinctly put it, its aim was 'to lay the foundation for a new European security system with NATO at the centre' (Borawski, 1995: 235). Over the course of the next two decades, the PfP served its purpose well and went on to envelop virtually the whole of postcommunist Europe. In essence, the PfP came to serve as a network built to co-opt states from the former Eastern Bloc, not only future members, into a NATO centred web of liberal security governance. Thus, it became one of the key links in the eastward expansion of the liberal security community.

The geographical expansion of the Euro-Atlantic security community occurred in parallel with the conceptual widening of the meaning of security. Although the roots of this process can be traced backed to the *détente* of the 1970s (Buzan, 1983; Ullman, 1983), conceptual widening gained significant momentum after the end of the Cold War (Buzan et al., 1998; Buzan and Hansen, 2009). In its 1991 Strategic Document, NATO also endorsed a 'multi-faceted' and 'multi-directional' understanding of security (Council, 1991). The widening of the concept of security beyond the traditional state centric military approach required the gradual involvement of civil society in practical security policy making, especially in the former communist countries. However, 10 years after the fall of the Iron Curtain there was still very little independent civilian expertise on security matters in postcommunist Europe. Newly appointed security policy makers lacked both the conceptual and the practical knowledge necessary for democratic and cooperative security sector governance. Moreover, once out of office, former security policy makers would disappear from the public scene, usually never to return. Across postcommunist Europe, civil society was either disinterested in security issues or lacked the expert knowledge necessary for active participation in security sector governance at the outset of transition (cf. Caparini, 2004; Caparini et al., 2006). The lack of a civilian security policy community prevented the consolidation of new institutional memory within the security and defence sectors in postcommunist Europe, and thus impeded its evolution from an embryonic to an ascendant security community. This problem also hampered Serbia's progress towards Euro-Atlantic security community (Ejdus, 2007; see also: Glišić, 2007).

The PfPC as an international network of scholars, practitioners and civil society activists came into existence as a solution to exactly this problem. As Christman observes, 'the PfP Consortium was conceived to enlist Eastern Europeans in the creation of a multinational "community of practice" within the Euro-Atlantic defense community' (Christman, 2008: 18). During the meeting of Euro-Atlantic Partnership Council (EAPC) defence ministers held in June 1998, American Defense Secretary William Cohen and his German opposite number Volker Rühe jointly sponsored the establishment of the PfPC. The vision to reach out beyond governments was confirmed in the summary statement which the group of defence ministers issued in June 1998:

> In addition to Government Defense Academic Institutions and Security Studies Institutes; non-governmental institutes, universities and other similar bodies, particularly those with a focus on national security and foreign and defense policy, will also have a valuable potential part to play in this work.[4]

The strategic goal of the PfPC is the same as that of the PfP program: to extend the Euro-Atlantic security community eastwards. Its goal is to foster cooperative practices in education and research in the field of security 'in the spirit of PfP'.[5] Although there is no precise definition of what the 'spirit of PfP' means, in essence, as one PfPC participants from Sarajevo put it, 'it means that all those countries are determined to foster those hard-to-achieve values, and that at least they will never wage war against each other.'[6] The Swiss Ambassador to NATO, Jean-Jacques de Dardel, aptly described the role of the PfPC:

> it contributes to the emergence of a wider Euro-Atlantic security community, where both *security* and *community* gain a more comprehensive meaning and scope of action.... Sporadic exchanges they enable contribute to the store of shared knowledge and foster a certain feeling of belonging to a wider security community. But it is the extended network created by the Consortium, and the form of constant work it implies, that really weaves a close-knit security community.
>
> *(De Dardel, 2008: 12, 14)*

The PfPC aims to achieve this strategic goal through defence and security education and research. According to the initial concept paper devised by the US Defence Department, 'the Consortium's primary purpose is to strengthen defense civilian and military professionalism through enhanced institutional cooperation among the 44 nations'.[7] One of its more concrete goals was to 'provide a forum to assist private foundations, "think tanks", governmental and non-governmental agencies to offer practical assistance' in security education and research.[8] The rationale behind the creation of the PfPC was, as one veteran of the consortium put it, 'to capture the minds' of people from across the former communist Europe in strategic positions in security research and education. As he vividly explains: 'The PfPC started out as a tool for opening academic brains to Western security thinking'.[9] One of the basic premises of this thinking has been the assumption that, as another participant from Bulgaria put it: 'the happiness of societies does not take place because of success in wars'.[10] In sum, this newly created IPN was meant to co-opt a wide range of civil society organizations as well as security and defence institutions into the Euro-Atlantic security community through education and research. From the very beginning, therefore, its goal has been to extend the liberal security community eastward by socializing civil and military experts into the liberal thinking about security.

Over the years, the PfPC has become politically and institutionally stronger. At the Washington Summit held in April 1999, NATO endorsed the consortium and this has been reconfirmed at all subsequent NATO summits. In addition to annual conferences, over 50 smaller events are held each year throughout the Euro-Asian region under the auspices of the PfPC. The PfPC brings together into a policy network over 800 defence academies and security studies institutes from 59 countries. The very idea of a network in the service of the security community is graphically represented on PfPC's logo: the goddess Athena, companion of heroes and a symbol of civilization holds a spear in one hand and the helmet of a fallen soldier in the other against the backdrop of a mesh net. The PfPC also has a small international secretariat located at the George C. Marshall European Center for Security Studies in Garmisch-Partenkirchen. Its governance structure is composed of a Steering Committee, which is a forum for study group chairs, and its Senior Advisory Council, a donor platform which allocates resources and coordinates strategic inputs (Christman, 2008: 21). The PfPC also publishes the scholarly journal *Connections: the Quarterly Journal*, in both English and Russian, and *Athena Papers* (published since 2004), covering longer studies on particular issues pertinent to Euro-Atlantic security. All in all, over the years, the PfPC has grown into a thinly institutionalized international security policy network.

The PfPC has six main stakeholders: the USA, Germany, Switzerland, Austria, Canada and NATO's international staff, while most funding is provided by the USA. Although the initial idea was to finance the PfPC according to the 'costs lie where they fall' principle, most costs of the PfPC are covered by the USA and Germany (through the Warsaw Initiative Fund) and to a lesser extent Switzerland and Austria (Costigan et al., 2008: 53). As Costigan, Felberbauer and Foot observed, 'the work being done is clearly being sponsored for national reasons' (Costigan et al., 2008: 58). The brunt of the work is done within nine stakeholder-led work and study groups dealing with: security sector reform (Switzerland), advanced distributed learning (USA and Switzerland), combating terrorism (USA), conflict studies (USA and France), emerging security challenges (NATO and Switzerland), comprehensive approach (USA, Germany and Switzerland), defence education (USA and Canada), South Caucasus (Austria) and Southeast Europe (Austria).[11] Each stakeholder is a leader of the working groups which deal with its greatest foreign policy concerns. The preoccupation of the US administration with the war on terror, Switzerland's focus on SSR and Austria's prioritization of Southeast Europe are all telling examples of that.

Due to its informality, loose nature and mixed composition, the PfPC is characterized by a high level of organizational flexibility. This stands in stark contrast to the rigidity of standard channels of communications between security and defence establishments in Western and Eastern Europe alike. As another longstanding member of the network stated: 'When you have a PfP activity, all the PfP countries are invited. The "spirit of PfP" means that we can chose our partners.'[12] Representatives of certain European states will be invited to the table, while others will be excluded depending on the context at hand. This is something which is much more difficult to achieve in a multilateral setting of intergovernmental cooperation. Moreover, the ability to choose partners not only applies to states, but to non-state actors as well. In the view of another network participant from Turkey, the spirit of PfP means going beyond the conventional security paradigm, where the key actors are the diplomats and the military: 'But in this new approach, in the new spirit, academics and NGO representatives can also participate.'[13] Here too, the network builders or key stakeholders will select the participants who can constructively contribute to the PfPC's work. Most often, it is the participants who subscribe to the policy relevant liberal peace agenda who are being (re)invited to attend the meetings.

This 'organizational flexibility' is obviously an instrument of exclusion, which leads to the creation of a gated and elite centred policy network. However, this feature also helps the PfPC to achieve effectiveness and efficiency. In contrast to traditional 'mil to mil' cooperation schemes and track one diplomatic meetings, the IPN format doesn't demand long and complicated security vetting and administrative procedures. Moreover, the Chatham House rule allows participants to express themselves freely without being bound by official positions or dull party lines. In short, one reason why government representatives, security scholars and civil society activists working within the PfPC can achieve together what none can accomplish on their own is due to its extraordinary organizational flexibility.

The PfPC was by and large successful in 'opening the brains' of Eastern and Southeast Europe expert communities to Western security thinking. However, the attempt to involve Russia has failed time and again. The watershed moment was the fourth annual conference held in Moscow, appropriately entitled 'Building a Strategic Community through Education and Research'. As Costigan, Ferlerbauer and Foot attested, the conference held in Moscow in 2001 was

> by almost any standard, a failure. Inspired by good intentions about bringing the new Russia into the Euro-Atlantic family, it was bedeviled by the *nomenklatura* members who ran the Moscow State University, by Russian determination to make information security (or, rather, counter-espionage through the Internet) the theme of the conference, and by the need of former client states to make much of their newly-found independence.
>
> *(Costigan et al., 2008: 59)*

The failure to engage Russia did not stem from the consortium's weakness but rather was a direct reflection of a much wider process of worsening relations between NATO and Russia. Although the track record of these relations showed signs of an embryonic security community, the process was not accompanied by the development of 'we-feeling' or collective identification (Pouliot, 2010: 4–5). While the rest of postcommunist Europe was being gradually brought into the fold of the European security architecture, Russia was increasingly being excluded from it due to its growing great power ambitions. The deepening gap between the NATO-centred cooperative security field and Russia's revisionist habitus creates a deep symbolic struggle between the two sides (Neumann and Pouliot, 2011). Russia's annexation of Crimea in the spring of 2014 and the subsequent return of the language of enmity in Europe after a quarter of a century is unfortunately just the most recent and gravest case in point so far. However, the venture to spread security community into East and Southeast Europe has been more successful. In order to offer a thick description of this process, in the remainder of this section I focus on the quotidian unfolding of a PfPC study group dealing with Regional Stability in Southeast Europe (RSSEE).

The RSSEE study group

The PfPC was quick to expand its operations in the direction of Southeast Europe. As early as the second annual conference, held in Sofia in December 1999, the Austrian delegation proposed the establishment of a study group entitled Crisis Management in Southeast Europe. The study group was conceived by a group working on Balkan matters at the Austrian National Defence Academy, who not only wanted to expand their view of the region but also to have a leading role in shaping the PfPC. The study group was named Crisis Management as, following the recent war in Kosovo and the NATO bombing of Yugoslavia, it was thought that there was still potential for crises to erupt (and therefore manage as well) in the region. As one of the study group organizers explained, such a crisis 'would then need an intervention, first politically and sometimes militarily'.[14] The establishment of the study group was co-sponsored by the Austrian Ministry of Defence and Sports in 1999, with the aim of creating 'a platform for building confidence and as a "neutral" platform to facilitate the exchange of different views in politically sensitive circumstances' (Ferlerbauer et al., 2010: 94).

The title of the first workshop, 'Information Management in the Field of Security Policy in Southeast Europe', held at Reichenau Castle in October 2000, reflected well the key functions of the study group. In his introductory remarks, study group chairman Colonel Gustav E Gustenau invited participants 'to provide support to the improvement of the network in the field of Security Policy and consequently to help in creating a Strategic Community within the Southeast European Region' (Gustenau, 2000: 2). Thus, the Austrian defence policy community initiated the expansion of the PfPC in the direction of the Balkans, a region which was trying to catch up with the rest of the Eastern Europe following the devastating wars of the 1990s.

Why did Austria invest in building this particular IPN? First, its foreign policy interests in the region have a strong historic, political, economic and security background. Austria's security strategy clearly indicates its orientation towards the region:

> Due to its geo-political position and the degree to which its security is affected and in light of its expertise and networks, Austrian priorities will continue to lie first and foremost with missions in Southeast and Eastern Europe as well as in the Middle East.
>
> (Austrian Security Strategy, 2013: 15)

Another longstanding participant in the PfPC, and a retired military officer from NATO who participated in the international intervention in Yugoslavia in 1999, explains the launch of the study group:

> it is clearly a case of enlightened self-interest from the Austrians. Their memory might not go back 700 years, but they do remember that the gates of Vienna were under threat at one stage so they are interested in the region in foreign policy terms ... this is an exercise in soft power on their part and it is entirely understandable and of benefit to all, but it is their foreign policy.[15]

Similarly, one of the first coordinators of the working group agrees that 'It was a pure Austrian interest to introduce this working group' in that it both supported forces on the ground and complemented the work of the Austrian intelligence services. He explains that Austria was 'trying to establish a network with scientists, with different people from the region, to get direct contact but also gain direct influence on certain areas of society in the Balkans'.[16] Obviously, Austria has a deep interest in building lasting peace and stability in Southeast Europe. However, the overall rationale behind the development of this particular IPN clearly went beyond Austria's national interests. Another American member of the group explains that the 'ulterior motive' for establishing the group was 'broader than just trying to create an echo-chamber for interest' but implied 'building up, within potential member states or partner countries, the so called broader security community'.[17] In fact, Austria's national interests in the region have been to create a peaceful space, integrated economically, politically and security wise into wider Euro-Atlantic structures. The alternative to this was instability, loss of markets, immigration flows, organized crime and other negative spillover effects that could threaten Austria's interests.

Although the study group initially went through a period of soul-searching, it became increasingly competent over the years. One of the core members of the group says: 'I have to say that we needed three, four years before we managed to build a team and started to do some real work'.[18] In the early years it was difficult for people from the region's NGOs to get funding from the USA due to very complicated vetting procedures. The memory of conflict was also still fresh, and so

Austrian military policemen were present at meetings. With time, however, competence in the practice of track 1 ½ networking grew and the presence of military policemen became completely redundant. The selection of participants from the region became more successful as the network builders identified civil society activists, scholars and decision makers who were seen as intellectually inspiring but constructive. The study group also served as an instrument for promoting young up and coming decision makers, activists and academics from the region, who share liberal values and security policy views. According to one group member, one rationale behind the study group was to promote capable young people who could be Austria's strategic partners in the future. 'Who will be our strategic partners? Is it going to be the elites that waged war or it will be a totally different, normal generation that we can cooperate with?' he asked.[19] The study group was intended to support the identification and empowerment of this new generation of security experts who will contribute to the maturation of the region's security community. As a matter of fact, many of the group members from the Western Balkans, who closely socialised within the study group over the years, went on indeed to become highly positioned government officials.

During its first decade work, the study group managed to achieve huge outreach. It gathered more than 250 partner institutions and around 350 scholars, experts and practitioners (Ferlerbauer et al., 2010: 97; PfPC, 2012: 33). The study group brings together policy makers, the media, NGOs and academics. It has three co-chairs, one from Austria and two from the region.[20] The study group is led by Austria, but the lion's share of its financial wherewithal is provided by the USA through the Pentagon's Operation and Maintenance fund. Other sources include NATO and third-party contributions. Austria also contributes significantly to the working group through 'in kind' contributions (such as Reichenau Castle, soldiers and so on).[21]

Workshops are attended by approximately 40–50 people, of whom at least one third are always new to the consortium and study group. Approximately one third of the participants are state or IO officials, one third are academics and one third work for Civil Society Organisations (CSOs). Each meeting ends with the drafting of policy recommendations which are later published. Workshops are held twice a year under the Chatham House Rule and are structured in a standard way, starting with keynote lectures, continuing with panel discussions and ending with interactive debate about policy recommendations. As General Raimund Schittenhelm, Commandant of the Austrian National Defence Academy, testified: 'These workshops have provided an opportunity for civil society actors from the region to introduce practical conflict resolution ideas to each other and international actors alike' (Felberbauer et al., 2010: 5). As a result, the study group developed the status of a high-profile network for security and defence experts either coming from the region or interested in it.

The study group has been a site of asymmetric elite socialization in which participants from the region have gradually taken ownership. Initially, the agenda for discussion was set by the organisers from Austria's National Defence Academy.

Participants would share their views, sometimes very heatedly, but they took a back seat. As the years passed, the group developed a 'culture of dialogue' as participants from the region socialized into a standard model of policy related academic presentation and discussion of sensitive international issues. An important facet of this is 'conceptual interoperability'. One regular participant from Turkey describes this evolution of competence: 'When I went to Bulgaria in 1998, their security terminology was different from the security terminology that I used, that NATO country experts or academics use, but today they speak the same language.'[22] Rather than just discussing issues, in the later stages of the study group's development its participants were invited to devise policy recommendations jointly. Currently, as one veteran of the group put it, 'we are now in stage three, where the program is actively shaped by our partners'.[23] In sum, over the years participants from the region were gradually given increasing ownership in terms of agenda setting and invitation policy.

In addition to this, the study group has incessantly worked, either implicitly or explicitly, on the spread of the norm of self-restraint from the Euro-Atlantic community to Southeast Europe. This norm was built into most of the topics discussed at workshops, covering the widest gamut of issues relevant to liberal security community building including democratization, multi-ethnicity, state building, state weakness, regional cooperation, organized crime, economic security, international intervention, transformation of armed forces, human trafficking, peace building, security sector reform, Kosovo status, NATO and EU accession, post-conflict reconstruction of BiH, frozen conflicts, ICTY verdicts and many others.

The study group also served to manage, produce and diffuse knowledge about the region. This concerns, first and foremost, the question of what the region is and where its borders lie. The geographical focus was initially on Southeast Europe. With time, however, the group's interest narrowed to the Western Balkans, tied by security-political interdependence related to the unresolved problems in BiH, Serbia/Kosovo and Macedonia. As Romania and Bulgaria joined NATO and the EU, the only remaining part of the Balkan Peninsula left unabsorbed by the Euro-Atlantic security community was the Western Balkans. One veteran of the study group explains its shift of geographic focus:

> Regional stability now is a closer approach. As other countries like Hungary, Romania, Bulgaria and Greece are already members of the EU, the study group is only considering the Western Balkans ... the former Yugoslav republics plus Albania minus Slovenia is still the area where we are afraid of new conflicts.[24]

Arguably, the study group was not only acknowledging a wider objective reality about the Western Balkan region, it was actively participating in its discursive production. Moreover, the study group has been managing knowledge about the security dynamics that tie the region together. For example, in 2002 the study group changed its name from Crisis Management in Southeast Europe to Regional

Stability in Southeast Europe. The term 'crisis management' was replaced by 'regional stability' because the risk of military crises had been minimized, if not entirely overcome. One Bulgarian participant who had been part of the group since the very beginning explained the decision for the name change: 'Regional stability is the minimum that we can have without war. In crisis management you always consider the presence of an ongoing crisis.'[25] The change of name reflects wider developments in the region and the birth of a nascent security community. However, it is clear that the study group was actively participating in the desecuritization of the region, a discursive process that has been underway within western international society since the end of war in 1999.

The overall discourse within the study group matches the mainstream liberal peace paradigm. It is based on implicit assumptions that democracy, market economics and international cooperation are good for peace among nations. More specifically, the benefits of Euro-Atlantic integration are almost never openly questioned. The Western Balkans is represented as the 'other' to the Western 'self' but as ultimately capable of catching up and becoming a full member of the liberal society of states. Consequently, the region is routinely portrayed as a 'success story in the making', 'unfinished business' or a 'glass half full'. This reluctant optimism is based on the assumption that, in spite of all the challenges, the region is on a well-trodden path that will ultimately reorder it in the same way that Western Europe was reordered after the Second World War or Eastern Europe after the Cold War. Liberal peace, enforced by overwhelming external power and implemented by internationally socialized political elites, is expected to simultaneously build sovereign states and make them pool their sovereignty, thus gradually removing the deep roots of the erstwhile conflict. Illiberal ideas, although quite powerful in politics across the Western Balkans, are rarely if ever heard at the meetings. As one participant from Kosovo lamented: 'We never have nationalists in our discussions. At the same time, we know that they are the main policy makers and decision makers in our countries right now, unfortunately.'[26] From all the above, it is clear that the study group has built a gated and elite network devoted to the promotion of liberal norms and knowledge production.

But in spite of the fact that it is a gated and elite network, the study group's members often emphasize that it is not an 'ivory tower ... divorced from the realities on the ground' (Ferlerbauer et al., 2010: 94). Policy relevance is of paramount importance to any discussion, while theoretical considerations or scholarly references are rarely, if ever, made. What is more, history is rarely discussed at length during workshops. In his presentation about the study group, traditionally made at the beginning of each workshop, one participant from the Austrian National Defence Academy usually repeats that: 'We don't talk about history but about the future'. Such a future-oriented outlook was reiterated on a number of occasions during workshops as well as in interviews. For example, one participant from Bosnia and Hercegovina, confirms this: 'At the workshops that I attended, the issue of the 1990s was never brought up. Much more attention was paid to the recent past and to the vision of the future'.[27] If any historical references are made, it is usually for the purpose of making analogies. In other words, examples from the European past such as Franco-German reconciliation are employed strategically by speakers as historical analogies to convince the audience that liberal security policies should be retained or adopted. All in all, the study group has maintained a hands-on, policy-relevant and future-oriented approach to security policy challenges.

One of the key priorities of the study group has been to influence security policy. To that effect, the study group produces two types of publications: longer conference proceedings and shorter policy papers with recommendations consensually reached during workshops.[28] The Austrian Ministry of Defence and Sports publishes all conference proceedings and conclusions as part of its Study Group Information series. The aim of these publications is to diffuse the ideas produced in the study group and influence policy making.

Indirect influence, although quite diffuse and difficult to measure, has been most clearly visible within Austria's defence and security policy community. Its members regularly receive input from the study group's meetings through reports, policy papers, publications and personal contacts. The study group's publications have also attracted the attention of various state and non-state actors in the region and are expected to inform the policy making process of NATO, the EU and the USA. For instance, in December 2012, the study group's policy papers were marked as 'recommended reading' by the US Under Secretary of Defense for Policy (PfPC, 2012: 34).

Direct influence is more tangible but also rarer. One case in point was an idea born during the study group's meeting held in Priština in 2011. At the margins of the meeting, participants agreed to involve the OSCE in the organization of Serbia's 2012 parliamentary and presidential elections on the territory of Kosovo. The implementation of this idea helped to defuse tensions between Serbia and Kosovo, to prevent potential escalation and to clear the ground for political negotiations which ultimately led to the historic Brussels Agreement signed in April 2013. As this model proved to function well, the OSCE also fairly successfully facilitated the extremely challenging municipal elections held in North Kosovo in November 2013, the first to be held according to Kosovo law (Ejdus et al., 2013).

The study group's format enabled great organizational flexibility and effectiveness. It allowed the Austrian National Defence Academy to circumvent the standard operating procedures associated with 'track one' diplomacy or mil to mil cooperation. It has been both easier and more effective for the Austrian National Defence Academy to work with NGOs and think tanks from the region. This is because the Academy was able to circumvent complicated bureaucratic procedures that would be unavoidable if regional counterparts were governmental institutions. Put another way, if the workshops were to be organized by the Austrian National Defence Academy and its opposite numbers in the region, organizing them would have taken much longer and been bureaucratically more complicated. One of the study group's architects argues that such a track 1 ½ model allowed them much greater freedom of movement:

> It is very, very difficult to deal with ministries of defence because you have these long lines, you have to go down, you have to invite them. It takes too much time and normally the outcome is zero or almost zero ... it's a lot simpler to work with organizations, with NGOs, with scientific society than to work with the government. Of course we can invite members of governments ... but to deal with them directly as partners is a problem.[29]

Moreover, the 'track 1 ½' format has also been much more effective in terms of the quality of discussions. When governmental agencies organize workshops of this type, the outcome is the reiteration of party lines rather than an open and critical discussion. However, the workshops within the study group are set up by the Austrian National Defence Academy together with NGOs and think tanks from the region. As a result, the organization and composition of the meetings are much more flexible and inclusive, while the discussions seem to be more open and substantial. As one of the founders of the study group explained, Austria was 'interested in the opinion of scientists and civil-society', which is:

> normally an opinion that is totally different from the opinions of diplomats, but also different from the opinions of the military ... and we had the feeling that the information we were receiving from our intelligence services is always filtered and not covering this side.[30]

The PfPC and the Austrian foreign and defence policy community consider the RSSEE study group to be a great success story. Encouraged by its success, and drawing on the experience of 'track 1 ½' networking gained through the RSSEE study group, the Austrian National Defence Academy decided to initiate a similar network in the Southern Caucasus. For a variety of reasons, the security landscape in that region is quite different from that which characterized Southeast Europe at the outset of the twenty first century, not least because of a stronger geopolitical presence of Russia. However, the assumption behind this endeavour is that the liberal peace project can draw lessons from one region and apply them elsewhere, with slight modifications. One of the network's architects explains the logic in the following way: 'We hope that we can transfer the model, as well as the lessons learned from Southeast Europe, to the South Caucasus, because both NATO and the European Union are strongly upping their engagement in this region.'[31] Whether the capillary power of the Euro-Atlantic community can properly function under the conditions of frozen conflicts and fierce geopolitical struggle remains to be seen.

Conclusion

In this article, I have focussed on the role of IPNs in security community building, something which the scholarly community has so far largely ignored. Drawing on my personal experience in one such network (PfPC) I have argued that IPNs play an important role as building blocks of transition from the *nascent* to the *ascendant* phase, during which state elites and civil societies are expected to be involved in the densifying patterns of amity and trust. In my ethnographic case study, I depicted the PfPC as a constellation of IPNs established in the late 1990s under the auspices of NATO with the aim of extending the Euro-Atlantic security community eastwards. In particular, I have demonstrated how an Austrian led study group on Southeast Europe has contributed to peaceful region building in the Western Balkans through knowledge management, norm diffusion, policy influence and organizational flexibility. This particular IPN was built to serve Austria's foreign security interests and promote its values in the Western Balkans. However, it is also meant to transform it from a conflict zone to a region of peace and stability and integrate it within the wider Euro-Atlantic security community.

Further research could extend the analysis to the histories, causes, dynamics and consequences of the extraordinary institutional isomorphism which exists among the various IPNs involved in peace building. Especially interesting is the recent mushrooming of so-called security forums in the region, including the Belgrade Security Forum, Globsec in Bratislava, Germia Hill in Priština, the Riga Conference, the Bled Strategic Forum, 2BS in Podgorica and the Sofia Forum. Modelled after the famous Munich Security Forum, these flagship events are increasingly becoming the must have symbols of prestige and relevance across East and Southeast Europe. It would also be useful to map and systematically study the overlapping of various IPNs involved in these events, their connection to various states, IOs and donors, as well as their role in macroregional security dynamics. Also, further investigation could reveal the role of the private sector in security community building (as drivers or spoilers), especially the military industrial complex and the information technology sector. Finally, it would be interesting to trace the direction and dynamics of policy transfer and the role of learning and knowledge production in the process. In sum, in addition to professional and epistemic communities, the study of IPNs promises to be an extraordinary way to shed light on aspects of security community building in Europe (and beyond) that have so far gone largely unnoticed in IR.

Notes

1 As a co-chair, I have continued to attend PfPC events ever since and I have conducted numerous additional conversations.
2 http://marshallcenter.contentdm.oclc.org/cdm/ref/collection/p16378coll10/id/32 (accessed 3 April 2014).
3 www.marshallcenter.org/mcpublicweb/en/nav-main-explore-gcmc-history-en.html#history-of-the-marshall-center (accessed 3 April 2014).
4 1st annual conference proceedings, Networking Security Institutions in the Information Age and the Way Ahead for the PfP Consortium 19–21 October 1998, Zurich, Switzerland. Source: https://members.marshallcenter.org/resource/1st-annual-conference-proceedings
5 Vision statement of the PfPC: www.pfpconsortium.com/#!untitled/cjg9 (accessed 3 April 2014).
6 Interview conducted on 28 May 2012 in Opatija, Croatia.
7 1st annual conference proceedings, Networking Security Institutions in the Information Age and the Way Ahead for the PfP Consortium 19–21 October 1998, Zurich,

Switzerland. Source: https://members.marshallcenter.org/resource/1st-annual-conference-proceedings
8 Ibid.
9 Interview conducted on 19 June 2012 in Tbilisi, Georgia.
10 Interview conducted on 5 May 2012 in Reichenau, Austria.
11 The names, numbers and composition of study and working groups have varied in the past.
12 Interview conducted on 29 September 2012 in Skopje, Macedonia.
13 Interview conducted on 4 May 2012 in Reichenau, Austria.
14 Interview conducted on 19 June 2012 in Tbilisi, Georgia.
15 Interview conducted on 4 May 2012 in Reichenau, Austria.
16 Interview conducted on 29 September 2012 in Skopje, Macedonia.
17 Interview conducted on 29 September 2012 in Skopje, Macedonia.
18 Interview conducted on 18 June 2012 in Tbilisi, Georgia.
19 Interview conducted on 18 June 2012 in Tbilisi, Georgia.
20 Since 2010 I have served as the co-chair from Serbia and in that capacity I have attended all of the meetings. This includes all the public meetings plus the preparatory track meetings that usually take place each December at the National Defence Academy in Vienna.
21 Interview conducted on 29 September 2012 in Skopje, Macedonia.
22 Interview conducted on 4 May 2012 in Reichenau, Austria.
23 Interview conducted on 18 June 2012 in Tbilisi, Georgia
24 Interview conducted on 4 May 2012 in Reichenau, Austria.
25 Interview conducted on 5 May 2012 in Reichenau, Austria.
26 Interview conducted on 6 May 2012 in Reichenau, Austria.
27 Interview conducted on 28 May 2012 in Opatija, Croatia.
28 All publications produced by the study group can be downloaded from www.bmlv.gv.at/wissen-forschung/publikationen/doktyp.php?id=7
29 Interview conducted on 29 September 2012 in Skopje, Macedonia.
30 Interview conducted on 29 September 2012 in Skopje, Macedonia.
31 Interview conducted on 18 June 2012 in Tbilisi, Georgia

Bibliography

Adler, E, *Communitarian International Relations: The Epistemic Foundations of International Relations*, Routledge, 2005.
Adler, E, "The Spread of Security Communities: Communities of Practice, Self-Restraint and NATO's Post-Cold War Transformation" in *European Journal of International Relations* 14:2 (2008): 195–230.
Adler, E and Barnett, M, *Security Communities*, Cambridge University Press, 1998.
Anderson, L, "Analytic Autoethnography" in *Journal of Contemporary Ethnography* 35:4 (2006): 373–395.
Andrieu, K, "Civilizing Peacebuilding: Transitional Justice, Civil Society and the Liberal Paradigm" in *Security Dialogue* 41:5 (2010): 537–558.
Austrian Security Strategy: Security in a New Decade, Shaping Security, Austria: Federal Chancellery, 2013.
Aydinli, E and Yoen, H, "Transgovernmentalism Meets Security: Police Liaison Officers, Terrorism, and Statist Transnationalism" in *Governance* 24:1 (2011): 55–84.
Bartelson, J, "Making Sense of Global Civil Society" in *European Journal of International Relations* 12:3 (2006): 371–395.
Belloni, R, "Civil Society and Peacebuilding in Bosnia and Herzegovina" in *Journal of Peace Research* 38:2 (2001): 163–180.

Bieber, F, "Aid dependency in Bosnian politics and civil society: Failures and successes of post-war peacebuilding in Bosnia-Herzegovina" in *Croatian International Relations Review* 8:26/27 (2002): 25–29.

Borawski, J, "Partnership for Peace and Beyond" in *International Affairs (Royal Institute of International Affairs 1944-)* 71:2 (1995): 233–246.

Bueger, C, "Counter-Piracy, Communities of Practice and New Security Alignments" in *Journal of Regional Security* 8:3 (2013): 49–62.

Buzan, B, *People, States and Fear: The National Security Problem in International Relations*, Boulder CO: Wheatsheaf Books Brighton, 1983.

Buzan, B and Hansen, L, *The Evolution of International Security Studies*, Cambridge, UK; New York: Cambridge University Press, 2009.

Buzan, B, Wæver, O and De Wilde, J, *Security: A New Framework for Analysis*, Boulder CO: Lynne Rienner Publishers, 1998.

Caparini, M, "Civil Society and Democratic Oversight of the Security Sector: a Preliminary Investigation" in *Sourcebook on Security Sector Reform*, Belgrade: DCAF, CCMR, 2004, 171–192.

Caparini, M, Fluri, P and Molná, F, *Civil Society and the Security Sector: Concepts and Practices in New Democracies*, LIT Verlag Münster, 2006.

Chandler, D, "The Limits of Peacebuilding: International Regulation and Civil Society Development in Bosnia" in *International Peacekeeping* 6:1 (1999): 109–125.

Christman, WL, "The PfP Consortium 'Community of Experts' Approach to International Security Cooperation" in *Connections: The Quarterly Journal* 7:3 (2008): 15–30.

Costigan, S, Felberbauer, E and Foot, P, "The Challenges of Being Ten: Reflections on the Uniqueness of the PfP Consortium" in *Connections: The Quarterly Journal* 7:3 (2008): 52–61.

Cross, MKD, *Security Integration in Europe: How Knowledge-Based Networks are Transforming the European Union*, Ann Arbor: University of Michigan Press, 2011.

De Dardel, J-J, "PfP, EAPC, and the PfP Consortium: Key Elements of the Euro-Atlantic Security Community" in *Connections: The Quarterly Journal* 7:3 (2008): 1–15.

Dupont, B, "Security in the Age of Networks" in *Policing and Society* 14:1 (2004): 76–91.

Ejdus, F, "Talking Truth to Power: Do Educational Infrastructures in Serbia Meet the Needs for New Generations of Security Specialists?" in *Western Balkans Security Observer* 6 – English Edition (2007): 55–62.

Ejdus, F, Malazogu, L and Nic, M, *Municipal Elections in Northern Kosovo: Towards a New Balance?*Bratislava: Institute CEP (2013).

Elias, N, *The Civilizing Process*, New York: Pantheon Books, 1982.

Felberbauer, E, Grimm, K, Halo, A, et al., *Policy Recommendations on Regional Stability in South East Europe – An Anthology*, Vienna (2010).

Ferlerbauer, E, Jureković, P and Labarre, F, "Advice and Advocacy: Ten Years of the Regional Stability in South East Europe Study Group" in *Connections* 9:3 (2010): 95–106.

Glišić, J, "In the Need for New Generation of Security Specialists: Belgrade School of Security Studies" in *Western Balkans Security Observer* 6 – English Edition (2007): 63–79.

Grillot, SR and Cruise, RJ, "Regional Security Community in the Western Balkans: A Cross-Comparative Analysis" in *Journal of Regional Security* 3 (2013): 7–24.

Gustenau, G, *Information Management in the Field of Security Policy in SEE – 1st Workshop of the Study Group "Crisis Management in South East Europe" – Proceedings*, Vienna, 2000.

Haas, PM, "Do Regimes Matter? Epistemic communities and Mediterranean Pollution Control" in *International Organization* 43:3 (1989): 377–403.

Jackson, PT, "Can Ethnographic Techniques Tell Us Distinctive Things About World Politics?" in *International Political Sociology* 2:1 (2008): 91–93.

Kavalski, E, *Extending the European Security Community: Constructing Peace in the Balkans*, IB Tauris & Company, 2008.
Kaye, DD, "Track Two Diplomacy and Regional Security in the Middle East" in *International Negotiation* 6:1 (2001): 49–77.
Keck, ME, and Sikkink, K, *Activists Beyond Borders: Advocacy Networks in International Politics*, Cambridge University Press, 1998.
Koneska, C, "Regional Identity: The Missing Element in Western Balkans Security Cooperation" in *Western Balkans Security Observer* 7–8 – English Edition (2007): 82–89.
Kraft, HJS, "The Autonomy Dilemma of Track Two Diplomacy in Southeast Asia" in *Security Dialogue* 31:3 (2000): 343–356.
Krahmann, E, "Security Governance and Networks: New Theoretical Perspectives in Transatlantic Security" in *Cambridge Review of International Affairs* 18:1 (2005): 15–30.
McDonald, JW, "Further exploration of track two diplomacy" in Kriesberg, L and Thorson, SJ, *Timing the De-escalation of International Conflicts*, Syracuse University Press, 1991, 201–220.
Mérand, F, Hofmann, SC and Irondelle, B, "Governance and State Power: a Network Analysis of European Security" in *JCMS: Journal of Common Market Studies* 49:1 (2011): 121–147.
Neumann, IB, "A Region-Building Approach to Northern Europe" in *Review of International Studies* 20 (1994): 53–53.
Neumann, IB and Pouliot, V, "Untimely Russia: Hysteresis in Russian-Western Relations over the Past Millennium" in *Security Studies* 20:1 (2011): 105–137.
North Atlantic Council, *The Alliance's New Strategic Concept*, 1991.
Orjuela, C, "Building Peace in Sri Lanka: A Role for Civil Society?" in *Journal of Peace Research* 40:2 (2003): 195–212.
Perkin, E and Court, J, *Networks and Policy Processes in International Development: A Literature Review*, London: Overseas Development Institute, 2005.
PfPC, *Annual Report*, Garmisch-Partenkirchen, 2012.
Pouligny, B, "Civil Society and Post-Conflict Peacebuilding: Ambiguities of International Programmes Aimed at Building 'New' Societies" in *Security Dialogue* 36:4 (2005): 495–510.
Pouliot, V, "The Logic of Practicality: A Theory of Practice of Security Communities" in *International Organization* 62:2 (2008) 257–288.
Pouliot, V, *International Security in Practice: The Politics of NATO-Russia Diplomacy* Cambridge University Press, 2010.
Reinicke, W, "The Other World Wide Web: Global Public Policy Networks" in *Foreign Policy* (Washington) 117 (2000) 44–57.
Slaughter, A-M, "The Accountability of Government Networks" in *Indiana Journal of Global Legal Studies* 8:2 (2000) 347–367.
Subotić, J, "The Past Is Not Yet Over: Remembrance, Justice and Security Community in the Western Balkans" in *Journal of Regional Security* 2 (2012): 107–118.
Ullman, RH, "Redefining Security" in *International Security* 8:1 (1983): 129–153.
Vučetić, S, "The Stability Pact for South Eastern Europe as a Security Community-Building Institution" in *Southeast European Politics* 2:2 (2001): 109–134.
Walker, RB, *Inside/Outside: International Relations as Political Theory*, Cambridge University Press, 1993.
Wenger, E, *Communities of Practice: Learning, Meaning, and Identity*, Cambridge University Press, 1998.

9

CONCLUSION

Security communities of practice between national and regional fields

Sonja Stojanović Gajić

This book has set out to study security community building below and beyond the level of states and international organisations. Across seven chapters, the authors have analysed the dynamics driving the transformation of inter-state relations in the Western Balkans, from conflict to peace, over a period spanning less than two decades since the end of the last armed conflicts in Macedonia, in 2001.

The original feature of this book is its focus on the everyday practices of professionals from key security and foreign policy institutions. These cases are relevant to understanding the transformation of sovereignty as the selected professions traditionally embody the state by defending its territorial integrity (military), maintaining internal order (police) or representing its interests abroad (diplomacy). They are also 'the face of the state' (Silver, 1967) to its domestic population (police), potential enemy (military) and external others worth negotiating with (diplomats). Therefore, the selected professional communities are relevant cases for the study of transformation of sovereignty practices in the field of security. The selection of security professionals is also relevant to understanding the transformation of Western Balkan inter-state relations as the majority of the professions examined here have experienced participation in armed conflict against their neighbours. Examples of such professions studied in this collection are: the Armed Forces of Bosnia and Herzegovina, composed of two formerly conflicting militaries,[1] as well as the police forces of Croatia, Kosovo, Montenegro and Macedonia.[2] The case of regional cooperation practiced by Albanian diplomats does not fall into the category of professions that experienced armed conflict but is nevertheless an interesting case as it analyses the return of Albanian diplomats to multilateral diplomacy, including regional cooperation, after a period of self-isolation lasting several decades, since the split of the Warsaw Pact with China. The book also includes the control case of the International Policy Network (IPN) that is composed of members from different professions and different countries both from within and outside the region, who share common values and policy ideas but not necessarily causal belief.[3]

The eleven authors contributing to this collection chose to analyse security community building processes 'from below', from the perspective of national professional communities which, although embedded in broader national identities, have distinct professional *habitus*. *Habitus* is understood in the Bourdieusian tradition as a 'shared set of dispositions that orient agents in the particular field' based on past experiences and history (Madsen, 2017:114). Simply put, is the self-evident 'sense of game' which 'inclines actors towards one or another practice' but that is based on the 'position that the individual occupies in the field' (Pouiliot and Mernard, in Adler-Nisson, 2013: 29). By field, we adopt Bourdieu's definition as 'a social space structured along three principal dimensions: power relations, objects of struggle, and the rules taken for granted within the field' (Bourdieu 1993: 72–77 quoted by Pouiliot and Merand in Adler-Nissen, 2013: 30). By using the category of field, we can analyse how security and foreign policy professionals take different positions in a social space of interactions based on dominant capital for that field (economic, cultural, bureaucratic, etc.). The main analysis in this chapter is focused on the question of how a common professional 'sense of game' (*habitus*) interacts in different fields – the national, regional and international – to sometimes produce cooperative security practices and at other times exclusionary security practices. The control case was the study by Filip Ejdus (Chapter 8) who undertook analysis 'from above', looking at the formation, functioning and influencing potential of the International Policy Network. Following the practices of different agents, the eleven authors examined the transformation of inter-state relations in the Western Balkans through semi-structured interviews, participant observation, content analysis of documents produced within the IPN and studied institutions and two surveys on cooperation within different regional networks in Bosnia and Herzegovina and Macedonia. This approach was inspired by the *sobjective methodology* developed by Pouliot (2007) aimed at inductive, interpretative and historical analysis of practices.

By looking at practices, the authors analysed how patterns of cooperation changed and were experienced and lived by security and diplomatic professionals and the International Policy Network (IPN). The main unit of analysis was security practices focusing 'less on how people represent one another [and more] on what practitioners actually do when they interact' (Pouliot, 2010: 5). In this way, using practice theory, we can study those implicit understandings between group members that are specific to a profession or *habitus* understood as a common 'sense of game' (Madsen, 2017: 114).

Through this empirical study of regional cooperation in the Western Balkans we wanted to examine whether Adler and Pouliot's claim, that practices are 'able to change the physical environment as well as the ideas that individually and collectively people hold about the world' (Adler and Pouliot, 2011a: 7), is relevant in the case of inter-state relations in the post-conflict Western Balkan region. In particular, we wanted to check if and when the practice of non-violent interaction between security professionals who share a similar collective, professional history and 'sense of game' (*habitus*) result in a practical sense of trust or 'believing despite uncertainty' as a second component of the security community (Pouliot, 2010: 40). In the case of the International Policy Network, Ejdus analysed if and how the interaction practices within this heterogeneous network composed of individuals with diverse professional backgrounds contributes to security community-building.

This book does not aim to reach conclusions on causal relationships between observed 'micro-practices and macroregional patterns of peaceful resolution of conflicts in Southeastern Europe' (Ejdus, this volume: p. 103), but 'to describe the quotidian involvement of this particular IPN [and studied security professionals] in the evolution of a security community and theorize this activity' (ibid.: 103). In this way, we hope to contribute to the literature on security communities from the Bourdieusian inspired perspective of international political sociology (Pouliot, 2010; Adler-Nissen, 2013; Balzacq et al., 2010) applied to post-conflict regions.

Outline

This concluding chapter provides comparative insights from seven case studies presented in this book: experience of regional cooperation by Albanian diplomats; the armed forces of Bosnia and Herzegovina; the police services of Croatia, Kosovo, Macedonia and Montenegro; and the International Policy Network of the Study Group for Regional Stability in Southeast Europe (RSSEE). The main finding of this study is that security and foreign policy professions practice cooperative security across national borders in line with the models within which they were socialised both as members of older former Yugoslav communities of practice and through participation in new transnational regional networks externally imposed by the EU and NATO. Post-conflict de-securitisation of inter-state relations took place through socialisation via a new categorisation of threats as predominantly non-military and transnational (definition of *joint enterprise*) and the learning of new competencies in policing, defence and diplomacy through cooperative security practices developed within the EU and NATO (*shared repertoire of practices*). While much regional cooperation developed as an instrument to join the larger regional communities within the EU and NATO, some communities of practice (Wenger, 1998; Adler, 2008) developed internally to the Western Balkan region based on common professional *habitus* and the definition of joint enterprises that sometimes differed from official national foreign and security policy.

Cooperative security practices are, however, functional only on issues that have not been subjected to securitisation at the national political level. This confirms earlier findings that 'battles for categorization take place nationally' (Madsen, 2017). The embeddedness of professional identity in national identity is seen through informally created sub-regions based on national perceptions of threat as well as language-grouping practices. The logic of sovereignty and a more exclusive understanding of threats prevails when professional autonomy is confronted with the authority of politicians. The case of the International Policy Network shows, however, that one of the key advantages of this transnational network composed of a heterogeneous group of professionals and civil society is flexibility in expanding the boundaries of the possible through track II diplomacy.

The text of the book is broadly divided into two parts, each with a number of sub-sections. In the first part, we described how practices of self-restraint and cooperation are developed among former enemies by external actors through support for communities of practice and the IPN (Wenger, 1998; Adler, 2008). Here we analysed how important the provision of sites for interaction, joint enterprise and shared repertoire of practices is for building new competent practices of self-restraint and 'we-feeling' through situated learning among participants from Western Balkan countries. In the second part, we described key limitations towards developing predictable 'belief despite uncertainty' among peers from neighbouring countries due to the embeddedness of professional *habitus* to societal categorisation of threats and sub-ordination to political actors at the national level. While observations made in the studied empirical cases cannot be generalised to other geographical and historical contexts, they can help us understand the interplay between professional *habitus* and its positioning in different fields.

The transformation of inter-state relations in the Western Balkans

The main empirical finding is that inter-state relations among Western Balkan states have transformed to a normalised practice of diplomacy in resolution of disputes and that security professionals who have been participants of armed conflicts are now accustomed to peaceful resolution of conflicts. This is also true for Albanian diplomacy, self-excluded from multilateral fora during the Enver Hoxha era to the point of having almost no communication with neighbouring countries. Consensus has been reached among the authors of the case studies in this collection that diplomacy has become a normalised practice but it still has not become the self-evident practice in all situations. They disagree whether regional security practices are best described by Pouilot's concept of a *non-war community* or different phases of Adler and Barnett's scale of security community intensity: *nascent* (Dyrmishi and Qeseraku, this volume) or *ascendant* (Ejdus, this volume). All of these categories have in common a great quantity and intensity of peaceful interactions and diplomacy as accepted practice but the ingredient that is not represented in adequate quantities is trust or 'believing despite uncertainty'. In the following sections, we will describe how the practice of self-restraint and cooperation is developed among former enemies by external actors through support for communities of practice and the IPN (Wenger, 1998; Adler, 2008). Most importantly, this study will document when cooperative practices are supported by common professional *habitus*, or 'sense of game', and when it is mediated by embeddedness of professional *habitus* in national societies or its sub-ordination to political actors at the national level.

The drivers of peaceful conflict resolution

All seven studies presented in the collection cite external influences, particularly those of the EU and NATO.[4] as a major reason for improvements in inter-state relations due to the conditionality they instil and the cooperative security they promote as a condition for membership of the broader Euro-Atlantic security community. This is in line with the findings of earlier studies of inter-state relations in the region (Vučetić, 2001; Kavalski, 2008) that the socialisation into new norms of cooperative security occurred in the context of asymmetrical power relations, where Western actors backed their model of security governance with military presence in the region as guarantors of peace agreements, as well as through political conditionality for EU and NATO membership. Regional cooperation was put forward as a key condition within the Stabilisation and Association Process established to socialise the Western Balkans during EU accession (Bechev, 2006) and was followed up by the creation of new multilateral agreements, fora and networks designed to facilitate cooperation among former enemies. Many of the studies in this volume (Dyrmishi and Qesaraku; Koneska; Knezović et al.) also confirm Vučetić's finding (2001) that initial regional cooperation was not motivated by the prospect of building a regional security community, but 'the process is driven by the desire to become part of security communities that extend beyond the Western Balkan region. Thus, regional integration is perceived as a temporary process rather than the end goal' (Dyrmishi and Qesaraku, this volume: p. 25).

The 'socialization by' external actors of political elites and diplomats through conditionality (Kavalski) opened the doors for interaction among security professionals. Solioz and Stubbs (2009: 5) also confirms that the regional cooperation architecture put in place by the EU, through creation of the Stability Pact, created 'the space between ... interstate diplomacy, technocratic policymaking and networked policy entrepreneurship'. The example of the IPN shows that socialisation of academics and civil society as knowledge intermediaries served 'to capture the minds' of people in strategic positions in research and education 'to extend the liberal security community eastward' (Ejdus, this volume: p. 107).

Interaction within regional networks, despite initially being externally imposed, has created some communities of practice among security and foreign policy professionals defined as 'like-minded groups of professionals linked informally and contextually by a shared interest in learning and applying common practice' (Wenger, 1998; Adler, 2008). These communities of practice have not, however, overlapped with institutional and formal boundaries of regional cooperation fora but were created and reproduced in practice. In order to describe the dynamics that give rise to regional communities of practice, three dimensions of communities of practice will be examined in analysing the state of cooperation in the Western Balkans: mutual engagement, joint enterprise and shared repertoire of practices (Wenger, 1998: 72).

Mutual engagement

The external actors provided for *mutual engagement* between former enemies through the creation of formal, regional, inter-state cooperation initiatives and networks. In this way, the external actors initiated the regular gathering of security and foreign policy professionals from the region, as well as between state officials and civil society representatives through looser networks such as the Regional Study Group for Stability in Southeast Europe (RSSEE) analysed by Ejdus in this volume (Chapter 8). All of the examined countries are regular members of different regional security and justice initiatives[5] while Kosovo was (until 2014) excluded from these multilateral fora due to Serbian objections, it has since been allowed to participate as an observer. The different inter-state regional initiatives facilitated first contact between policy and operational-level professionals and provided sites for socialisation in new ways of performing core professional tasks. As evident from Ejdus's chapter, the initial interactions happened in an atmosphere of distrust and the fear of the organisers was evident from the presence of Austrian military police at the initial meetings of the RSSEE but these early concerns were slowly transformed into fear-free interactions.

One of the observations made during this study was that a formal context for interaction is less conducive to building trust than informal interaction among security and foreign policy professionals, as well as with civil society in the case of the IPN. It is the unofficial part of programme and informal interactions during breaks at regional events and training sessions that were valued most, by the interviewed security practitioners and diplomats, as a way to build personal contacts that are later used to overcome bureaucratic obstacles. This was reported both by top-level professional decision-makers, in the context of the Southeast European Police Chief Association (SEPCA), as well as by more mid-level and rank-and-file participants involved in the participant observation of regional military training in the chapter on Bosnian and Herzegovina and the conferences and training programmes described in the chapters on Montenegro and Macedonia. Due to the importance police culture places on prompt and unhindered reaction to security problems, informal contacts were valued as they enabled rapid response in cases where an alarm is raised about the whereabouts of a felon or of a planned illegal operation, replacing long, formal procedures of requests between two interior ministries. Informality plays an important role also in the case of the IPN, where the track II diplomacy helps state officials interact with civil society and avoid the traditional bureaucratic obstacles present in track one processes, such as adherence to hierarchies and protocols. Creating an informal setting through the use of Chatham House rules has enabled a broadening of the boundaries of possible interaction. As Ejdus puts it, it 'allowed participants to express freely without being bound by official positions or dull party lines' (Ejdus, this volume: 109). Ejdus highlights the composition and flexibility of IPNs as a key advantage over other diplomatic formats, enabling them to serve as a policy transmission belt towards the national community: 'when a security community needs to evolve from an embryonic phase, in which state elites engage in rudimentary cooperative practices, to the ascendant phase, characterized by wider societal trust and we-feeling' (ibid.: 101). Importantly, he lists how informality allows for creativity or 'thinking outside the box' (ibid.: 115) through the example of how the participants of the RSSEE came up with the idea to engage the OSCE as an independent election monitor during the first elections held under Kosovo legislation in four Serbian-majority municipalities in northern Kosovo in 2013.

Most importantly, the cases studied show that informality creates the context for stepping out from the framework of official foreign policy. This was documented in the difference in interactions between Serbian and Kosovan diplomats in an official setting and during the unofficial part of program in a pub, as reported in Albania case study. '*When the Kosovar diplomat gave his business card to his Serbian colleague, the latter refused to accept it [...] but later on in the pub the Serb told the Kosovar 'I'm sorry for earlier... but you know, I have nothing against you ... it's state policy*" (MD7, June 15, 2012). Qehaja and Bekaj (Chapter 5) also mention that Serbian and Kosovan police have experience of cooperating without formal recognition, through informal exchange of data and even handover of suspects to the other side, subsequently registered as a deportation as there were no formal arrangements in place to organise formal extradition (Kursani, 2015: 7–8). Importantly, the precursor for this practice was the establishment of professional contacts through the Austria-led and EU-sponsored project on establishing International Law Enforcement Coordination Units (ibid.).

Interaction practices during unofficial parts of events have, however, led to the informal creation of sub-security communities whose boundaries do not overlap with the externally imposed categories of the Western Balkans and Southeast Europe. The most commonly noted re-grouping was that based on a common language – into the Slavic language sub-community and Albanian language sub-community. The role of non-formal contacts, facilitated by the absence of a language barrier among sub-groups in the region, was very frequently mentioned by respondents as a crucial element of cooperation. While this could be linked also to the embeddedness of professional *habitus* in broader societal identities, the language-based re-grouping frequently fails to overlap with the official foreign policy priorities of the studied countries. An example of this was the experience of Croatia, whose primary partners were other members of Adriatic Charter, the countries from the region that shared the ambition to become part of NATO (Macedonia and Albania), while actual security cooperation was more intensive with Serbia and Bosnia. This finding confirms Wenger's point that communities of practice are not 'congruent with reified structures of institutional affiliations, divisions and boundaries' (Wenger, 1998, 118–119).

Joint enterprises

The key component for building trust is undoubtedly the second component of communities of practice – *joint enterprises* or *domain*. Our research confirmed that identification of joint enterprise occurred more easily in groups composed of members of the same professional background as they used same categories to comprehend the problems. Brčvak and Kalač quote a Montenegrin police officer who classifies his peers based on common purpose: 'they do not speak of Albanians, Serbs or Croats; rather they speak of fellow colleagues, of professionals. They are interested in achieving the same goal – making their communities as secure as possible, thus, they share a common purpose' (this volume: 48). Some of these shared goals and purposes were found in situated problem solving, especially in contexts where, not only competent performance, but sometimes lives depended on cooperation with colleagues. Dautović (Chapter 3) cites the example of cross-national unity of Balkan militaries during deployment in multinational operations or among military professionals in mine-clearance units and aviation. Also, the practices such as joint border patrols developed a sense of common purpose, as reported in the chapter on Montenegro.

More importantly, a major change seems to have taken place through a deliberate strategy employed by the EU and NATO, which tried to de-securitise inter-state relations among Western Balkan countries by socialising security and foreign policy professionals from the region into a new categorisation of professional problems. The EU and NATO implicitly justified cooperation among former enemies by introducing priority and prestige to the addressing of transboundary and non-military risks such as organised crime, terrorism and disaster response. Even in the case of militaries, the emphasis has been shifted from the task of territorial defence towards provision of support to civilian authorities and peace-supporting operations in other regions. This is evident from the mantra of 'threats not recognising borders', quoted by a number of interlocutors in this volume. This re-definition of professional tasks has led to a blurring of the divide between internal and external security, exposing Western Balkan police services to enhanced inter-state cooperation than they were previously used to and, at the same time, putting diplomats in a position to discuss issues which were previously exclusively dealt with as a part of internal politics – such as 'organised crime, money laundry, finances and electoral reform' (Dyrmishi and Qeseraku, this volume: 23).

In this way, more powerful actors such as EU and NATO re-defined the 'objects of struggle' in the regional security field, from defence of national territories towards response to transnational threats. This was to serve the role of re-positioning national actors in the field not one against each other but against a borderless, external 'other'. The foreign policy orientation of Western Balkan countries created an environment in which security professionals were authorised to learn re-classification of security problems in line with post-sovereign European security practices. This socialisation by external actors was most successful in those cases where interactions were run by peer security and foreign policy professionals or allowed working together with colleagues from the EU and NATO on common practical problem solving for prolonged periods of time.

While we are going to explain later that the strategy of socialisation into privileging transnational problems was only partially successful, as much categorisation of threats still takes place at the national level, it is important to note the change in implicit understanding of priority professional problems is the first step in building security community. As Bremberg (2015: 677) explains, the practice-based theory of security community emphasises that 'common practice precedes common identity in security community-building'. The assumption behind this claim is 'that shared practical understanding can evolve through social interaction even though actors' understandings of self and other(s) might be unaltered. From the perspective of practice, what is important in terms of processes of (security) community-building is not that they first create a common identity, but whether actors learn to do something in a new way' (ibid.).

Shared repertoire

This brings us to the third component of security community of practice, a *shared repertoire* of routines, tools and methods. As Adler highlights, the spreading of 'background knowledge' through capacity-building activities, 'enables practitioners to share similar beliefs related to their practices, to entertain similar reasons and to act with common sense' (Adler 2008: 201). The authors list two of the most frequent ways common background knowledge was developed as a part of common *habitus*. In the cases of Macedonian and Montenegrin police services, as well as the Bosnia and Herzegovina military, background knowledge is based on joint training and socialisation in standard operating procedures that took place during the Yugoslav era. Socialisation into new ways of policing, diplomacy and defence, as promoted by the EU and NATO, is listed as a central experience through which regional professionals and IPN have adopted new competent practices. Through participation in regional capacity-building, different communities of practice were created within and across distinct professions focused on solving problems in line with new models of doing core business promoted by the EU and NATO. Some new ways of doing things documented in this study have been interoperability in joint deployments in line with NATO military standards, multilateralism for diplomacy and a number of new security practices based on EU models of police cooperation – such as integrated border management, cross-border hot pursuits, joint patrolling etc. Ejdus's study of the RSSEE (Chapter 8) shows how an International Policy Network is built and its members are socialised in liberal security practices, 'such as democratic control of the armed forces, security sector reform, peaceful resolution of conflicts, human security, transparency and accountability, security cooperation and integration' (p. 104), through selection of these topics on agenda and the use of language in line with NATO standards during discussion.

The adoption of new repertoires was possible due to the practice of avoiding discussion of sensitive topics, such as the causes of recent conflicts or experiences of the recent past. This practice of avoidance of divisive issues was documented in the participant observation of regional military training at the Peace Support Operations Centre by Dautović (Chapter 3) and in Ejdus's study of IPN (Chapter 8). This especially refers to the discussion of the past, as quoted in Ejdus's study: 'we do not discuss history, only the future' (p. 114). Similarly, Ejdus quotes one of the participants as stating that when historical references are made, 'it is usually for the purpose of making analogies. In other words, examples from the European past such as Franco-German reconciliation are employed strategically by speakers as historical analogies' (p. 115).

Another interesting example of tacit knowledge that influences interaction among members of the same professional *habitus* is documented in participant observation in Macedonian and Montenegrin chapters. This is exclusionary and defensive practice directed toward a common 'other' as perceived from within the professional in-group. In Koneska's (Chapter 7) observation of a regional conference, Macedonian police distancing from local Macedonian civil society was used as a police-to-police signal that they share common institutional cultures and values, including similar distrust of civil society. Brčvak and Kalač's (Chapter 4) Montenegrin interviewees reported that there is frequently grouping among Western Balkan police officers during breaks at courses also attended by 'officers from a wider geographical area' (p. 50).[6]

To summarise the first part of this analysis, we have observed that the EU and NATO influenced the creation of security communities of practice in the Western Balkan region by establishing sites for mutual engagement among former enemies and for situated learning of a new definition of security problems and a shared repertoire of new ways of doing policing, defence and diplomacy. In this way, the EU and NATO used their dominant positions in the field to partially re-configure the positions of local professional actors, the key struggles and the rules taken for granted in the field of regional security in the Western Balkans. The context of informal interactions, focus on problem-solving and avoidance of discussions of divisive issues of the past were some of the practices that contributed to development of cooperative practices among security and diplomatic professionals, as well as within IPN. This has sometimes taken place in spite of national foreign policies. The regional security communities of practice were established across national borders not necessarily overlapping with formal regional initiatives created by the EU and NATO or by national foreign policy.

The limits of security communities of practice

This research has, however, confirmed the Bourdieusian point that, 'battles of categorization [of problems] take place nationally as most of agents, even the most international ones, make most parts of their careers nationally and are educated nationally' (quoted in Madsen, 2017: 107). Therefore, it makes sense to analyse processes of the securitisation and de-securitisation of inter-state relations by looking at the routine practices of national-level actors and their re-positioning regarding other actors within the national and regional fields.

The embeddedness of security professions in national/social securitisations

First, cooperative security practices are functional on the issues that have not been securitised in the national political arena. This means that security and foreign policy professionals have greater autonomy to work across the borders on issues that are not controversial within their political community at home.

Nationally classified threats were seen in these studies through the preference for bilateral security cooperation over the multilateral, despite the recognition of transnational threats. Most interviewed police officers expressed the need for cooperation with countries their country physically shares borders with, thus excluding other parts of the externally imposed Western Balkan region. Examples of prioritising cooperation are illustrated in Knezović et al.'s (Chapter 6) study of Croatian police where preference is given to cooperation with EU neighbours and other EU member states over cooperation with non-EU Balkan neighbours.

The national level of trust and distrust is translated into a professional hierarchy of trust through the use/deployment of different policing techniques. Our research showed that police valued operational cooperation and the exchange of personal data on suspects and victims over more general joint training and conferences. Therefore, the difference in categorisation of professional counterparts is seen through different levels of intensity of developed cooperation, as well as the tools used for cooperation. Qehaja and Bekaj (Chapter 5) give an example of significant 'trust despite uncertainty' between Kosovo and Albanian police who jointly police Kosovo citizens on holiday deep inside Albania. Performing joint patrols of borders and managing joint border crossing points were other examples of closeness and trust developed between two police services. A contrast to this has been the reluctance by Macedonian police to deploy new police tactics available after signing the Convention for Police Cooperation in Southeast Europe, such as hot pursuits of suspects across borders, due to a lack of trust in neighbouring police.

Regional imagination in practice

Our study has also shown that promotion of security communities by external actors has its limits, as it is further interpreted by national-level dynamics transferring through practices into different sub-regions. The geographical boundaries of professional communities of practice do not necessarily overlap with the externally imposed category of the Western Balkan region (Bechev, 2011) or with institutional boundaries of different intergovernmental security organisations/initiatives. The empirical research indicated that within existing formal regional cooperation, informal sub-regions formed on the basis of language and common institutional legacy (e.g. former Yugoslav or Slavic language-speaking vs. Albanian-speaking sub-regions), as well as on the basis of the level of integration into other security initiatives (e.g. NATO-members vs. PfP). While many Kosovo Police still speak Serbo-Croatian, they sometimes chose not to use it in formal regional events to signal separation from former home country, Serbia, while they exhibit a greater willingness to use it in everyday communication with Serbian, Montenegrin and Macedonian colleagues in on resolution of practical problems. There are positive practices of the overcoming language barriers when there is a common professional interest, such as catching smugglers in the case of cooperation of Montenegrin and Albanian maritime police units. Brčvak and Kalač (Chapter 4) mention Montenegrin maritime police using a note in Albanian meaning 'something of security interest' to retype and warn the Albanian police commander on the other side of a potential impending risk.

The integration of ethnic minorities has also helped transform relations with neighbours. In the case of Macedonia, the transformation of the role the police play in society after the 2001 internal conflict has helped facilitate inter-national cooperation. After the Ohrid Framework Agreement, the Macedonian police service has become more inclusive of the internal ethnic 'other' Albanian minority within its ranks, facilitating cooperation with neighbouring Albania and Kosovo. Also, in both Kosovo and Serbia, police have used members of minorities to serve at borders/boundary lines so as to facilitate cooperation and exchange with people crossing these lines, as reported in Qehaja and Bekaj's chapter (Chapter 5).

Besides language, another informal differentiation was made based on the level of integration into larger Euro-Atlantic security community. This was most evident in the case of the Croatian police service, which highlighted that their progress in integrating and implementing international norms and standards hinders the development of cooperation with neighbours. The example provided was that other Balkan countries not having the same level of protection of privacy of data as Croatia was able to build during the accession process to the EU, prevents it from sharing sensitive data with its neighbours. For example, in becoming an EU member state, Croatia was obligated to adopt border control standards adhered to by all other member states, while other countries in the region do not have this type of border control, which presents an obstacle to border police on both sides.

An inter-state conflict in the professional imagination

Diplomacy has become dominant and common-sensical practice in professional interactions in the Western Balkans. Some interviews cited it as the only possible practice once Serbia and Kosovo, the last remaining unresolved conflicted parties, have started being worked through diplomatic negotiations. The 'trust [in their colleagues'] beyond doubt' (Pouliot, 2008: 278) has not, however, been fully internalised, as imaginings of potential inter-state conflicts are still present in the interviews. While conflict has not been imaginable in the short-term, it was imaginable in the long term as a fear legitimately expressed in a few scenarios.

Distrust of the regional agency of communities of practice is evident from the fear that the international forces will one day withdraw. External 'others' were simultaneously perceived not only as guarantors of peace but also as potential spoilers of regional dynamics by potentially siding with some regional actor (Dautović, this volume). The second reason frequently mentioned was the difficulties of breaking with the past — and resistance to specify which factors from the past. This was proven by Albanian diplomats who claimed that it is easier to use diplomacy as a means of dealing with issues pertaining to current developments or future prospects than to tackle issues which are rooted in the past. An example of divisive issue from Dautović's text is prosecution of war criminals, especially because some of them could be affiliated to integrated ethnic militaries within the Armed Forces of BiH. The coping practice observed in this case was that the course participants were observed to handle this sensitive topic by simply avoiding it as described earlier.

Professional habitus *in relation to national political authority*

The last, but most frequently mentioned potential cause of conflicts are the narrow interests of politicians. The boundaries of the possible interactions in regional field are constantly tacitly negotiated in relations between security professionals and politicians at home. All cases document that it is the politicians who decide which issues are purely technical and therefore left to professionals to resolve (Dautović, Chapter 3; Dyrmishi and Qesaraku, Chapter 2) and which are transferred to the political domain. This shows that we need to study the positioning of security professionals not only in relation to their counterparts from other countries but also in relation to politicians as dominant actors domestically.

The influence of politicians has been differently mediated and interpreted in different countries based on the role of a particular profession and institution in political transition that shaped the *habitus* of professions studied in this book. For example, the Kosovo case is illustrative of how this origin of a particular professional *habitus* influences its positioning within the national and international field. As quoted in the Bekaj and Qehaja's chapter, the line between politicians and police has been blurred since 1999 and frequently leads to a 'switch from uniform to political party' (p. 65).

The transformation of relations between politicians and professionals, creating greater autonomy for professional rationality during democratization in each of studied countries was supportive of more regional professional cooperation (e.g. Montenegro, BiH, Macedonia). Dyrmishi and Qeseraku (Chapter 2) highlight that improved interpersonal ties between diplomats in the region only occasionally contribute to the pace of communication and interactions, as the influence of diplomats still remains weak in terms of influence over the course of actions taken by governments. However, most of communities of practice have limited professional autonomy in respect to problem solving that runs counter to the interest of politicians (e.g. corruption) due to their weak professional autonomy. Professional *habitus* in the region lacks autonomy due to the politicisation of governance over professional matters, not only through the appointment of personnel but also through meddling in the investigation of cases that are perceived as sensitive. Many of routine practices exercised by security professionals out of view of the public is still not autonomous, due to political interference in the day-to-day work of these services. This is in contrast to much of the literature on internal affairs cooperation within the EU, where security professionals were able to exercise more autonomy in routine practices of securitisation due to their expert knowledge. While police are allowed to pursue cooperation on issues that are perceived as apolitical, their room to manoeuvre is limited for the issues that are perceived as having the potential to hurt politicians. These cases are often securitised by politicians as a matter protecting national sovereignty. Brčvak and Kalač (Chapter 4) give an example of how the Montenegrin police service lacked the professional autonomy needed to continue cooperation in the high-profile Šarić case, which could potentially incriminate political elites and expose their suspected links with organised crime.

In conclusion to the second part of the analysis, the logic of sovereignty prevails when professional autonomy is confronted with political authority in the national security field. Believing despite uncertainty (Pouliot) among professionals is effectively translated into practice around issues that are not at stake for politicians. The security fields in the Western Balkans have been dominated by politicians overruling security professionals and thus also influencing the potential for regional interaction.

Conclusion

This empirical ethnographic study analysed security community building from below and beyond the level of states and international organisations. By focussing on what security and foreign policy professionals and the members of IPN do together and how are things done informally, we were able to arrive at a more nuanced picture of regional cooperation dynamics in the Western Balkans since the end of armed conflicts in the first half of the 2000s. The conclusions presented in this book are not to be understood as laws applicable to all cases of current and future security cooperation and resolution of the conflicts in the Western Balkans, but as observations relevant for particular historical moment.

The main finding of this study is that security and foreign policy professions practice cooperative security across national borders in line with the models within which they were socialised both as members of older former Yugoslav communities of practice and through participation in new transnational regional networks externally imposed by the EU and NATO. The EU and NATO influenced the creation of security communities of practice in the Western Balkan region by establishing sites for mutual engagement among former enemies and for situated learning of new definitions of security problems and a shared repertoire of doing policing, defence and diplomacy. In this way, as the most powerful actors in regional security field, the EU and NATO re-defined the 'objects of struggle' in the regional security field from defence of national territories towards the response to transnational threats. This was to serve the role of re-positioning of national actors in the field not against one another but against borderless external 'other'. The foreign policy orientation of Western Balkan countries created an environment in which security professionals were authorised to learn re-classification of security problems in line with post-sovereign European security practices. The context of informal interactions, focus on problem-solving and avoidance of divisive issues from the past were some of the practices that contributed to the development of cooperative practices among security and diplomatic professionals, as well as within IPN. This has taken place sometimes in spite of national foreign policies.

Cooperative security practices are, however, functional only on issues that have not been subjected to securitisation at the national political level. This confirms earlier findings that 'battles for categorization take place nationally' (Madsen, 2017). The embeddedness of professional identity in national identity is seen through informally created sub-regions based on national perceptions of threat as well as language-grouping practices, not necessarily overlapping with formal regional initiatives created by the EU and NATO. The logic of sovereignty and a more exclusive understanding of threats prevails when professional autonomy is confronted with political authority in the national security field. Politicians, rather than security professionals, have dominated the national security fields in the Western Balkans, thus also influencing the room for manoeuvre security and foreign policy professional have in regional interactions. Therefore, 'believing despite uncertainty' (Pouliot) among professionals is effectively translated into practice only around those issues not at stake for politicians. The case of the International Policy Network shows, however, that one of the key advantages of this transnational network composed of a heterogeneous group of professionals and civil society is flexibility in expanding the boundaries of the possible through track II diplomacy.

In conclusion, communities of practice are the most effective way to develop practices of trust and peaceful conflict resolution among national security and foreign policy professionals. Through development of implicit common classification of problems at stake, as well as doing something in new way among the members of groups that share the same *habitus*, the 'shared practical can evolve through social interaction even though actors' understandings of self and other(s) might be unaltered' (Bremberg, 2015: 677). The reach of regional communities of practice is mediated by the position its national members have in the national level security field. Their manoeuvring space for autonomous professional action is, however, most seriously limited by the dominance of politicians in national security field. The IPN shows looser connections but more flexibility in exerting influence on regional dynamics due to a free-riding position within the regional security field.

Notes

1 The Armed Forces of BiH were formed through the unification of two ethnically based militaries previously engaged in a civil war against one another: the Army of Federation of BiH (with two separate command chains for Bosniak and Bosnian Croat forces) and the Army of Republika Srpska.
2 The book is missing a study of the Serbian police which took part in conflicts in Croatia, Bosnia and Herzegovina and Kosovo due to that country's Ministry of Interior refusing to allow interviews with its employees. The remaining police services studied have varied levels of experience in armed conflict and differing institutional legacies pertaining to

their wartime role. In Croatia and Montenegro, police services were seen as primary state-building institutions due to their role as the only armed forces during conflicts for independence. A significant number of Croatian police officers has experience of war, while a limited number of Montenegrin police officers took part in combat during Yugoslav wars. While the Kosovo Police has not been built on the legacy of the Kosovo Liberation Army (KLA), a number of its members are veterans with strong links to political leaders who emerged from this insurgency group. The Macedonian police has experience of internal conflict against the 2001 Albanian insurgency.
3 Ejdus mentions that IPN are communities of practice but different from epistemic communities due to the level of cohesion within the group.
4 In this chapter, when we refer to the EU and NATO we refer both to the collective entities and the member states that promote EU and NATO security practices.
5 For an overview of key security and justice initiatives in the region see: www.rcc.int/pages/35/rcc-and-regional-initiatives-and-task-forces-in-south-east-europe
6 In this context this refers to officers from beyond the Western Balkans.

Bibliography

Adler, E, "The Emergence of Cooperation: National Epistemic Communities and the International Evolution of the Idea of Nuclear Arms Control" in *International Organization* 46:1 (1992): 101–145.

Adler, E, *Communitarian International Relations: The Epistemic Foundations of International Relations*, Routledge, 2005.

Adler, E, "The Spread of Security Communities: Communities of Practice, Self-Restraint, and NATO's Post-Cold War Transformation" in *European Journal of International Relations* 14: 2 (2008): 195–230.

Adler, E. and Barnett, M. (eds), *Security Communities*, Cambridge University Press, 1998.

Adler, E. and Pouliot, V, "International Practices" in *International Theory* 3:1 (2011a): 1–36.

Adler, E. and Pouliot, V, (eds), *International Practices*, Cambridge University Press, 2011b.

Adler-Nissen, R, (ed.), *Bourdieu in International Relations*, Routledge, 2013.

Balzacq, T, Basara, T, Bigo, D.Guittet, E-P and Olsson, C, "Security Practices", in Denemark, RA (ed.), *International Studies Encyclopaedia Online*, Blackwell, 2010, pp.1–30.

Bechev, D, "Carrots, Sticks and Norms: the EU and Regional Cooperation in Southeast Europe" in *Journal of Southern Europe and the Balkans* 8:1 (2006): 27–43.

Bechev, D, *Constructing South East Europe – The Politics of Balkan Regional Cooperation*, Palgrave Macmillan, 2011.

Bremberg, N, "The European Union as Security Community-Building Institution: Venues, Networks and Cooperative Security Practices" in *Journal of Common Market Studies* 53:3 (2015): 674–692.

Kavalski, E, *Extending the European Security Community: Constructing Peace in the Balkans*, IB Tauris & Company, 2008.

Kursani, S. *Police Cooperation between Kosovo and Serbia*, BCSP and KCSS, 2015.

Madsen, MK, "Transnational fields and power elites: Reassembling the international with Bourdieu and practice theory" in BasaranT. et al. *International Political Sociology – Transversal Lines*, Routledge (2017): 106–125.

Pouliot, V, "Subjectivism: Toward a Constructivist Methodology" in *International Studies Quarterly* 51:2 (2007): 359–384.

Pouliot, V, "The Logic of Practicality: A Theory of Practice of Security Communities" in *International Organization* 62:2 (2008): 257.

Pouliot, V, *International Security in Practice: The Politics of NATO-Russia Diplomacy*, Cambridge University Press, 2010.
Silver, A, "The Demand for Order in Civil Society: A Review of Some Themes in the History of Urban Crime, Police and Riots" in *The Police: Six Sociological Essays*, New York, 1967.
Solioz, C and Stubbs, P, "Emergent regional co-operation in South East Europe: towards 'open regionalism'?" in *Southeast European and Black Sea Studies* 9:1 (2009) 1–16.
Vučetić, S, "The Stability Pact for South Eastern Europe as a Security Community-Building Institution" in *Southeast European Politics* 2 (2001): 109–134.
Wenger, E, *Communities of practice. Learning, meaning, and identity*, Cambridge, NY: Cambridge University Press, 1998.
Wenger, E, McDermott, R and Snyder, W, *Cultivating Communities of Practice: A Guide to Managing Knowledge*, Harvard Business School Press, 2002.

INDEX

Abbott, A. 6, 57, 74
Adler, Emanuel 6, 7, 10,15, 18, 25, 39, 47, 74, 103–4, 129; & Barnett, Michael 2, 4, 7, 10, 25, 28, 30–1, 31, 32, 37, 39, 40, 66, 124; & Pouliot, V. 6, 7, 11, 31, 37, 43, 122
Adler-Nissen, R. 122, 123
Adriatic Charter (2003) 21
Albania: linguistic isolation 32; moderating influence of 20; NATO membership 3, 13; Sarajevo embassy 22
Albanian diplomacy: changes in practice 17; communist era 17, 22; data collection 16; international norms 18; postcommunist era 17–18, 124; and practice theory 16; and regional identity 23; regional interactions 18, 23
Albanian diplomats: interviews with 16; perception of neighbours 20–1; professional values 23; training 18
Albanian language 60, 127
Armed Forces of Bosnia and Herzegovina (AFBiH): formation 135n1; professional solidarity 34; regional cooperation 39; research on 29, 39n1
Austria, sponsorship of RSSEE study group 110–11, 117

Balkan Route 78, 81, 86n5
Balkans *see* Eastern Balkans; Western Balkans
Barnes, B. 16
Belgrade Agreement (2003) 45

Benson, R.W. 63
Berridge, G.R. 14
Bosnia and Herzegovina (BiH): Croatia, border 79; Dayton Peace Agreement (1995) 3, 35; ethnic peoples 35; regional cooperation 35; war (1992–5) 3; *see also* Armed Forces of Bosnia and Herzegovina (AFBiH)
Bourdieu, Pierre 31, 41; Bourdieu and Wacquant 31; Bourdieusian tradition 122, 123, 130
Bremberg, N. 129
Brussels Agreement (2013) 3, 66–7, 69, 115
Bueger, Christian 102
Buzan, Barry 48, 60, 106; Buzan and Hansen 106;

Carr-Saunders, A.M. & Wilson, P.A., *The Professions* 5
Civil Society 1, 49, 94, 102–9, 112, 116, 124, 125, 126, 130, 135
Cohen, William 107
Communities of Practice (CoP): 9, 41, 129; and corporate practices 31; creation of 125; definition 6, 59; and International Policy Network 102, 107; in international relations 6–7; militaries 28, 30, 39; and practice turn 6; *see also* epistemic communities
corporate practices, and Communities of Practice (CoP) 31
corporateness, military profession 30

Index

crime 1, 43, 52, 134; and borders 52; and diplomats 128; and police 44, 46; threats 72, 78, 97, 111; war crimes 33; *see* organised crime
Croatia: BiH, border 79; Erdut Peace Agreement (1995) 3; EU membership 3, 13, 80, 81; Euro-Atlanticism 80; Law on Internal Affairs 75, 76, 77; National Guard 76; NATO membership 3, 13, 80; self-perception 85; Slovenia, border dispute 22; war (1991–5) 3
Croatia-Serbia, cooperation 82
Croatian nation 35
Croatian police service: development 75–7; EU influence 76, 77; interviews with 77–8; Law on Police Affairs and Authorities (2009) 76; Police Academy 76; Police Act (2011) 76; and politics 82; regional cooperation 78; research on 73, 77–84
Cyber Crime Conference, Montenegro (2012) 43, 49

Danube Strategy, EU 83
Dautović, Kenan 8, 130, 133
Dayton Peace Agreement, BiH (1995) 3, 35
Deutsch, Karl 2, 4, 15, 25, 29, 32, 60, 66, 69, 73, 75, 99
diplomacy: and common projects 22; embodiment of 19; informal, IPNs 104–5, 124, 126–7, 135; as international institution 15; in Italian city-states 14; NATO-Russia 15; as normalizing factor 21–2; prevalence, in WB 19, 124, 132; as profession 14–16; Vienna Convention (1961) 15; *see also* Albanian diplomacy
diplomats, Albanian *see* Albanian diplomats
Djukanović, Milo 45
DPS party, Montenegro 44
Dyrmishi, Arjan & Qesaraku, Mariola 7, 133

Eastern Balkans 3; *see also* Western Balkans
Ejdus, Filip 122, 123, 126
Elias, Norbert 103
epistemic communities 5; definition 7, 58; Haas's notion 7, 58; and IPNs 102; and police 7, 57, 58, 59, 97; principles and practices 58–9; *see also* Communities of Practice (CoP)
Erdut Peace Agreement, Croatia (1995) 3
ethnic minorities, integration 132
ethnicity, relevance of 24
ethnography, autoethnography, 101, 103, 118; ethnographic study 9,10, 119, 134; non-causal ethnographic account 103

EU: Croatian membership 3, 13, 80; Danube Strategy 83; and regional cooperation 79, 83; as security community 14; Stabilisation and Association Process 46, 125; Stability Pact 3, 4, 125
Euro-Atlantic: integration 13, 23, 32, 132; structures 33, 111
Euro-Atlantic Partnership Council (EAPC) 107
Euro-Atlantic security community 2, 5, 39, 78, 125; eastward expansion 106, 117
European Council meetings, Santa Maria de Deira (2000) 3

field 31; definition 122; positioning in fields 124, 128, 133, 134, 135; security field 128, 134, 135
forensic science 86n7

George C. Marshall European Center for Security Studies 105
Goode, W.J. 53, 74
Grillot, S.R., Cruise, R.J. & D'Eman, V.J. 5

Haas, Peter, epistemic communities notion 7, 58
habitus 31, 46, 53, 110, 124, 135; Bourdieusian definition 122; embeddedness in social identity, 125, 127; examples 130; professional 123, 124, 129, 130;, and political influence on 133–4; and security practices 122
Harries-Jenkins, G. 30
Helsinki Process 59
Huntington, S. 30

identity: shared identity as a component of security community 59, 73, 74, 84, 85, 88, 102, 129; Southeast Europe (SEE) 4; trust 39; *see also* national identity; professional identity, state identity
international Organizations (IOs) 1
International Policy Networks (IPNs) 122; definition 9; and epistemic communities 102; functions 101, 103–4; growth 117; informal diplomacy 104–5, 124, 126–7, 135; knowledge diffusers 104, 116–17; membership 102–3; and security community building 101, 102–5, 125; security policymaking, influence on 104; and self-restraint norm 103–4; *see also* Partnership for Peace Consortium (PfPC)

interoperability, militaries 28, 39, 81, 129; 'conceptual interoperability' 113

Jackson, Patrick Thaddeus 103
Jahjaga, Atifete 64–5
Janowitz, M. 30
joint enterprises 9, 123, 127–9

Kalač, Emir & Brčvak, Dženita 8
Kavalski, Emilian 4–5, 10, 75, 125
Knezović, Sandro & Cvrtila, Vlatko, & Vučinović, Zrinka 8
Koneska, Cvete 8–9, 130
Kosovo: independence 64; Kumanovo Military-Technical Agreement (1999) 3; UNMIK 60–1; UNSC Resolution 1244 3; *see also* Kosovo police service; Serbia-Kosovo
Kosovo Liberation Army (KLA): disbandment 61; *see also* Kosovo Protection Corps (KPC)
Kosovo police service: cohesiveness problems 62; composition 57; elites 65; establishment 57, 61; high turnover 65; identity 63; international practices 63, 64; KLA legacy 62–3; numbers 61; personnel categories 61–2; police culture 62–3; and politics 64–5, 66, 67, 69; public trust 66; in regional security cooperation 66–7; research data on 60; standard operating procedures 63; use of Serbo-Croat 131–2
Kosovo Protection Corps (KPC) 61; *see also* Kosovo Liberation Army (KLA)
Kosovo-Serbia: Integrated Border Management 67; normalisation process (2013) 3; war (1999) 3, 4

Language: barrier 32, 50, 82, 85, 132; body 32; of enmity 110; language-grouping 124, 127, 135; practice 94, 105, 129; shared/common 15, 21, 32, 49, 53, 113; trust 68; sub-communities/sub-regions: Albanian 60, 68, 127, 131; Slavic 127, 131;

Macedonia: EU membership bid 92, 93, 97; Faculty of Security (Police Academy) 96–7; NATO membership bid 22, 92; Ohrid Framework Agreement (2001) 3; war (2001) 3
Macedonian police service: education 96–8; hierarchical practices 94; independence role 92; norms' transmission 89; popular perceptions of 90–1; and practice theory 91; professional identity 93; regional security cooperation 89, 90, 94–6, 97, 98; research on 93
Malmström, Cecilia 68
militaries: as communities of practices 28; interoperability 28; and regional cooperation 34–5
military profession 28–30, 34; corporateness 30; essentialist model 30; officership 30
Mobile Training Teams: activities 38; and regional cooperation 38
Montenegrin police service 41–2; as defence mechanism 44; joint border patrols 50–1; like-mindedness, creation of 47; militarization 4, 45; Police Academy 47; Police Law (2005) 45; professional autonomy 45; professional identity 46; regional cooperation 48–9, 50; regional security cooperation 48–9, 50; research data on 43; socialization process 46–7; as state-building actor 45; studies on 43
Montenegro: coalition government 45; criminality 44–5; Cyber Crime Conference (2012) 43, 49; DPS party 44, 45; SDP party 45; sovereignty 42, 44, 45; union with Serbia 44
Moskos, C. 30

national identity, professional identity in 123–4
national interest, and regional cooperation 32–3
nationalism, Western Balkans 20
NATO: Croatian membership 3, 13, 80; as security community 3, 14, 15; Strategic Concept (1999) 78; Western Balkans members 3, 20
NATO-Russia: Council 15; diplomacy 15
Neumann, I.B. 6, 14, 15, 16, 91, 104; Neumann and Pouliot 110; Neumann and Williams 2

officership, military profession 30
Ohrid Framework Agreement, Macedonia (2001) 3, 132
Operation Balkan Warrior 46; jurisdiction issues 51–2; *Listing* Affair 52
Organisation for Security and Cooperation in Europe (OSCE), election monitors 115, 127
organised crime 44, 45, 46, 72, 81, 83, 85; and diplomats 23; regional cooperation 42, 78–9, 79–80, 81, 134

Paoline, E. 62
Partnership for Peace Consortium (PfPC) 101; activities 108; establishment 107; organisational flexibility 109; rationale 107–8; role 107; Russia, failure to involve 109–10; secretariat 108; stakeholders 108; work and study groups 108; *see also* Regional Stability in Southeast Europe (RSSEE)
Partnership for Peace (PfP) program 3, 4, 106
Peace Support Operations Training Centre (PSOTC) 29, 130; courses 37; pros and cons 38; and regional cooperation 38
Perry, William 106
police competences, and regional cooperation 81
Police Cooperation in Southeast Europe, Convention 131
police profession 46, 47, 57, 62, 66, 69, 73, 76; definition 57
police work: common identity 83–4; regional cooperation 52–3, 80–1, 84; and security cooperation 43; trust issues 68; *see also* Croatian police service; Kosovo police service; Montenegrin police service
Pouliot, Vincent, 2, 6, 13, 15, 16, 19, 24, 31, 37, 41, 102, 110, 122, 132, 134, 135; *sobjective* methodology 122
poverty, and regional cooperation 33
practice theory 16, 31, 32, 41, 42, 122; Albanian diplomacy 16; elements of 31; and the Macedonian police service 91; security communities 31; and study of police 47, 90
practice turn, 6, 10; and CoPs 6
practices (international): 1, 4; definition 6, 16; as performances 6; research on 6–7; Western 5; violent, 15; *see also* security practices and professional practices
profession: 34; Balkan military 38; Bosnian military 34; definition, 5–6, 29, 73–75; diplomacy as 14–15; embeddedness in national identity 123–4, 135; habitus 46, 122, 123, 124, 125, 130, 133; Kosovo Police 62, 63, 65; Macedonian police service 91, 93, 94; Montenegrin police service 46; police profession professional identity 42, 46, 53, 93, 123, 135; sub-professions 34; *see also* military profession;
professional 52; autonomy 41, 42, 45, 52, 124, 133, 134, 135; background 128; communities 5, 9, 43, 49, 53, 60, 91, 99, 121, 122, 131; contacts 50, 127;
cooperation 52, 53, 67, 78; culture 61, 63, 64, 89; elites 90; hierarchy 94, 95, 131; imagination 132; interests 41, 132; level 24, 93; networks 52, 53; norms 92, 93, 95, 96, 98, 99; practices 4, 5, 7, 34, 91, 94, 95, 121; problems 128, 129; solidarity 34; values 23, 92
professionalism 18, 34, 41, 51, 69, 108
professionals 1, 4, 33, 34, 35, 41, 43, 49, 83, 89, 121, 124, 125, 126, 133; and IPN 122
professionalization 45, 58, 59, 64, 66, 74, 76, 77
professions: behaviour 6; definitions 5–6, 74–5; practice turn 6; *see also* security professions

Qehaja, Florijan & Bekaj, Armend 8, 127, 131

regional cooperation: AFBiH 39; Bosnia and Herzegovina 35; Croatian police service 78; and EU 79, 83; external drivers 32, 79–80, 89, 125, 126, 130; informal settings 126; internal drivers 32; military role 34–5; and MTT 38; and national interest 32–3; obstacles to 33; and organised crime 78, 78–9, 79–80, 81; and police competences 81; police work 52–3, 80–1, 84; political initiatives 36; and poverty 33; as process 33; and PSOTC 38; purpose 32; strategic initiatives 36; tactical initiatives 36–7; and trust 32; *see also* regional security cooperation
regional security complex 48
regional security cooperation 20, 21, 24, 42; achievements 22; assessment 88; development 73, 83–4; Kosovo police service 66–7; Macedonian police service 89, 90, 94–6, 97, 98; Montenegrin police service 48–9, 50; and national priorities 131, 135; and police work 43; regional initiatives 48; and security communities 60
Regional Stability in Southeast Europe (RSSEE) 101, 126, 129; optimism 114
Regional Stability in Southeast Europe (RSSEE) study group 110–16; achievements 112; Austrian sponsorship 110–11, 117; 'culture of dialogue' 113; diplomatic flexibility 115–16; finance 112; future orientation 114–15; knowledge diffusion 113; name change 113–14; publications 115; topics discussed

113; transferability of model 116; workshops 112, 116
Reiner, R. 64, 69
Rühe, Volker 107
Russia: Crimean annexation 110; great power ambitions 110; non-involvement in PfPC 109–10

Šarić, Darko: case 51–2; *Listing* affair 52
securitisation 9, 123, 130, 131, 134, 135; de-securitisation 123, 130
security, post-Cold War meaning 106
security communities: ascendant 60, 66, 103, 124; as CoPs 74; definition 60, 74; formation 1; geographical spread 2; mature 60, 66; nascent 60, 66, 103, 124; practice theory 31; and regional security cooperation 60; and security professions 75; and trust 31; types 2, 60; *see also* Communities of Practice (CoP)
security community: concept 14; definition 2, 66, 99; EU as 14; Euro-Atlantic 2, 5, 39; NATO as 3, 14, 15; norms 4; WB as 3–5, 14, 18, 24–5, 41, 84, 88; *see also* Euro-Atlantic security community
security community building: 29; and IPNs 101, 102–5, 123, 125; joint enterprises 127–9; mutual engagement 126–7; and peace building 1; professional practices 5–7, 122; research 134; shared repertoire 129–30
security interdependence, WB 48–9, 123
security policymaking, IPNs' influence on 104
security practices 122, 124, 128, 129, 135, 136; cooperative 74, 122, 123, 131, 135; examples 104; exclusionary 122; and *habitus* 122; liberal 107, 129;
security professions: in national/social securitisations 131; and security communities 75
Security Sector Reform (SSR) 61
self-restraint norm, 15, 59, 74, 101, 103, 113; and IPNs 9, 103–4; practices of, 74, 85, 104, 124
Selimi, Behar 63, 64
Serbia, union with Montenegro 44
Serbia-Croatia, cooperation 82
Serbia-Kosovo: diplomacy 19; Integrated Border Management 67; normalisation process (2013) 3; war (1999) 3, 4
Serbian nation 35
Serbian police service, interview refusal 135n2

Serbo-Croat, use by Kosovo police service 131–2
Slavic solidarity, Western Balkans 24
Slovenia: Croatia, border dispute 22; war (1991) 3
sobjective methodology 122
socialization, of WB elites 2, 4, 5, 88, 89, 93, 112; of diplomats 21, 23; IPN 102; of military 39; of police 42, 46–49, 50, 59, 96, 98; of professionals 96; 'socialization by' 4, 125; 'socialization within' 4;
Solioz, C. & Stubbs, P. 125
Southeast Europe Police Chiefs Association (SEPCA) 82, 83; informal contacts 126
Southeast Europe (SEE) 3; identity 4
sovereignty: IPN 114; logic of sovereignty 124, 134, 135; Macedonia, 89, 90, 92, 95, 96, 98, 99; and Montenegrin police service 42, 44, 45; Montenegro 42, 44, 45; transformation of sovereignty 121; and the WB 88
Stabilisation and Association Process, EU 46, 125
Stability Pact, EU 3, 4, 125
State 7, 9; communist state 17, 22, 71; diplomacy 14, 15, 121; EU member states 68, 80, 81, 83, 97, 131, 132, 136; federal state/state union 3, 44, 45, 48; inter-state relations 4, 7, 13, 14, 17, 19, 21, 22, 52, 79, 102, 103, 121, 122, 124, 128; the level of analysis 4, 5, 9, 72, 101, 106, 121, 134; military 28, 29, 30, 31, 34, 121; new state 42, 72, 78, 86, 90; non-state actors 109, 105; police 42, 43, 45, 57, 76, 83, 90, 91, 121; potential members 111; security community 1, 2, 5, 7, 13, 16, 40, 102; state border 45, 78, 88, 95, 99; state elites 4, 5, 103, 104, 105, 117; state identity 38, 44; state learning/socialisation 4, 5, 46, 47, 88, 96, 123, 125, 128; state level in Bosnia and Herzegovina 34, 35; state practice 22; state security 89, 90, 91, 92, 95, 96; state-building 45, 57, 113, 136; statehood 88; weak state 78, 81, 113; Western Balkan states 3, 77, 85, 96;
Stojanović Gajić, Sonja 55, 121–137
Sudgen, J. 58

trust: diplomats 16; hierarchy of trust 131; mistrust/distrust 9, 22, 46, 89, 91, 93, 94, 99, 126, 130, 132; police work 62, 68, 94, 96, 131; regional cooperation 32; security communities 1, 5, 13, 31, 59, 80, 89, 105, 117, 127; trust practices 32,

39, 94,123, 124, 135; trust-building 22, 33, 90, 127

UN Interim Administration Mission in Kosovo (UNMIK) 60–1

van Wagenen, Richard 30
Veljović, Veselin 45
Vienna, Congress of (1815) 15
Vienna Convention on Diplomatic Relations (1961) 15
violence: exclusion of, in WB 19, 20; experience of violence 72, 91; fear of 13, 19, 24; management of violence, 30, 31; non-war community 19; restraint from 15, 103; war community 19
Vučetić, Srdjan 4, 59, 60, 67, 125

war criminals 133
Wenger, E. 6, 30, 102, 124, 125, 127
Western Balkans (WB) 1; diplomacy, prevalence of 19, 124, 132; military cooperation 39; and national sovereignty 88; nationalism 20; NATO members 3, 20, 22; normalizing factors 21; regional cooperation 20; as security community 3–5, 14, 18, 24–5, 41, 84, 88; security interdependence 48–9; Slavic solidarity 24; violence, exclusion of 19, 20; *see also* Albania; Bosnia-Herzegovina; Croatia; Eastern Balkans; Kosovo; Macedonia; Montenegro; Serbia

Yugoslav Succession, Wars of 3
Yugoslavia: amalgamated security community 14; break-up 3, 72; cooperation of diplomats 22; cooperation of police from succession states 49; Federal Republic of Yugoslavia 44, 45; formal cessation 45, 66, 72; former security structures of Yugoslavia in Kosovo 61; institutional legacy 75; intervention 110, 111

Zagreb Summit (2000) 3

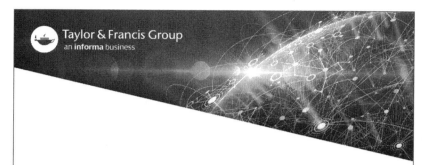